Ethical Hermeneutics

ETHICAL HERMENEUTICS

Rationality in Enrique Dussel's
Philosophy of Liberation

by

MICHAEL BARBER

Fordham University Press
New York
1998

Copyright © 1998 by FORDHAM UNIVERSITY PRESS
All rights reserved.
LC 96–37190
ISBN 8232–1703–5 (*hardcover*)
ISBN 8232–1704–0 (*paperback*)
ISSN 1089–3938
Perspectives in Continental Philosophy, No. 2

Library of Congress Cataloging-in-Publication Data

Barber, Michael D., 1949–
    Ethical hermeneutics : rationality in Enrique Dussel's Philosophy
of liberation / by Michael Barber.
        p.   cm.—(Perspectives in continental philosophy : no 2)
    Includes bibliographical references and index.
    ISBN 0–8232–1703–5 (hardcover).—ISBN 0–8232–1704–3 (pbk.)
    1. Dussel, Enrique D.—Ethics.   2. Ethics—Latin America.
3. Ethics, Modern—20th century.   4. Social ethics.
5. Hermeneutics.   6. Reason.   7. Liberation theology.
8. Lévinas, Emmanuel.   I. Title.   II. Series.
BJ414.D87333B37   1998
199'.8—dc21   96-37190
                                                                          CIP

Printed in the United States of America

To Tim and Sean
Terry, Maryanne, Luke, and Matthew

CONTENTS

PREFACE

Enrique Dussel's philosophy of liberation has gained worldwide prominence. He has published more than two hundred articles and more than forty-five books, principally in philosophy but also in history and theology, including three widely acclaimed volumes on Marx based on a thorough reading of the manuscripts underlying *Capital.* He has participated in a one-on-one dialogue with Paul Ricoeur, and he has met for several years with Karl-Otto Apel in what has come to be known as the North–South Dialogue. Critical, scholarly articles on his philosophy of liberation have appeared in Spanish, French, Portuguese, German, and English circles, and book-length studies of his corpus have recently appeared in Spanish and German. To my knowledge, this is the first full-length book in English on the entirety of his philosophy.

One of the major tasks of this book, then, is to introduce Dussel's thought to an English-speaking audience, but such a presentation requires creative interpretation. In my opinion, the substance of Dussel's philosophy can be grasped through the idea of an "ethical hermeneutics" that seeks to interpret reality from the viewpoint of the "Other," as philosopher Emmanuel Levinas presents him or her. For Levinas, the category of the Other includes the poor, the stranger, the widow, or the orphan of the Jewish scriptures as well as contemporary analogates—those who are vanquished, forgotten, or excluded in any way from existing sociopolitical or cultural systems ("totalities," in Levinas's terminology). To substantiate this interpretation, I trace Dussel's development toward Levinas's philosophy through his early anthropological writings, his discussion of the Hegelian dialectic, and, finally, the stages of his own ethical theory. Dussel originally sought to overcome the ethics of modernity through a Heideggerian version of natural law ethics before passing on to Levinas, but his subsequent ethical hermeneutics continued to employ Heideggerian hermeneutical principles in the ethical service of Levinas's Other. Incidentally, his turn from natural law to Levinas permits a reconciliation with modernity, particularly critical theory.

But not only does Dussel appropriate Levinas's thought, he also transforms it by both transposing it to a Latin American setting and developing his own analectical method, which begins with the Other, recognizes the analogical character of the Other's word, unmasks false universals imposed upon the Other, and expands rationality through exposure to the Other. Dussel's transmutation of Levinas's thought enables him to explain the distinctiveness of Latin American philosophy, which is analogous to but not univocal with European philosophy. In addition, this Latin Americanizing of Levinas results in a philosophy that Dussel himself describes as "transmodern." This is so, on the one hand, because Dussel cannot afford to share the comfortable skepticism at times characterizing postmodernity, because he requires rationally based universal norms of justice to denounce the poverty and violations of human rights inflicted on Latin Americans. On the other hand, he cannot wholeheartedly partake of the Frankfurt School's optimism about the project of modernity, since Latin America's history of oppression, from the conquest of Mexico to present-day economic dependency, has so frequently been justified in the name of "rational," "modern," or "universal" values which have turned out to be only Eurocentric or North American. Ethical responsibility to the Other prohibits either the abandonment or the uncritical acceptance of universal norms and judgments.

To conclude this exposition of Dussel's thought, I show the relevance of his ethical hermeneutics to the domains of history, economics, and theology. Dussel's historical writings, admittedly perspectival in character but without being relativistic, seek objectivity by recovering the forgotten Other of history, as exemplified in his analysis of the discovery of America and the conquest of Mexico. On the basis of this analysis, Dussel relocates the origin of modernity in these worldwide events and thereby highlights the violent, exploitative underside of modernity, in contrast to those, such as Jürgen Habermas, who envision the more flattering, intra-European events of the Renaissance and Reformation as the origin of modernity. As regards economics, Dussel's careful reading of all Marx's pre-*Capital* manuscripts has yielded a new, philosophical Marx, one engaged in an ethical hermeneutics of the capitalist system. This Marx interprets capitalism in terms of its origin in and impact upon living labor—labor outside the system, in sheer destitution and yet the origin of value, coming to sell itself to the capitalist and discarded in economic crises. Although Marx allows Hegel's logic to describe the interior unfolding of capitalism's moments, Marx's main focus, in Dussel's novel interpretation, lies in the Other outside the system to whom one is ethically bound. Dussel, in effect, reads Marx along the lines more of Levinas or Schelling than of Hegel. He also shows how this "unknown" Marx is relevant, in the current predicament of Latin America, for avoiding the dangers of totalitarianism, economicism, and historical determinism that have plagued Marxism. Finally, he illustrates how even theology can avoid ideology by opening itself to the viewpoint of the Other.

The second major task of this book involves assessing a series of criticisms of Dussel's thought. American critics, such as Mexico's Horacio Cerutti Guldberg and the United States's Ofelia Schutte, attack Dussel for holding a "first philosophy" preeminent over the sciences and lacking any rational demonstration, for uncritically supporting Catholic Church positions and fascist forms of populism, and for advocating blind heteronomy in the face of the Other. Though I acknowledge Schutte's critique of Dussel's sexual ethics, I argue that Cerutti's and Schutte's criticisms, which portray him as indulging in irrationalism, can be adequately answered by referring to his Levinasian roots—roots which he himself often does not acknowledge. The rationality of Dussel's position cannot be understood, I believe, without understanding the rationality of Levinas's. To facilitate that understanding, an initial chapter situates Levinas within the prorational phenomenological tradition, since Levinas, too, explores the taken-for-granted horizons of theory itself, engages in a type of phenomenological description (unlike other kinds of description, though), and philosophizes self-reflectively about his own very peculiar type of philosophy.

Karl-Otto Apel raises pertinent criticisms as well. Though he tries to subsume the philosophy of liberation under his own tran-

scendental pragmatics, by presenting it as a mere application of
transcendental pragmatics, such a move fails to appreciate the
distinctiveness of Dussel's position. I suggest, instead, a division
of philosophical labor in which the philosophy of liberation and
transcendental pragmatics use their different methods for different purposes as part of the talk of a single rationality. This single
rationality owns up to its own often-overlooked presuppositions,
as it uncovers at a pretranscendental level the origins of theory
itself in the face-to-face, and reflects at the transcendental level
on the presupposed conditions of argument itself. Apel further
argues that Dussel's turn to Marx is utopian and anachronistic,
given the recent collapse of Eastern-bloc socialism. Although the
situation of Third World nations would mandate that Apel move
toward more economic planning in line with his ethics of responsibility, Dussel, it would seem, cannot avoid markets and their
inevitable alienation, even within such planned economies. But
Dussel's novel interpretation of Marx in intersubjective terms, as
seeking to reassert the rights of capitalism's forgotten Other,
undercuts the Frankfurt School's usual interpretation of Marx as
depending on German idealism's philosophy of the isolated consciousness triumphantly exerting its power over inert matter.
    Dussel's philosophy of liberation stands, then, at the intersec-
tion of a number of contemporary crossroads. In his thought,
several tensions, many of them unresolved and more polarized in
the North Atlantic philosophical community, play themselves out.
For instance, one can find in his work the opposition between
phenomenology and the Frankfurt School, between the universality of philosophy and its national/cultural distinctiveness, between natural law and modern ethics, between modernity and
postmodernity, between the situations of Latin America and those
of Eastern Europe, between the new Marx and the old Marx, and
between philosophy and other disciplines such as history, theology, economics, and the natural and social sciences. In my opinion, the question of rationality runs as a common thread through
all these antagonisms. My account of the rationality of Dussel's
thought, understood as an ethical hermeneutics at a pretranscendental level in the tradition of Levinas, can resolve many of these
tensions. It can also enable the philosophy of liberation to withstand most of the criticisms advanced against it by critics from

both sides of the Atlantic who accuse it of succumbing to forms of irrationality.

Finally, it is difficult to write a book on a living philosopher because one no sooner finishes the book than the philosopher has moved in new directions. This book presents the bases of Dussel's thought so that the reader will be able to understand his future progress, even though that progress might involve modifying or even retracting earlier positions. For instance, in a recent collection of essays entitled *The Underside of Modernity*, the reader can see Dussel moving out from the philosophy of liberation to engage the positions of Paul Ricoeur, Richard Rorty, and Charles Taylor, as well as Karl-Otto Apel. In addition, Dussel has just completed a major work, *Ética de la liberación en la edad de la globalización y de la exclusión* (Ethics of liberation in the age of globalization and exclusion), that subsumes the valid philosophical contributions of formal pragmatics and critical theory within a broader liberationist architectonic. Familiarity with the trajectory of Dussel's development, presented here, will equip the reader to understand more fully these subsequent extensions of his thought. Furthermore, it may well be that some of the critical suggestions advanced here will be recognized and incorporated in future works by Enrique Dussel, as he pursues his own historical evolution.

The author would like to thank Professors Bohrman, Caputo, Dussel, Marsh, and Punzo for their suggestions; the Department of Philosophy at St. Louis University and Rev. Theodore Vitali, C.P., for their support; the College of Arts and Sciences at St. Louis University for a generous Mellon Grant; Mr. Ollie Roundtree for his assistance; and the Leo Brown Jesuit Community for its patience and encouragement.

INTRODUCTION

In order to explore the theme of rationality in the thought of Enrique Dussel, in the first chapter I examine that same theme in the thought of Emmanuel Levinas, the philosopher on whom Dussel relies more than on any other. This question of rationality in Levinas is inseparably linked with the question of whether Levinas is actually doing phenomenology. Hence, the first chapter makes the case, against competing interpretations, that he is indeed a phenomenologist, albeit a unique kind, in the service of rationality, as was his predecessor Edmund Husserl. Like the later Husserl and the post-Husserlian generations of phenomenologists, Levinas criticizes theory by exploring its horizons, not in order to discredit it, but to make it more self-aware and, therefore, rational. Moreover, in his descriptions of the Other coming to appearance in ethico-practical relationships, Levinas struggles to recover an originary, forgotten experience overlain with uncriticized traditions and theories—as all phenomenology does. This Other, who commands from a height instead of being an equal, interchangeable term in a formal logical relationship, enhances rationality by initiating self-critique, inviting rational discourse in the first place, and thus impugning one-sided notions of rationality and expanding them. The ultimate test of the rationality of Levinas's position depends, however, on reflection on his methodology. Although his Other defies all phenomenological categories (and thus is not given as noema, intentional object, etc.), I argue that some kind of phenomenology must be at play in order to recognize positively who this Other is who does not submit to usual phenomenological categories. Jean François Lyotard's reading of Levinas helps clarify the latter's methodology by claiming that he depicts the attitude of one who receives a prescription (a "prescriptive") as opposed to one who comments on or reflects on the experience in order to test the prescription's validity (and so produces "denotatives"). However, since Levinas is depicting prescriptives, he is actually at a denotative, philosophical level, at one remove from the experience of receiving a prescriptive. In response to Derrida's radicalization of the question of Levinas's methodology—namely, that one must use language to get at what lies beyond language and to philosophize about what lies beyond philosophy—Levinas acknowledges that the very use of language to describe the Other both reveals and conceals the Other, who is "given" as a trace. In an ultimate self-reflective moment in *Otherwise Than Being*, Levinas admits that his own philosophizing— and he *is* philosophizing—inevitably brings the Other within the scope of Being and thus betrays the saying in the said. In a move reminiscent of transcendental phenomenology, Levinas attempts to redefine philosophy itself—as the task of continually reducing the betrayal of the saying in the said and of submitting to self-critique in the presence of the Other. The Other that phenomenology pushes to discover throws that very phenomenology off-balance and brings it to the severest self-criticism and rationality—which had been its dream all along.

Chapter 2 begins my critical exposition of the development of Dussel's philosophy of liberation and its implications, which extends into the next two chapters. In Chapter 2 I explain how Dussel, starting from a rather traditional education, arrives at a Levinasian position through studies of diverse philosophical anthropologies (the Hellenic and Semitic, for example) and the Hegelian dialectic and through the collapse of his Heideggerian version of natural law ethics. An effort at a Heideggerian retrieval of the Christian-Semitic unified anthropology—similar to Heidegger's own nondualist existential descriptions—from its Hellenic dualistic superimpositions leads Dussel to discover the unity of the human person as a "supplicating carnality." This unified anthropology reflects Hebraic-Semitic categories marked by an ethics of alterity, like Levinas's, beyond institutionalized Christendom and even Heidegger himself. Such an exercise in Heideggerian retrieval does not reject Hellenic rationalism, but shows that same rationalism correcting its own errors, reflexively appropriating its own past, destroying inauthentic history, and rendering historiography more rational. Though appreciating the valuable aspects of Hegel's dialectical method, Dussel rejects his Absolute, because it represents the subject of modernity "elevated to actual infinity which englobes everything in an absolute immanence without exteriority." In his flight into consciousness, Hegel forgets the point of embarkation that the post-Hegelians and Levinas have finally recovered: the ethico-practical relationship with the concrete Other. In restoring to Hegel what Hegel himself presupposes without admitting, one makes Hegel the archrationalist even more rational. Finally, in his early ethics, Dussel fuses the natural law tradition of ethics with fundamental Heideggerian ontology in such a way that moral conscience appears as the voice of Being summoning one to heed one's authentic nature and to adopt responsibly and resolutely one's own fundamental project instead of mindlessly conforming to the pressures of *das Man*. From this perspective, Dussel attacks modern ethics, which, because of its focus from Descartes to Kant on the subject, independent of ontology, "hangs in the air," forfeits any check on arbitrary subjectivity, and thus climaxes in Nietzsche's will-to-power. But through his exposure to Levinas, Dussel comes to see that Heidegger really presents, not an ethics, but the ethically neutral conditions of the possibility of good and evil. Levinas, on the contrary, provides him with an ethical context situating Heideggerian ontology, placing all Heideggerian categories under an index of orientation toward the Other, and revealing authentic Otherness beyond *Mitsein*. This turn to Levinas enables Dussel to separate ethics from ontology, embrace the modern tradition's separation of the 'is' from the 'ought,' and pinpoint his difference with modernity in a fear of the arbitrariness of the subject that is lacking to modernity. I argue, though, that Kant and particularly dialogic (as opposed to monologic) critical theory in the Kantian tradition are also aware of this arbitrariness and battle against it. This criticism and my rebuttals to several other of Dussel's criticisms of Kant pave the way for a possible reconciliation between the philosophy of liberation and modernity, particularly critical theory, provided the distinctiveness of their levels, methods, and tasks within a common rational architectonic is preserved.

Dussel appropriates Levinas's theory but also transforms it, as Chapter 3 illustrates, by setting it in a Latin American context and developing a unique *analectical method* that begins with the Other and discovers the *analogical* word of the Other. The metaphysi-

cally distinct Other, whose alterity exceeds that of the ontologically different, calls for an apprenticeship of listening and trust in
which one resists reducing the analogical word of the Other to
univocity with one's own. The Eurocentric proclivity to see in all
philosophy that employs Western philosophical categories, such
as Dussel's, merely an extension or application of itself engages
in such reductionism to the univocal. In spite of Dussel's exalta-
tion of the universal at the expense of the particular prior to his
discovery of Levinas, and in spite of his faulty universalizations
particularly in the domain of sexual ethics, the later Dussel employs his analectic method to unmask false processes of universalization. Such false "univocation" becomes evident in modes of
political and economic domination—in the conquest of Mexico,
for example, or in contemporary economic theories of development, in Eurocentric patterns of cultural understanding from Aristotle's politics to Rousseau's pedagogy to Freud's erotics, in
certain Roman Catholic practices and teachings, in brands of
theological research, and in dialectics and negative dialectics,
swirling in their own own vortices instead of beginning with a
positive affirmation of the Other. Even science, whose objects are
constituted within praxis, could profit from Dussel's heuristic of
ethically oriented suspicion, since contact with the frequently
overlooked exteriority heightens objectivity. The illumination
sought after in taking up the hermeneutic position of the oppressed suggests that Dussel is doing more than skeptically uncovering false universals: he is engaging in a hermeneutics ethically
bound to the Other—an ethical hermeneutics—that improves
prospects of knowledge. When one adopts an ethos of liberation,
one enhances rationality by bringing to light unnoticed values
and emphases, opening horizons of the possible constitution of
objects, deculturating oneself, deepening in self-criticism, facing
anomalies that force paradigm revision, ensuring more thorough
correspondence with the real, and even exposing the Other and
other cultures to critique undertaken respectfully and for their
sake. The prorational character of Dussel's work becomes clear
in his *1492: El encubrimiento del Otro—Hacia el origen del "Mito de
modernidad"* (1492: The covering over of the Other—Toward the
origin of the "myth of modernity"), in which he attacks, not reason, but the irrational myth accompanying modernity and justify-

INTRODUCTION xix

ing its violence in the name of development or civilization. Not as
disdainful of rationality as is postmodernity and not as optimistic
about the modern project as is modernity, Dussel concludes the
volume by classifying himself as a "transmodernist." Both his
skepticism and his rationalism derive from his ethical hermeneutics, which interprets events of history and structures of society
from the perspective of the poor and outcast Other and thus fuses
Levinas's ethical passion with the hermeneutics of Martin Heidegger, whose earlier impact on Dussel has never been totally neutral-
ized.

Chapter 4 traces the implications of Dussel's ethical hermeneutics for history, economics, and theology. Dussel's historical writings use a nonpositivistic methodology that recognizes the
perspectival nature of history writing, while seeking to ensure objectivity through retrieving the viewpoint of the forgotten Other
of history. His *1492: El encubrimiento del Otro* exemplifies this eth-
ico-hermeneutical approach to the writing of history. Tracing the
history of the "discovery of America" from the landing on Guanahaní (San Salvador) to the conquest of Mexico, it describes the
diverse worldviews of the Spanish and the indigenous peoples,
highlighting the viewpoint of Moctezuma, the vanquished and
discredited emperor of the oppressed indigenous peoples. Dussel
also uses this work to correct a false periodification of history
which would locate the origin of modernity in the intra-European
and Europe-flattering events of the Renaissance and the Reformation. He argues, instead, that modernity began with the worldwide
event of the conquest of the Americas, in which the European
ego practically constituted itself prior to Descartes's theoretical
ego cogito and the other face of modernity—its irrationality, violence, and exploitativeness—becomes evident. As regards the
economy, Dussel, who had lambasted Marx in his earlier writings,
undertakes a more sympathetic evaluation of Marx's interpretation of capitalism. Dussel's reading of all the pre-*Capital* manuscripts revealed to him a philosophical Marx (Althusser's
interpretation notwithstanding) focused on living labor, which,
exterior to the capitalist system, has at one and the same time
absolute poverty as an object and the universal possibility of
wealth as an active subject. In Dussel's view, Marx undertakes an
ethical hermeneutics of capitalism, interpreting it in terms of its

origin in and impact upon living labor. With great originality, Dussel reconstrues the Hegel/Marx relationship by placing the point of Marx's rupture with Hegel in his focus on exteriority, on living labor beyond the system. Although Hegel's logic can be used to describe the internal moments of capital, Dussel's Marx is really interested in the ethical relationship with the Other beyond that system, and so begins to appear much less like Hegel and much more like Schelling or Levinas. On the basis of this fresh reading of Marx, Dussel illustrates how capitalists, their theoreticians, the workers themselves, and even the Marxist theoretical tradition from Lukács to Habermas have fallen into hermeneutical errors. Marx's ethical hermeneutics forms an interpretive framework or heuristic focused on the forgotten Other of the economy—just as it concentrated on the forgotten Other of history—a framework seeking to provide a higher-level context for empirical research in the tradition of German *Wissenschaft*. This Levinasian Marx has great significance for interpreting the Latin American situation and for evading the dangers of totalitarianism, rigid economicism, and historical determinism of previous Marxism. Finally, Dussel's ethical hermeneutics can preclude any use of theology as an ideological support for the status quo, as becomes clear in his critique of the "Documento de consulta" (Document of consultation) for Puebla.

In Chapters 5 and 6 I assess Dussel's philosophy of liberation in the face of criticisms advanced by his American critics Horacio Cerutti Guldberg and Ofelia Schutte and by Karl-Otto Apel. Cerutti and Schutte find Dussel engaging in self-righteous moral superiority, holding a first philosophy for which he provides no rational demonstration, assuming preeminence over the sciences (and, as a result, for instance, neglecting the multicausal character of international economic dependence), claiming to have surpassed all European rationality and previous Latin American thought, being driven by unacknowledged religious commitments (to the point of reduplicating the Church's teachings, even the condemnation of divorce), supporting Perón's fascist populism, and fostering uncritical heteronomy before the Other. Most of these criticisms center in the accusation that Dussel is an irrationalist, and flow from Cerutti's and Schutte's own positive valuation of rationality and its mandates to avoid dogmatism, give an account of oneself, remain open to maximal possible self-criticism, and test all validity claims, even those originating from the Other, instead of committing the genetic fallacy by arguing that origin proves validity. Although I agree with Schutte that Dussel's sexual ethics reflects an inadequate attention to alterity, many of Cerutti's and Schutte's criticisms betray a lack of familiarity with Dussel's Levinasian bases, perhaps because Dussel is often reluctant to acknowledge them. To understand adequately both the nature of Dussel's "foundation" and its "indemonstrability," and his seemingly arrogant claims of having surpassed European rationality or earlier Latin American thought, one needs to have a more thorough grasp of Levinas's method of phenomenological description, its unearthing of the presuppositions of "proof" itself, the relationship between Levinas's phenomenology and the sciences, and the meaning of ethics as first philosophy in Levinas. The charge of uncritical heteronomy overlooks numerous texts of Dussel's and fails to consider the autonomy of the I that is upheld by Levinas's phenomenological starting point as well as by such key notions as separation, enjoyment and identity, interiority, apology, discourse, and election. Though Dussel himself, in my opinion, has responded adequately to the attack that he supported Peronist fascism, a retrieval of his Levinasian roots makes possible a response to the many trenchant criticisms that Schutte and Cerutti have raised. Such a response would indicate that Dussel could agree as well with the positive endorsement of rationality underlying their negative verdict on him.

In Chapter 6, I present Karl-Otto Apel's two penetrating criticisms of Dussel's philosophy of liberation: (*a*) that Apel's transcendental pragmatics achieves the same solidarity and openness to the Other as the philosophy of liberation does and so can replace it, with the philosophy of liberation fulfilling the subordinate role of removing the barriers to the implementation (at level B of Apel's theory) of transcendental pragmatics; and (*b*) that Dussel's reappropriation of Marx is anachronistic, given the collapse of Eastern-bloc socialism. In response to the first criticism, I argue that Apel overlooks differences between himself and Dussel and that Dussel's theory could accommodate Apel's through Levinas's concept of the Third. In place of a competition in which transcendental pragmatics and the philosophy of liberation each seek to subsume the other, I suggest a division of philosophical labor in which Dussel and Apel operate with different methodologies for different purposes within a common architectonic. The philosophy of liberation and transcendental pragmatics are the work of a single rationality, authentically owning up to what it usually bypasses or ignores, whether reflecting on the horizons prior to the origin of theory or on the operative but unadmitted presuppositions of argumentation itself. Without the philosophy of liberation, one would lose sight of an account of origins; of the constant challenge that the Other, as exterior to every totality, poses for hermeneutics, validity claims, and contractual agreements; and of the motivation on which selfless, daring, and heroic emancipation relies. Regarding Apel's second criticism, it is necessary to understand that Dussel reads Marx in the tradition of German *Wissenschaft* and therefore construes him as constructing an ethical hermeneutics of the capitalist economy in order to keep clearly in sight the forgotten Other of capitalism, living labor. Although such a hermeneutics never ought to contradict economic facts, no empirical phenomena of the economy can refute this hermenuetical framework, any more than individual historical facts can abolish the decision to interpret history by focusing on its suppressed Other. I further contend that Apel's critique of Dussel's dependence theory fails to grasp the abstract level of Dussel's analysis. In reaction to Apel's charge that Dussel should be reformist instead of utopian, I explain how in a Third World setting Apel's reformism would have to move toward a more revolutionary stance and a more thoroughly planned economy in keeping with Apel's endorsement of an ethics of responsibility at level B of his own theory. On the other hand, following Franz Hinkelammert, I do not see how Dussel can avoid the existence of a market even in revolutionary settings, with the inevitable alienation that follows. Finally, Dussel's interpretation of Marx in Levinasian/Schellingian intersubjective terms offsets critical theory's attack on Marx's theories of alienation, surplus value, and history as being bound within the parameters of German idealism's philosophy of isolated consciousness.

A word of caution: throughout this book, references will be made to Dussel's theological writings basically in order to illustrate the implications of his philosophical positions. There is no expectation that the reader share Dussel's religious faith, and no demonstration of God's existence is given here. However, when one seeks to understand an author fully, it seems somewhat artificial to isolate completely that author's philosophy from the rest of his (in this case, historical and theological) writings, even if one does not share the fundamental presuppositions of those writings.

1

Emmanuel Levinas's Phenomenology and the Allegiance to Reason

EMMANUEL LEVINAS'S RELATIONSHIP to phenomenology and its commitment to rationality would appear ambiguous. On the one hand, commentators speak of his anti-phenomenology and anti-ontology, describe him as struggling *against* philosophy, and pit him against the rationally oriented universal pragmatics of Jürgen Habermas and Karl-Otto Apel. Even Levinas himself comes close to belittling the rigorous philosophical method characteristic of phenomenology and philosophical rationality:

> There you have my response to the question of method. I would also say to you that I know no more about it. I do not believe that there is a possible transparency in method or that philosophy is possible as transparency. Those who have spent their lives on methodology have written many books to replace the more interesting books they would have been able to write. Too bad for the march in the sun without shadows that philosophy would be.[1]

On the other hand, Levinas at times acknowledges that, from the point of view of philosophical method and discipline, he remains to this day a phenomenologist. He admits that his analyses are in the spirit of Husserlian philosophy, even if he does not follow it to the letter. For him, the presentation and development of notions employed in *Totality and Infinity* "owe everything to the phenomenological method." Theodore de Boer considers Levinas's philosophy as combining transcendental, phenomenological method with the dialogical method developed by Martin Buber and Franz Rosenzweig.[2]

A careful study of whether or in what sense Levinas is or is not a phenomenologist will provide us with insight into his unique

meaning of "rationality," and will prepare us to grasp the notion
of rationality underlying the works of Enrique Dussel, who, in
spite of many original modifications of Levinas's thought, nevertheless relies heavily on it.

THE CRITIQUE OF THEORY: THE HORIZONS OF THEORY

As is well known, Husserl's phenomenological reflections at the
time of *Cartesian Meditations* were moving in the direction of a
transcendental idealism. Heidegger reacted against Husserl's idealism by emphasizing the modes of existence pertaining to prere-
flexive being-in-the-world, from which theoretical thought arose.
Hence, Heidegger described the pragmatic relationships with
things (*Zuhandenheit*) that precede any consideration of them as
objects, independent of their usefulness for us (*Vorhandenheit*).
Existentialism followed Heidegger by focusing on how human existence, the lived body, substitutes for the transcendental ego.
Concurring with many of these developments, Levinas notes that
contemporary phenomenologists tend to move from what is
thought toward the plenitude of that which is thought, discovering new dimensions of meaning. Levinas observes ironically,
though, that several of these critics of Husserl made use of his
insights and methods in their own phenomenologies. In fact,
apart from these criticisms and even in reaction to them, Husserl
indicates in his own writings that representative consciousness,
which isolates what is given into distinct objects, is embedded in
horizons of nonobjectifying consciousness. Husserl, anticipating
many of his successors, recognized that conditions of corporate
or cultural existence lie beneath and beyond representation.[3]

Husserl's recognition of this fact becomes evident in *The Crisis
of European Sciences and Transcendental Phenomenology*, written years
after Heidegger's *Being and Time*. There Husserl charges those
who would establish a completely self-sufficient logic with naïveté,
since this logic's

> self-evidence lacks scientific grounding in the universal life-world a
> priori, which it always presupposes in the form of things taken for
> granted, which are never scientifically, universally formulated,
> never put in the general form proper to a science of essence. Only

when this radical, fundamental science exists can such a logic itself become a science. Before this it hangs in mid-air, without support, and is, as it has been up to now, so very naïve that it is not even aware of the task which attaches to every objective logic, every a priori science in the usual sense, namely, that of discovering how this logic itself is to be grounded, hence no longer "logically" but by being traced back to the universal prelogical a priori through which everything logical, the total edifice of objective theory in all its methodological forms, demonstrates its legitimate sense and from which, then, all logic itself must receive its norms.[4]

As this excerpt illustrates, Husserl saw clearly that the very dynamism of reason leads beyond the limits of "the total edifice of objective theory" to explore horizons taken for granted in different branches of that edifice. In "The Vienna Lecture," he traces the resolve to examine these horizons and not to accept unquestioningly any pregiven opinion or tradition back to the universality of the Greek critical stance at the origin of philosophy. Husserl chides mathematical natural science as *lacking in rationality* for its forgetting and refusing to investigate the intuitively given surrounding world and the nature of the consciousness that undertakes natural science.[5]

Vestiges of this same Husserlian zeal for giving a rational account surface in Levinas's preface to *Totality and Infinity* after he acknowledges his debt to Franz Rosenzweig's *Stern der Erlösung* and to the phenomenological method, to which the presentation and development of his notions owe everything.

> Intentional analysis is the search for the concrete. Notions held under the direct gaze of the thought that defines them are, nevertheless, unbeknown to this naïve thought, revealed to be implanted in horizons unsuspected by this thought. What does it matter if in the Husserlian phenomenology taken literally these unsuspected horizons are in their turn interpreted as thoughts aiming at objects! What counts is the idea of the overflowing of objectifying thought by a forgotten experience from which it lives.[6]

Levinas's enterprise seems, then, to parallel Husserl's return to the life-world horizons underlying theory, although these horizons will not be found to contain "thoughts aiming at objects." The direction of his analysis partakes of that search, typical of post-Husserl generations, to dig beneath theory in order to turn

up theory's own preconditions. But is Levinas anti-phenomeno-
logical or anti-rational in adopting this orientation? Is his turn to
the pretheoretical actually in the interests of a more comprehensive rationality, leaving no presuppositions unexamined, as Husserl's was? Is his pretheoretical in fact protheoretical, as Husserl's
was? Such questions can be answered only after we discuss what
Levinas finds as he turns to these forgotten horizons.

The Phenomenology of the Other and
the Struggle to Be Rational

Levinas's regressive uncovering of the forgotten experiences from
which theory arises depicts how the Other appears in dyadic relationships to a "me," that is, to Levinas the phenomenologist and,
Levinas hopes, to the reader following his text. According to this
fresh phenomenological description, which can be fully recap-
tured only by presenting Levinas's major works in their entirety,
the irreducible Other calls into question my spontaneity and appears as a Master who judges me, who is not on the same plane as
I am, who commands me from a position of height, who speaks
to me as a first word, "You shall not commit murder," who offers
me the resistance of what has no resistance—ethical resistance—
and who demands not to be left without food. In *Otherwise Than
Being*, Levinas describes this practical human relationship as occurring at the level of bodily sensibility that, like Merleau-Ponty's
analysis of bodiliness, is not constituted by a Cartesian consciousness first deciding to establish a relationship with one's own body
or with the Other. This sensibility consists, rather, in exposure to
others, vulnerability to them, and responsibility in proximity to
them prior to thematization, apophansis, willed responses, and
consciousness conscious of consciousness.[7]

The height from which the Other commands—not as my equal,
not as identical or interchangeable with me—is leveled out when
I consider human relationships through the prism of formal
logic, in which terms are reversible, read indifferently from left
to right and from right to left. In formal logic, instead of taking
account of how the Other appears to me as I stand face to face
with him, I remove myself from the direct face-to-face and "from

above" look upon myself as a neutral A in relation to the Other as B, who is equally related to me as A. In this extrinsic, third-person perspective, in which A and B appear interchangeably related, I distance myself from the ethical demands that I experience when face to face with B. The extrinsic, logical description from a third-person perspective hides the ethical inequalities and disequilibria intrinsically present in the face-to-face. In Levinas's terms, I replace the face-to-face with the "alongside of."[8]

Similarly, in *Otherwise Than Being*, Levinas finds the contents of propositions, the said, obscuring the underlying saying activity, the ethico-practical relationship to an Other whose hostage I am. Should I formulate this relationship itself in propositions within the said, I would again speak of the Other and myself from a third-person perspective, as if we were two objects in the same discourse. All the while, I would be distracted from the nonreciprocity of my utter responsibility for the Other to whom I am saying these propositions. Similarly, Levinas notes that the experience of being vulnerable to the Other, "on the surface of the skin characteristic of sensibility," is "anaesthetized" in the process of knowing.[9]

Formal-logical processes, the utilization of language within the said, and the process of knowing itself effectively obscure the radically demanding features of the face-to-face. Only a disciplined effort to let those features appear in their authenticity can disclose them. Levinas describes his own disciplined effort in phenomenological terms: "One has to go back to that hither side, starting from the trace retained by the said, in which everything shows itself. The movement back to the saying is the phenomenological reduction."[10]

Levinas mentions several other major presuppositions of the Western philosophical tradition that must be overcome if one is to recognize the exigencies accompanying the Other's appearance, particularly the presupposition that one must always begin philosophizing with the freedom of the ego concerned only for itself. Because of this presupposed starting point, people insist that they cannot be held to answer when they have not done anything; they feel that it is questionable whether they are really their brother's or sister's keeper; they look on every Other as a limitation inviting war, domination, and precaution; and, finally, like Hobbes, they believe that society commences with a war of all against all. In addition to these presuppositions, there is another major philosophical prejudice that Levinas withstands in his effort to return to what precedes all theory: namely, that ethics is a mere problematic addition to the more fundamental philosophical disciplines of epistemology and ontology.[11]

If the guiding principle of Husserlian phenomenology is the refusal to accept unexamined cultural and philosophical prejudices so that the things themselves might come to appearance more clearly, then Levinas remains faithful to the spirit of phenomenology. Levinas himself readily acknowledges, though, that he has not implemented phenomenological reduction according to Husserl's rules and has not respected the entirety of Husserlian methodology. For Husserl, to the extent that logical positivism partakes of the prejudice that all judgments be based on empirical experience without first studying the essential types of judgment and the domains they treat, it is less than rational. For Husserl, to the extent that the natural sciences refuse to give any account of the intuitively surrounding world from which they arise, they succumb to prejudice and irrationality. Even in trying to bring to light the authentic features of human intersubjectivity at the origin of theory, encrusted over as they have been with mistaken assumptions, Levinas too is attempting to render theory, philosophical or otherwise, more rational.[12]

Not only is the rationality of Levinas's position shown in the fact that he uncovers the forgotten Other, but this very Other itself also augments rationality by initiating self-criticism. By engaging in theoretical processes, I show that I am not abandoned to my drives and impulsive movements; on the contrary, I distrust myself. In putting myself in question in this way, I act "unnaturally." Levinas refuses to trace this self-critical stance back to my aggressive spontaneity's discovery of its limits and its desperate search to circumvent these limits. To locate the origin of reflective self-criticism here would leave my spontaneity both unchallenged at its root and intact. Rather, self-critique is born in the Other, who calls my spontaneity itself into question. "The essence of reason consists not in securing for man a foundation and powers, but in calling him in question and in inviting him to justice." The demand for theoretical self-critique reflects prior ethical exigencies sedimented within it.[13]

Furthermore, one embarks upon discourse and gives reasons because some Other has asked an account; rational discourse itself is an ethical response.

> Thus I cannot evade by silence the discourse with the epiphany that occurs as a face opens, as Thrasymachus, irritated, tries to do in the first book of the *Republic*. . . . The face opens the primordial discourse whose first word is obligation, which no "interiority" permits avoiding. It is that discourse that obliges the entering into discourse, the commencement of discourse rationalism prays for, a "force" that convinces even "the people who do not wish to listen," and thus founds the true universality of reason.[14]

Levinas repeatedly tries to situate the search for truth in the context of a relationship with an Other who requests a response. For instance, in the preface to *Totality and Infinity*, he struggles to show that eschatological judgment of the Other upon the truth of the totality does not lead to irrationalism and subjectivism. In Section I, parts B ("Separation and Discourse") and C ("Truth and Justice") of *Totality and Infinity*, he presents the pursuit of truth unfolding within relationships under the mandate to be just. The subsection "Ethics and the Face" in Section III of the same work begins with ethics and ends with a discussion of reason. The ethical relationship is not, then, contrary to truth, but accomplishes the very intention that animates the movement into truth. Speech lies at the origin of truth, not Heideggerian disclosure, which takes place within the solitude of vision.[15]

This Other teaches and introduces something new into thought. "The absolutely foreign alone can instruct us." This Other issues a challenge, to any "Rationality" that is capable of attributing "order" to a world where one sells "the poor person for a pair of sandals." Thus, the Other, outside of reigning systems of rationality, opens the way for more authentic and comprehensive notions of rationality. Of course, we do not heed the Other's ethical appeal solely in order to enrich our fund of knowledge, since that would be to subordinate the Other to our investigative purposes, to our *telos*, to our totality, within which we would nevertheless remain entrapped. Paradoxically, one learns most where one gives oneself over to the Other without taking thought for how one might intellectually profit from this giving over.[16]

It is clearly a mistake to place Levinas in the camp of anti-phe-nomenological or anti-rational postmodernists. He imitates Hus-serl's philosophical rigor in exploring forgotten horizons, in criticizing taken-for-granted presuppositions, and in illuminating phenomena never before seen clearly. The pretheoretical that he elucidates, the Other, induces self-critique, ushers in discourse and rational processes, and impugns one-sided notions of ratio-nality and expands them. Like Husserl, Levinas's pretheoretical would appear to be protheoretical. But we must not rest content too soon, for other considerations point to ways in which Levi-nas's thought seems to undermine phenomenology and head for irrationality.

PHENOMENOLOGY AND RATIONALITY IN LEVINAS

The Other who comes to appearance in the ethico-practical rela-tionship described by Levinas's phenomenological endeavor de-fies usual phenomenological categories. The Other is not a noema. When the Other gives meaning to his or her presence, an event irreducible to evidence occurs, which does not enter into an intuition. This revelation by Others constitutes a "veritable inversion" of any objectifying cognition. The mode in which the face is given does not consist in figuring as a theme under our gaze, in spreading itself forth as a set of qualities forming an image; rather, the knowledge that thematizes is subverted here and turned into conversation. Whereas things have no meaning of their own apart from our *Sinngebung*, the face of the Other signifies before we have projected light upon it. In *Otherwise Than Being*, Levinas defines intentionality as "an aspiration to be filled and fulfillment, the centripetal movement of a consciousness that coincides with itself, recovers, and rediscovers itself without age-ing, rests in self-certainty, confirms itself, doubles itself up, consol-idates itself, thickens into substance."[17] Intentionality, so defined, ineptly apprehends the proximity of the Other, who, for Levinas, cannot be confined within a "consciousness of" and who inverts intentionality. Given the fact that Husserlian intentionality bears the trace of the voluntary and the teleological, Levinas refuses to describe the subject on the basis of intentionality, representational activity, objectification, or freedom and will. Rather than starting with subjectivity as intentionality, founded on auto-affection, Levinas approaches the subject in terms of the passivity of time, a lapse of time, irrecuperable and outside all will, the exact contrary of intentionality. The Other appears to this subject, not as phenomena or an apparition in the full light, but as a trace and an enigma that disturb phenomena.[18]

This strange Other, given as an "object" in the face-to-face relationship and yet given totally differently from any object, evokes conflicting assessments of Levinas's project on the part of commentators. De Boer, for instance, holds that Levinas's method is not the intuitive, explicating disclosure of the phenomenologists. Similarly, Adriaan Peperzak insists that the Other is not a new sort of phenomenon that can be located among and conjoined with other kinds of phenomena. But Alphonso Lingis believes that in *Totality and Infinity* Levinas works out the phenomenological analysis of facing and that in *Otherwise Than Being* alterity takes form and "becomes a phenomenon in the face of another."[19]

To resolve this question of Levinas's phenomenology, one must pay attention to the way he focuses on the Other as an "object" over against the subject, which this Other overwhelms and whose intentionality this Other disrupts.

> The idea of infinity hence does not proceed from the I, nor from a need in the I gauging exactly its own voids; here the movement proceeds from what is thought and not from the thinker. It is the unique knowledge that presents this inversion—a knowledge without a priori. . . . desire is an aspiration that the Desirable animates; it originates from its "object"; it is revelation—whereas need is a void of the Soul; it proceeds from the subject.[20]

Levinas reaffirms this preeminence of the Other over against the subject in *Otherwise Than Being* when he notes that responsibility for the Other does not begin in my commitment, but comes, rather, from the hither side of my freedom, from a "prior to every memory," an "ulterior to every accomplishment." Just as for Husserl the objects of diverse regional ontologies prescribe rules for the manifolds of appearances and distinctive modes of investigation (including distinctive phenomenologies), so for Levinas this "object" unlike any other object, the Other, dictates a unique method of approach, irreducible to other approaches, irreducible even to previous modes of phenomenology. Hence, the Other resists being subsumed under previous phenomenological categories (such as intentionality, noema, etc.).[21]

But how is it possible that Levinas can point out the ways in which the Other eludes such phenomenological categorizations? Has he not apprehended the Other at least sufficiently enough to recognize that all these phenomenological characterizations fall short of or distort the true sense of the Other? Levinas, it would seem, must presuppose a type of phenomenological reflection to which the Other is given enough that one can determine the unsuitability of all previous phenomenological conceptions to this given. As Husserl utilized phenomenological theory to go beyond theory itself to phenomenological theory, Levinas's phenomenology probes even more radically, even to the point of unsettling phenomenology itself. By being absolutely phenomenological and returning to the "things themselves," Levinas penetrates into a domain where phenomenology itself no longer works. As such, he proves himself the eminent phenomenologist he is. Levinas himself, speaking of philosophy in general, highlights this paradox: "The fact that philosophy cannot fully totalize the alterity of meaning in some final presence or simultaneity is not for me a deficiency or fault. Or to put it another way, the best thing about philosophy is that it fails. It is better that philosophy fail to totalize meaning—even though, as ontology, it has attempted just this—for it thereby remains open to the irreducible otherness of transcendence."[22]

Of further relevance to this question of the phenomenological character of Levinas's work is Jean-François Lyotard's essay "Levinas' Logic." Lyotard detects similarities between Levinas and Kant in that both were interested in safeguarding the specificity of prescriptive discourse. Just as Levinas understands ethical expressions such as "Welcome the alien" as having their own authority in themselves, so Kant argues that the principles of practical reason are independent of those of theoretic reason and that one cannot draw the principle of prescriptive reason from any object language. It is, however, the differences between Kant and Levinas that are most instructive.[23]

Lyotard distinguishes between prescriptive and denotative statements. Prescriptions issue a straightforward order, such as "Close the door," and ask not to be commented on but to be executed. Denotations involve commentary on orders, descriptions, explanations. Commentators, instead of going to close the door, might ask how it is possible for a prescriptive statement to produce an act instead of (or as well as) its intellection, and in so doing they transform an immediate prescriptive into a "metalinguistic 'image' of the expression." Denotative transcriptions effectively neutralize the executive force of an order. Recipients and executors of commands are mere addressees, but when they assume the role of commentator on these commands, they become addressers. When philosophers embark on such commentary on prescriptives, even when they find such prescriptives valid, they dissolve ethics by making it pass under the jurisdiction of the true. Readers, in confronting commentaries such as Kant's *Critique of Practical Reason*, find themselves addressed by denotative propositions requiring them to understand and assent or dissent, but not to do. They read, not orders, but declarations that certain orders are valid norms. As Lyotard sums it up, "the statement of an obligation is not an obligation."[24]

But, Lyotard points out, Kant does not and cannot sufficiently ensure the specificity of prescriptive statements. The addressee of the moral law ceases to be in the position of the Thou to whom the prescription is addressed once that addressee partakes in Kant's discourse. Rather, the addressee now becomes the I who delivers an opinion as to whether a prescription is or is not universalizable. In effect, Levinas focuses his attention on the experience of the prescriptive statement as it confronts us, before our later description and analysis of the prescription will test whether we can convert that prescription into a universal norm. Prescriptions can become norms only if they can be rewritten as universal norms, and, of course, philosophical reflection is absolutely necessary to establish such universality and to distinguish rational from irrational prescriptions. But two different attitudes are at play when one receives a prescription and when one reflects on whether that prescription is validly universalizable. For Levinas, "the simplest prescription, instructively empty but pragmatically affirmative, at one stroke situates the one to whom it is addressed outside the universe of knowledge."[25]

Lyotard's essay clarifies a new dimension of Levinas's thought, beyond his careful and original exposure of the unique way in which the Other, the "*object*," comes to appearance, underneath the theoretical constructs that level out the Other's height. The *subject*, faced with the Other's prescription, has the experience of being bound to the Other, seized by the presence of a Thou, before the subject ever begins to reflect upon that prescription. This attitude on the part of the subject differs radically from the attitude of reflection on prescriptions in which one enters a universe of denotative propositions, weighs the grounds for universalizing such prescriptions, and issues statements requiring their address-ees not to act but to understand and to agree or offer counterar-guments. Levinas, with Lyotard's exposition, would seem to be engaging in the delicate phenomenological process of disentan-gling the differing subjective attitudes through which objects present themselves, correlative, of course, to different objects ap-pearing to those attitudes. Here again, Levinas's effort is analo-gous to Husserl's endeavor to specify the kinds of rational procedures and modes of apprehending appropriate to different regional ontologies.[26]

But one might still take exception to Lyotard's contrast of Kant and Levinas. After all, isn't Levinas *describing* the Other and the obediential attitude the Other evokes? Isn't Levinas, like Kant, bringing the prescriptive under the dominion of denotative dis-course? For all his revealing insights, doesn't Levinas's very dis-course neutralize and conceal the force of the Other's solicitation? Does the very form of the discourse betray the very topic it discusses? Jacques Derrida poses several of these questions to Levinas and thereby exacts the ultimate and most profound self-reflection on Levinas's own project and its phenomenologi-cal/rational nature.

Derrida formulates many of these questions in his critique of *Totality and Infinity* in his famous essay "Violence and Metaphys-ics." He interprets Levinas as attempting to open toward the be-yond of philosophical discourse by means of philosophy. But Levinas encounters problems when he attempts to express his findings in language. Since Levinas feels compelled to renounce all language as totalizing, Derrida charges that he cannot speak positively of Infinity as infinite alterity and cannot employ even the words "infinite" and "Other." Since the Other cannot be translated into the rational coherence of language, thought appears stifled in the region of the origin of language as dialogue and difference. "This origin, as the concrete condition of rationality, is nothing less than 'irrational,' but it could not be 'included' in language." Derrida classifies Levinas as an empiricist, who dreams of a pure presentation of the purely given—as Hegel presented empiricism in his *Encyclopedia*, a dream which must vanish at daybreak, as soon as language awakens. In addition, Levinas appears to be caught in a dilemma with respect to phenomenology. Either he deprives himself of the very foundation and possibility of his own language by not permitting the infinitely Other to be given through an intentional modification of the ego, as Husserl does—that is, with reference to any transcendental perspective. Or his metaphysics presupposes the very transcendental philosophy that it seeks to put into question.[27]

Levinas clearly took account of these questions before writing *Otherwise Than Being*, although, as Robert Bernasconi observes, he never explicitly recognizes Derrida's contribution. Levinas admits quite freely that he thematizes that which eludes thematization, subsuming under being that which is otherwise than being: "The very discussion which we are at the moment elaborating about signification, diachrony and the transcendence of the approach beyond being, a discussion that means to be philosophy, is a thematizing, a synchronizing of terms, a recourse to systematic language, a constant use of the verb being, a bringing back into the bosom of being all signification allegedly conceived beyond being."[28]

Our descriptions of the Other never grasps the Other; it grasps only a "trace" in which the Other is both revealed and hidden, in which the Other obsesses the subject without staying in correlation with the subject. The Other orders me before appearing. When faced by the inscrutable Other, all language stands "under erasure," as Derrida would put it. A presence is given which is the shadow of itself; that which is absence comes to pseudo-presence; a being lurks in its trace. Just as the trace escapes the dilemma of

either revealing or concealing by doing both, so Levinas's phenomenology is a hybrid, both phenomenology and not phenomenology, because of the Other facing it. Levinas pushes
phenomenology to its extreme and thereby uncovers that which
revises the significance of all phenomenological categories. This
very undoing of phenomenology depends on the rigorous application of the phenomenological spirit.[29]

In fact, these paradoxes lead Levinas to conceive philosophy
itself in novel terms. What is shown in the said is shown by betraying its meaning, but philosophy's task now becomes that of reducing that betrayal.

> It [God or the Other] is non-thematizable, and even here is a
> theme only because in a said everything is conveyed before us, even
> the ineffable, at the price of a betrayal which philosophy is called
> upon to reduce. Philosophy is called upon to conceive ambiva-
> lence, to conceive it several times. Even if it is called to thought by
> justice, it still synchronizes in the said the diachrony of the differ-
> ence between the one and the other, and remains the servant of
> the saying that signifies the difference between the one and the
> other as the one for the other, as non-indifference to the other.
> Philosophy is the wisdom of love at the service of love.[30]

Husserl, as we have seen, found himself driven by a demand for
rational accountability to go beyond the theories of science and
logic to uncover the horizons of those theories, the life-world.
Reason's own desire for accountability impelled him to describe
the conditions for these other theories through a new theory—
phenomenological theory. Levinas, compelled by a similar urge
for accountability, finds himself prodding phenomenology itself
to its limits, until it arrives at the Other who evokes, conditions,
and questions all theory, including phenomenology itself. This
Other, which phenomenology finds, this "object," throws every
theoretical attempt to come to grips with it off-balance. What Levinas has unveiled is an "object" that shows the unsuitability of
every framework and theoretical attitude for comprehending it.
This unique object revolutionizes philosophy, shattering its pretensions and prescribing for it the humble but ever vigilant role of
reducing the betrayal of the saying in the said and of conceiving
ambivalence over and over again. Who would not recognize in

these paradoxical findings of Levinas's the spirit that animated Husserlian rationalism? One is to return to the things themselves without presuppositions and allow those things to dictate the appropriate theoretical-philosophical outlook through which they are to be approached. This self-reflection on the "access through which" takes two different directions in the phenomenologies of Husserl and Levinas. Phenomenology for Husserl constitutes the ultimate self-reflective posture, for it becomes aware of the presuppositions taken for granted by other theories and aware of itself as the only theory capable of clarifying those presuppositions. Levinas, too, shows an ultimate kind of self-awareness, an awareness that all one's efforts will never be enough, that one must remain perpetually vigilant about one's own unavoidable tendencies to betray the saying and to obscure the Other. While Husserl's self-reflection heads toward a master science, Levinas's directs us toward unending, ruthless self-critique in the presence of the Other and for the sake of the Other. Could Levinas's rational standards be set higher?

NOTES

1. Steven G. Smith, "Reason as One for Another: Moral and Theoretical Argument in the Philosophy of Levinas," in *Face to Face with Levinas*, ed. Richard A. Cohen (Albany: State University of New York Press, 1986), pp. 56–62. David E. Klemm, "Levinas's Phenomenology of the Other and Language as the Other of Phenomenology," *Man and World*, 22 (1989), 410. Michael J. MacDonald, "Jewgreek and Greekjew: The Concept of the Trace in Derrida and Levinas," *Philosophy Today*, 35 (Fall 1991), 225. Emmanuel Levinas, *De Dieu qui vient à l'idée* (Paris: J. Vrin, 1982), p. 143.

2. Emmanuel Levinas and Richard Kearney, "Dialogue with Emmanuel Levinas," in *Face to Face with Levinas*, ed. Richard A. Cohen (Albany: State University of New York Press, 1986), p. 14. Emmanuel Levinas, *Otherwise Than Being, or, Beyond Essence*, trans. Alphonso Lingis (The Hague: Martinus Nijhoff, 1981), p. 183. Emmanuel Levinas, *Totality and Infinity: An Essay on Exteriority*, trans. Alphonso Lingis (The Hague: Martinus Nijhoff, 1979), p. 28. Theodore De Boer, "An Ethical Transcendental Philosophy," in *Face to Face with Levinas*, ed. Richard A. Cohen (Albany: State University of New York Press, 1986), p. 83.

3. De Boer, "Ethical Transcendental Philosophy," pp. 86, 89, 104, 105, 106. Levinas, *Totality and Infinity*, pp. 110, 129. Levinas, *De Dieu qui vient à l'idée*, pp. 139–40. Emmanuel Levinas, *En decouvrant l'existence avec Husserl et Heidegger* (Paris: J. Vrin, 1982), pp. 23–24.

4. Edmund Husserl, *The Crisis of European Sciences and Transcendental Phenomenology: An Introduction to Phenomenological Philosophy*, trans. David Carr (Evanston, Ill.: Northwestern University Press, 1970), p. 141.

5. "The Vienna Lecture," in ibid., pp. 286–87, 295–99.

6. *Totality and Infinity*, p. 28.

7. Ibid., pp. 43, 101, 199–201, 213–15. *Otherwise Than Being*, pp. 51, 53–54, 63–64, 66–69, 76–77, 80, 136, 150.

8. *Totality and Infinity*, pp. 35–36, 80–81, 289–90.

9. *Otherwise Than Being*, pp. 45, 53, 64.

10. Ibid., pp. 53, 45, 64. De Boer, "Ethical Transcendental Philosophy," p. 107.

11. *Otherwise than Being*, pp. 117, 119, 121, 159. Stephan Strasser, *Jenseits von Sein und Zeit: Eine Einführung in Emmanuel Levinas' Philosophie* (The Hague: Martinus Nijhoff, 1978), p. 10.

12. *De Dieu qui vient à l'idée*, pp. 139–40. "Vienna Lecture," p. 286. Edmund Husserl, *Cartesian Meditations: An Introduction to Phenomenology*, trans. Dorion Cairns (The Hague: Martinus Nijhoff, 1960), pp. 1–6, 11. Edmund Husserl, *Ideas: General Introduction to Pure Phenomenology*, trans. W. R. Boyce Gibson (New York: Collier; London: Collier Macmillan, 1931), pp. 74–88.

13. *Totality and Infinity*, pp. 82–88.

14. Ibid., p. 201.

15. Ibid., pp. 53–100, 194–219 (particularly 99–100, 201–203, 218, 219). *Otherwise Than Being*, p. 121.

16. *Totality and Infinity*, pp. 73, 219. *De Dieu qui vient à l'idée*, p. 19.

17. *Otherwise Than Being*, p. 48.

18. *Totality and Infinity*, pp. 50–51, 66–67, 74, 90. *Otherwise Than Being*, pp. 47–48, 53, 96, 111. Emmanuel Levinas, "Phenomenon and Enigma," *Collected Philosophical Papers*, trans. Alphonso Lingis (Dordrecht, The Netherlands: Martinus Nijhoff, 1987), p. 70. De Boer, "Ethical Transcendental Philosophy," pp. 105–106.

19. De Boer, "Ethical Transcendental Philosophy," pp. 105–106. Adriaan Peperzak, "Some Remarks on Hegel, Kant, and Levinas" in *Face to Face with Levinas*, p. 210. Alphonso Lingis, "The Sensuality and the Sensitivity," in *Face to Face with Levinas*, p. 227.

20. *Totality and Infinity*, pp, 61–62.

21. *Otherwise than Being*, pp. 10, 15. See *En decouvrant l'existence avec Husserl et Heidegger*, pp. 27–28, 115, where Levinas repeats the fundamen-

tal principle of phenomenology that objects prescribe methods of investigation. Husserl, *Ideas*, pp. 389–90.

22. Levinas and Kearney, "Dialogue with Emmanuel Levinas," p. 22.

23. Jean-François Lyotard, "Levinas' Logic," in *Face to Face with Levinas*, pp. 131–33, 152.

24. Ibid., pp. 125–26, 130, 144, 145, 152.

25. Ibid., pp. 131, 142, 147, 153.

26. Ibid., p. 152.

27. Jacques Derrida, "Violence and Metaphysics," *Writing and Difference*, trans. Alan Bass (Chicago and London: The University of Chicago Press, 1978), pp. 110, 114, 125, 127–28, 133, 151.

28. *Otherwise Than Being*, p. 155.

29. Robert Bernasconi, "Scepticism in the Face of Philosophy," in *Rereading Levinas*, ed. Robert Bernasconi and Simon Critchley (Bloomington and Indianapolis: Indiana University Press, 1991), p. 159. *Otherwise Than Being*, pp. 90–94. Jan de Greef, "Scepticism and Reason," in *Face to Face with Levinas*, ed. Richard A. Cohen (Albany: State University of New York Press, 1987), pp. 167–68. J. Claude Evans, *Strategies of Deconstruction: Derrida and the Myth of the Voice* (Minneapolis: University of Minnesota Press, 1991), p. 54.

30. *Otherwise Than Being*, pp. 156, 162.

31. Husserl, *Cartesian Meditations*, pp. 152–54.

2

Dussel's Philosophy of Liberation: Discovery and Integration of Levinas's Thought

IN HIS AUTOBIOGRAPHICAL "Liberación latinoamericana y filosofía," Enrique Dussel describes both his philosophical development toward Emmanuel Levinas's thought and the gradual evolution of the philosophy of liberation. He admits the traditional character of his undergraduate work at the Universidad Nacional de Cuyo and classifies his subsequent doctorate in philosophy, finished in 1959 in Madrid, as falling "within the most traditional third period of Scholasticism." After spending time in the Middle East and completing doctorates in theology and history and further philosophical studies in Europe, Dussel still shows himself to be rather traditional. In his 1965 theological article "Hacía una historia de la Iglesia latinoamericana," he envisions the task of Christianity as forming elites so that it might insert itself into a technical and pluralist civilization, in imitation of the early Christians who were able to integrate themselves (*internarse*) into the Roman Empire, the secular culture of their day. Latin American Christians need to partake of the Universal Civilization (the capitals are Dussel's) of which Latin America is only one part. This early Dussel also praises Hernando Arias de Ugarte for his life of perpetual service to the Church and the king. Dussel even defends the Spanish evangelization of Latin America for avoiding syncretism, even though he admits that it neglected indigenous points of view. His earliest major philosophical article, "Situación problematica de la antropología filosófica," espouses traditional phenomenological positions opposed to forms of idealism and endorses phenomenological methods such as phenomenological reduction.[1]

From this starting point, Dussel will undergo a substantive series of transformations on the way to his own final philosophy of liberation, which derives from and transforms Levinas's philosophy. This chapter will show why Dussel found it necessary to turn to Levinas in the first place, and the next chapter will discuss his transformation of Levinas into his own unique philosophy of liberation. Following Dussel's own clues in the autobiographical material in "Liberación latinoamericana y filosofía," I will argue that there are three trajectories in his thought that led him to Levinas. (*a*) At the beginning of his career, Dussel wrote three works of what could be called a philosophically styled anthropology: *El humanismo semita* (begun in 1960 and published in 1969), *El humanismo helénico* (completed in 1963 and published in 1975), and a synthesis of these two works, *El dualismo en la antropología de la cristiandad* (finished in 1968 and published in 1974). (*b*) After the breakdown of his later project of founding an ethics on Heideggerian-hermeneutic grounds, Dussel devoted himself from 1970 to 1974 to a substantial study of Hegel which issued in *La dialéctica hegeliana* (1972) and a revised edition of that work, *Método para una filosofía de la liberación* (1974). (*c*) Dussel developed his own theory of ethics, extending from his attempt to base ethics on Heideggerian-hermeneutic grounds in *Para una de-strucción de la historia de la ética* (1970) to his five-volume *Para una ética de la liberación latinoamericana*, published from 1973 until 1980, with the first three volumes clearly manifesting the confrontation between Heidegger and Levinas in his thought. In this chapter, I will take up each of these three trajectories, and will demonstrate how each of them led to Levinas. Of course, I will be continually asking the question guiding this text: what is the meaning of rationality in Dussel's own philosophy of liberation?

LEVINAS AND DUSSEL'S ANTHROPOLOGICAL WORKS

Dussel understands his inquiries into the Semitic and Hellenistic worldviews and their synthesis in Christianity as propaedeutic to grasping the actual prephilosophical world of Latin America. Ac-

cording to Dussel, every culture possesses a "pre-position" toward
the world exercised in every experience, manifesting itself in the
anticipations and potentialities of the least perception of the most
humble thing. In more Heideggerian terms, being always takes
on meaning within the horizon of a certain precomprehension of
the world which varies from culture to culture. Paralleling the
later Husserl's recovery of the world of everyday life (*mundo de la
vida cotidiana*), Dussel believes that philosophy can question the
forgotten, prephilosophical approaches to the world out of which
philosophy itself arises.

> Even if Christian thought would not have arrived at presenting a
> philosophical discourse, that is to say, even if there would not have
> been a Christian philosophy, there existed effectively a pre-philo-
> sophical anthropo-logical structure at the existential level. Such a
> structure would be contained in the "world" of the Christian his-
> torically given. We are setting out, insofar as we are philosophers,
> necessarily contemporary ones at that, not only to discern the ele-
> ments of a philosophy, but also to study a structure, a pre-philo-
> sophical anthropo-logy, effectively given even before thought has
> situated its object reductively as an "entity" to be thematized. For
> that reason, it does not matter whether we dwell on philosophical
> documents or on expressions of everyday life, since every docu-
> ment will be of value for discerning in its contents the basic an-
> thropo-logical structures that are *implicit* and hidden beneath the
> clothing of a theological, literary, or historical question.[2]

This Heideggerian/phenomenological project of recovering
precomprehensions of the world and resolutely taking up one's
past unearths basic features characteristic of the Semitic and the
Hellenic cultures. The Semites attribute responsibility for evil to
human beings rather than to the gods or the structure of being.
Such a view sets God off as transcendent over the realm of nature,
and its emphasis on human responsibility posits the human being
as self-conscious and autonomous over against the things of nature. Yet there is no mind/body dualism among the Semites as
there is among the Greeks. Historicity is integral to the human
person, and Semites tend to rejoice in the adventure of the
changing and the phenomenal that scandalizes the Greeks.[3]

The Hellenic precomprehension of the world, including its
preclassical, classical, and Hellenistic stages, traces itself back to

the Western Eurasian steppes and the worldview of the Indo-European, understood not racially but culturally. For the Greeks, heirs of Indo-European culture, mind/body dualism constitutes an undiscussed dogma that implies the corollaries that the soul takes precedence and that salvation can be found only in freeing oneself from one's body. This anthropological dualism often accompanies an ontological monism in which all things return to a fundamental principle or emanate from an immanent divinity. Thus, Greek thought shows tendencies of an inability to assume the intransferable value of the concrete and to flee from the irreversible and unforeseeable in search of the security offered by immobile, eternal, first principles. The Greeks stress individual perfection and contemplation "outside the city," thereby assigning only secondary importance to intersubjectivity and the common good.[4]

Dussel examines the confluence of these two cultural streams in his *El dualismo en la antropología de la cristiandad*, acknowledging that his text focuses on the soul/body relation solely as it appears in the comprehension of humanity of early Christianity in its passage to its later, established form as Christendom. According to Dussel, the primitive Christian community carried with it a certain (Semitic) understanding of the human person as its universalistic impulses prompted it to reach out to Romanized Hellenism. The process of acculturation—that is, the passage from early Christianity to an established form of Christendom, culminating in Constantine's declaration of Christianity as the official religion of the empire—required expressing this Semitic understanding through the totality of mediations (language, logical instruments, economic, political, pedagogic, erotic systems) of Hellenic culture. For Dussel, it was the Christian Apologists (A.D. 120–180) who mediated this "dialogue to the death" between two giant cultures, and he advances abundant evidence to show how the proponents of the Semitic-Christian belief system struggled to uphold the unity of the person even though the very Greek categories they employed undermined their struggle. For example, even as Methodius of Olympia denies dualism and affirms synthesis, he admits the existence of two irreducible components: "The human being by nature is neither soul nor body . . . but rather the synthesis composed of the union of soul and body." In tracing this dualism down through the history of Western thought, Dussel observes that all Christian thinkers held the secret conviction that they were betraying something central to the Hebraic-Christian worldview expressed in the Old and New Testaments. The biblical comprehension of the human person was unitary; the philosophical expression turned dualistic. In Dussel's view, only Thomas Aquinas articulated a unitary vision of the human person by construing the soul not as a separate, incomplete substance, but as a *sui generis* substantial form, the direct recipient of the *esse* pertaining to the whole person, which is irreducible to the soul itself. Only by breaking with all previous philosophical categories could Aquinas successfully preserve the unity of the person.[5]

Dussel engages here in a Heideggerian venture of returning to the origins of Christianity to recover a lost unity, to escape from the trap of dualism into which Christianity fell in acculturating to Hellenism. Just as Heidegger criticized the metaphysical tradition for encrusting over and concealing originary experiences, Dussel turns to accounts and descriptions of existential situations of everyday life—a prephilosophical moment—distorted when they were thematized within Greek categories. In order to thematize adequately, one has to situate oneself existentially in an originary world, prior to the philosophical separation of the human being into soul and body. Not only is Dussel's method Heideggerian, but Heidegger's fundamental ontology also comes to represent the goal toward which the Western philosophical tradition has been approaching, however haltingly. Thus, near the end of *El dualismo*, Dussel recommends replacing the logico-analytic interpretation of human nature that has treated human nature merely ontically, as if it were a thing (composed of two subthings), with an existential description that would analyze human existentials. Corporality, animality, temporality, intersubjectivity—all constitute existentials of an ontological, structural, *a priori* unity before the appearance of any dualism. Dussel suggests that such an existential analysis of the fundamental ontological type exists effectively in the thought of Thomas Aquinas.[6]

Although Dussel's search for lost origins in *El dualismo* recovers a unity of the person approximating Heidegger's own philosophical anthropology, Dussel confesses in the foreword of that book that he had recently experienced a "theoretic rupture" with European ontology (including Heidegger's) that would require him to rewrite the entire book. Rather than undertake such major revisions, he decides to include additions expounding the origin of the notion of "person," the originary concept of a unified being, which philosophers and Christian thinkers in their attempted explanations subsequently bifurcated into separate substances of soul and body. The term "person" represents neither an entity nor an animal differentiated by rationality, but refers instead to alterity, the Other from whom the moral world is constituted. "Person" in the Old Testament signifies "face," not the mask through which a voice resounded as in Greek theater, but, rather, the face of the other as Other, exemplified when Moses spoke "face to face" with God. This notion of person designates a locus beyond the horizon of the world, of being, and even of ontology. This Other is given as a unity, as "a supplicating carnality" (*carnalidad suplicante*), who cries out "I am hungry," prior to any philosophical considerations of soul and body. Thus, the unity of the person, forgotten by the philosophical tradition except for Heidegger and Thomas Aquinas, itself derives from more fundamental ethical origins, prior to any ontological elucidation. Utilizing Heideggerian method to rescue Christian anthropology from Hellenistic superimpositions, Dussel is led beyond Heidegger and Heidegger's fundamental ontology and even beyond Christianity itself to Hebraic-Semitic categories marked by an ethical "logic of alterity." In brief, his anthropological studies utilize Heidegger only to lead beyond Heidegger to Levinas.[7]

This is not to say that all Dussel's interpretations of individual figures or groups are historically accurate. One might dispute his claim in *El humanismo helénico* that Heraclitus was too fixated on order. Similarly, it does not seem correct to assert that Aristotle emphasizes the species over the concrete and reduces the individual to no more than a subject/carrier of the universal, especially since Dussel never refutes the most powerful counterevidence to such assertions: namely, Aristotle's critique of Plato's theory of the forms. Moreover, Dussel frequently evinces a less than fair approach to Judaism. He repeatedly interprets the New Alliance in Christianity as the fulfillment of Judaism, a Christian reading offensive to Jews and repudiated in recent Christian documents.

Accepting all Jesus's words as authentic and ignoring the anti-Jewish polemic underlying Christian texts, Dussel presents Jesus as opposing the merely "carnal" practices of Judaism such as circumcision. Furthermore, when he claims that Israel was less open to pagans than Christianity was, Dussel neglects broad universalistic tendencies in the Prophets and in works such as the Book of Jonah. The criticism that Judaism never extended to the entire world because it would not deny its particularism and because it demanded of nations that they forfeit their own physionomy to become part of the people centered in Jerusalem smacks of hypocrisy, especially when one considers Christianity's traditional suppression of internal diversity and its age-old aggressive persecution of non-Christian religions, particularly Judaism. Rosemary Reuther has convincingly argued that Christianity's reproach of Jewish particularism in contrast to its own universalism has often concealed from Christians their own ruthless particularism.[8]

Dussel's preference for the Semitic current over the Hellenic might indicate an option against rationality and philosophy, which would seem to have done nothing more than misrepresent lived experience and create a pseudo-problematic (for example, dualism) plaguing the history of philosophy for more than two millennia. But the very anthropological inquiries disclosing the errors and limits of rationality are themselves the work of reason. Dussel's entire anthropological investigation is premised on the fact that we inherit much more than we are aware of from our parents in terms of race, character, culture, and home. Following Heidegger, Dussel observes that we are thrown (*arrojado*) into life with a (pregiven) meaning and direction within which we can freely choose. The cultural heritages of Latin America act upon its denizens more than they realize. Of course, even to be aware of one's thrownness requires self-reflection—a reflection requisite, in Dussel's view, for personal and cultural maturity.

> Someone might reproach us: In the present anguish of a Latin America that is debating about realizing a revolution that will establish a more just order, what sense does it make to lose time studying the far-distant Greeks? We ought only to respond that in order to understand truly the human edifice constructed in history, it is necessary to begin with the foundations in order to decipher the *mean-*

ing of our own present. One becomes an adult only through attaining reflexive consciousness of one's collective and historical existence. In this case, consciousness will be able to precede history, *orienting it.*[9]

The rational process of recovering one's own and one's cultural past in anthropology stands as the only alternative to remaining a child, a passive victim of one's own history, or a culture alienated within world history.[10]

Apart from its results, this Heideggerian-like "destruction" of history entails, as Dussel describes it, a "demystifying" (*dimitificar*) of history, with all the connotations of Weberian rationalization that that word carries. Dussel hopes to destroy inauthentic history and unveil its forgotten meanings, to rescue them from the dominant tradition, that is, the vulgar tradition of the mere traditionalists. Thus, his anthropological endeavor leads him to uncover the originary unified Semitic anthropology that has been overlaid with Hellenic dualisms. Dussel's restoration of the importance of the Apologists in the process of the constitution of Christian anthropologists runs counter to usual histories of philosophy, such as Gilson's, Fraile's, or Heimsoeth's that, after presenting the Ancients and the New Testament texts, leap to the Hellenists, Neoplatonists, and Augustine. Later, we shall see Dussel producing similar critico-destructive histories, such as his effort to recover the religious meanings of the indigenous people whose voice was drowned out in the Spanish conquest of Latin America. Dussel's writing of critico-destructive history is but an effort to make historiography itself more rational.[11]

We have teased out elements of rationality implicit in Dussel's own anthropological explorations. Of course, what those explorations ultimately find—the face of the Other as the basis of the unified notion of the person—ultimately invites us to a richer, more authentic notion of rationality, as the previous chapter argued. Nevertheless, Dussel's anthropological writings would leave us with the impression that Greek thought, and philosophy in particular, serve only to obscure originary experiences and blunt their ethical force. Only later will we be able to see whether Greek rationality provides riches that the philosophy of liberation has yet to tap in their fullness.

LEVINAS AND DUSSEL'S READING OF HEGEL

In "Liberación latinoamericana y filosofía," Dussel reports that after his *Para una de-strucción de la historia de la ética* he began to find Heideggerian terminology and hermeneutic instruments unsatisfactory and thus began an intense study of Hegel which would be the theme of his graduate seminars and occupy him from 1970 until 1974. Why Dussel found that terminology and those instruments unsatisfactory will be the theme of the next section. For now, though, we will discuss how he critically appropriated the Hegelian dialectic and why he felt impelled to move beyond Hegel to Levinas.[12]

Near the end of *La dialéctica hegeliana*, after tracing the development of the dialectic and its various meanings in the history of philosophy, Dussel discovers two valuable aspects of the dialectic: it denies the security and obviousness of everyday life, and it opens out on encompassing ontological structures, which are never exhaustively known. Later, in his *Para una ética de la liberación latinoamericana*, Dussel maintains his admiration for the dialectical method by admitting that it plays an important role even after an originary moment of analectic conversion to the Other. Philosophy then proceeds dialectically, borne along by the word of the Other.[13]

Most of Dussel's reactions to Hegel's thought, though, are negative. He sees in Hegel's Absolute merely the subjectivity of modernity "elevated to actual infinity which englobes everything in an absolute immanence without exteriority." In the dialectic of desire, the master–slave, and stoicism in Hegel, it is purely and simply the same self-conscious consciousness undergoing modifications, without any real Other. When in Hegel's philosophy of "identity and absolute knowing" the finite destroys itself, the elevation of the whole does not come from anything outside itself. Hegel's comment that "As opposed to the desire of the Absolute, the desire of other spirits of other particular peoples has no rights" constitutes a sacralization of the predominant order of the world. In Dussel's opinion, philosophy of the Hegelian type ends up justifying the elimination of the Other and thus serves as an "ontological cause" of such diverse phenomena as fascist concentration camps, Siberian forced labor, and the repression of African-Americans in the United States.[14]

Dussel contends, though, that the post-Hegelians overcame Hegel's dialectic, just as Levinas has overcome Heidegger's ontology, and so they, along with Levinas, make up the prehistory of Latin American philosophy. The young Schelling argued that beyond Hegel's identity of thought and being lies the positivity of the unthinkable—existence—a *prius* abandoned when Hegel pushed on to the level of consciousness. Feuerbach, continuing Schelling's line of thought, believed that atheism regarding the Hegelian totality led to the rediscovery of the other human being—sensible, corporal, fleshly—that Descartes had denied and that can be apprehended only in the true dialectic of a dialogue, not in the monologue of a solitary thinker. Marx reformulated Feuerbach's notion of the sensible to include human sensible action and praxis; and for Kierkegaard, who remained on the theological plane only, the Other appeared as incomprehensible and absurd, known only through the Other's free self-revelation. The later Schelling also reiterated this necessity for self-revelation on the part of a Creator, who produces an autonomous creation instead of a mere pantheistic emanation from that Creator's own self. In Dussel's view, Levinas recapitulates and surpasses this entire tradition by focusing on the human sensible Other's revealing itself and the Divine and provoking an *an-archic* concern for justice beyond what can be thought, beyond logos, beyond Hegel's identity. Dussel starkly contrasts the method of Hegel's dia-lectic with his own ana-lectic, which, though he develops it on the basis of Levinas's thought, is beyond it.

> The method of which we wish to speak, the *ana*-lectic, goes beyond, above; it derives from a level higher (*ana-*) than the mere *dia*-lectic method. The *dia*-lectic method is the path that the totality realizes within itself: from entities to the fundament and from the fundament to entities. What we are discussing now is a method (or the explicit dominion of the conditions of possibility) which begins from the Other as free, as one beyond the system of the totality; which begins, then, from the Other's word, from the revelation of the Other, and which, trusting in the Other's word, labors, works, serves, and creates.[15]

The criticism of Hegel here leads through the post-Hegelians to Levinas, just as Dussel's anthropological investigations lead beyond Hellenism to the Semitic notions of the unified person which are articulated better by Levinas's ethics than by even Heidegger's fundamental ontology. In recovering what Hegel's dialectic forgets and overlooks, the post-Hegelians and Levinas effectively make even the archrationalist more rational. But it is in Dussel's attempt to develop an ethics for Latin American liberation that he will turn most dramatically to Levinas and, as we shall see, sharpen modernity's own efforts at constructing a rational ethics.

LEVINAS AND THE ETHICS OF LATIN AMERICAN LIBERATION

In 1970, Dussel published *Para una de-strucción de la historia de la ética*, a Heideggerian and hermeneutically based ethics that he will find unsatisfactory and that will prompt him to embark on his study of Hegel before coming finally to write his five-volume *Para una ética de la liberación latinoamericana*. The 1970 work constitutes his critique of modernity's ethics, particularly Kant's, and in the latter work he criticizes the Heideggerian foundations of the earlier work. After examining these permutations in detail, we shall assess this entire project in ethics.

In the foreword to *Para una de-strucción*, Dussel informs us that he uses "destruction" in the Heideggerian sense of separating oneself from traditional interpretations, untying the transmitted hermeneutics, to recover the forgotten and open one's ears to what in the tradition addresses itself to us as the Being of being. Dussel believes that all the ethics ever written bring to light an ontological structure that already is an "ethic equally ontological." In this task of discovering, thinking, and expositing the ontological ethics, which Dussel says is actually an *ethica perennis*, there is no doubt that ethics and ontology go hand in hand. The synthesis of these two philosophical domains prompts Dussel's admiration of Aristotle and the natural law tradition:

> In conclusion, the being of humanity, which has begun through its being a physically given being from birth, will be, in the course of its existence, more and more, an *eidos proaireton*. The same human

being will go through life realizing its self effectively. That realization will not be a pure construction of its essence (as Sartre will think), but an effectuation *kata physin* (according to nature) by *discovery* (not through *invention*) of unforeseeable existential possibilities. Ethics is thus understood, not as a type of thinking posterior to ontology, but as one of the chapters of ontology; and it is normative, not through promulgation, but through elucidation: the discernment of the ethical being of humanity illuminates existential comprehension and interpretation.[16]

In agreement with Aristotle, Dussel describes the human being as tending toward its proper being, toward a "situating-in-one's-end" (*estar-en-su-fin*) that comes toward one (*le ad-viene*), in the sense that one does not arbitrarily invent one's *telos*, but finds it demanding ethical compliance. When discussing Thomas Aquinas, a principal proponent of natural law ethics, Dussel portrays this demand in very Heideggerian terms, stating that moral conscience is "the voice of being," showing us our "authentic possibility" and filling us with remorse when we fail to live up to it. Not to act in accordance with the end that approaches is to obnubilate one's own being, to lose one's way and the comprehension of one's authentic being. For Aquinas, the meaning of evil is "the silencing and obscuring" of being. The only rule, for Dussel and Aristotle, is that which an authentic human being would obey on the basis of a correct, comprehensive interpretation. This ontological ethics is situational, not determinable beforehand, and yet ontologically founded in being.[17]

The Heideggerian nature of Dussel's interpretation of natural law is evident not only from the overarching character of his project—namely, to reestablish "destructively" ontological ethics—but also from the terms he employs, such as "existential possibilities," "existential comprehension and interpretation," "the voice of being," and "authentic human being." Dussel himself acknowledges as much by claiming in his conclusion that in his approach to the first two sections of *Para una de-strucción*, on Aristotle and Aquinas, he read ancient works with new eyes and detected in them beyond any traditional interpretation a hidden ontological ethics. Ethics, he concludes, is only a final chapter of fundamental ontology.[18]

Armed with this Heideggerian reading of natural law, Dussel

goes to war with modernity, particularly Kant and Scheler. But before he discusses Kantian ethics, and following Max Scheler and Werner Sombart, Dussel depicts the modern world, in which Kant was immersed, as dominated by a capitalistic bourgeoisie interested no longer in contemplating the world but in dominating and transforming it in accord with the will-to-power. Symptoms of this modern worldview appear in the mathematicization of nature by the sciences and in particular in political theories premised on the belief that human beings as solitary individuals form social bonds only when they foresee that freely embraced contractual terms will procure their egoistic interests. Philosophically, such cultural strands express themselves in the representational theory of knowledge, according to which being is not discovered, but reduced to the objectivity of an object constituted by the synthetic unity of apprehension. Being is thus an "act of human subjectivity"; it is posited and even produced by representation. Following Descartes, who confused what Heidegger would later call the "human being who comprehends being" with the *ego cogito*, Kant succumbed to the same cultural blindness by denying to humanity the comprehension of the being that approaches (*del ser ad-viniente*) and by reducing the human being to being one who represents objects and is, thus, only a subject.[19]

Because he relies on the subject as the ultimate foundation of his ethics, Kant separates his ethics from ontology and pretends that it is independent of any ontology. For Dussel, Kant's ethics "remains in the air," appearing to be an autonomous discipline—the exact opposite of his own view that ethics is an inseparable chapter of fundamental ontology. *Homo faber* and technical humanity will thus no longer have any standard given through manifestation or discovery; rather, humanity itself will posit from itself as consciousness, as subject, its own rules. Artistic and technical production beginning from a goal or prototype freely invented by self-determined human representation replaces the hermeneutic discovery of being as approaching. Empiricist ethicians agree with Kant's founding ethics in the empire of the subject, since for them that action is moral which produces the most subjective happiness.[20]

Slowly the metaphysics of the subject, characteristic of the modern era, cut off from all ontology that might check its pretensions, leads to the arbitrariness characteristic of Nietzsche's will-to-power.

> This modern human being, which is an "I represent," "I constitute the meaning of objects," little by little will deteriorate into an "I order," "I organize and calculate the political, economic, or cultural event." In this "will-to-power," the human being has no measure, and nothing is able to serve as limit for its creative zeal. It is artistic *ethos*, if one understands by art a mere inventive, creative impulse in which the human being "takes from itself" (from its own subjectivity) what it places before its sight: the artistic creation by art itself. This technical, calculating ethos, made greater by science, can transform human beings into material for its unlimited creation. It is, therefore, the slavery of humanity as a machine and as an instrument of labor.[21]

Dussel sees Kant as the culmination of Descartes's tradition, with Hegel as its ultimate result, and Sartre, as one of its latest representatives. For Sartre, "there is being" because of human decisions, and what is fundamental is humanity, as opposed to the viewpoint of Heidegger and the natural law tradition in which "being gives itself to humanity" in such a way that what is essential is being, not humanity.[22]

Dussel develops at least three other criticisms of Kant in addition to the charge that he espoused an arbitrary metaphysics of the subject. First, Dussel opposes his formalism and *a priori* approach, which led Kant mistakenly to seek to found an ethics not only apart from ontology but also "totally isolated and without mixture with anything of anthropology, theology, physics, or hyperphysics." Dussel attributes this formalism to Galileo's call for a radical disregard of everyday experience of the contents of nature which are really written *in lingua matemática*. Second, relying on comments from the third part of Kant's *Grundlegung zur Metaphysik der Sitten* about the intelligible world behind phenomena, Dussel argues that for Kant all knowledge (*saber, Wissen*) ceases when it comes to the moral domain, which can be grasped only by rational faith (*fé racional, vernünftigen Glaubens*). Everything in the moral domain is a matter of faith, not knowledge. This very weak rational faith stands opposed to Dussel's stronger existential, ontological comprehension of the being that approaches and makes its ethical demand. Third, in his second formulation of the cate-

gorical imperative in the *Grundlegung*, Kant tests maxims by having the agent ask if the action the agent is about to perform could
become a universal law of nature. Dussel reads Kant as relapsing
here into an ontological ethics much like natural law and thereby
not restricting himself within the formal limits he himself speci-
fied for ethical theory. A similar relapse occurs when Kant posits
an unknowable kingdom of ends analogous to the kingdom of
nature. It is clear that in all these objections Dussel regards a
Heideggerian-based natural law theory as superior for eliminating
arbitrariness, for being more rationally comprehensible, for and
honestly owning up to its ontological suppositions from the beginning. Before we critically examine both these objections to
Kant and Dussel's entire anti-modern project, let us present Dussell's arguments against Heidegger in his *Para una ética de la liberación latinoamericana*, the very Heidegger who provides his bulwark
against Kant in this earlier work.[23]

Dussel's five-volume *Para una ética de la liberación latinoamericana*
comprises two initial volumes on his ethical foundations, a third
on liberation pedagogics and erotics, a fourth on economics and
politics, and a fifth on the philosophy of religion. Dussel comments repeatedly on the structure of the first six chapters of the
first two volumes—the section of the ethics that will concern us
here. The first chapter provides an ontological fundament (the
relation between *Dasein* and Being); the second, ontic possibilities
(possibilities, choice, praxis) flowing from that fundament. Dussel informs us that he wrote this part in 1970 while he was in the
Heideggerian tradition. In the third chapter, he introduces a new
metaphysical foundation, the face of the Other, and traces its implications through chapters four and five. Dussel credits Levinas
with influencing this new aspect of his thought, but also asserts
that he goes beyond Levinas. In the sixth and final chapter, Dussel
recapitulates the method of his ethics, stating that although the
ontological description may come first in the order of presentation, ethics is really first philosophy.[24]

Dussel's early antagonism toward the modern metaphysics of
the subject continues throughout his five-volume ethics. In his
view, Nietzsche, Sartre, and Husserl all belong to the tradition in
which the subject as will does not start from the horizon of being
that is discovered but, rather, transforms ethics into a doctrine of

logos or art in which the subject creates laws and values inventively and arbitrarily. For Dussel, on the contrary, ethics involves opening up to values and discovering possibilities founded in the previous dis-covery of being. At this early stage of his ethics, prior to the introduction of Levinas, Dussel still opts for Heidegger, who envisioned his own philosophy as overcoming phenomenology, which, by its focus on subjectivity and transcendental philosophy, had proved itself the final bastion of modern philosophy.[25]

A Heideggerian ethics such as Dussel's must begin where Heidegger himself does. Before the subject objectifies and constitutes values, the human being is already in the world as a comprehender and projector of being. For Dussel, existential comprehension as access to being makes the radical thematization of being possible, and this making explicit of what is implicit often depends on the passage to reflection effected by a crisis, an alienation, rupture, or separation that forces one to forsake the security of everyday life. Philosophy, as ontology, becomes here a matter of rupture, conversion, death to the mundane. In other places, Dussel speaks of a dialectic that opens onto being as the fundament. This phenomenological-like thematization of what is already implicitly comprehended specifies the task of ethics as highly descriptive (rather than prescriptive): "The task of ethics is justly to describe [*describir*] the ethical structure that the human being lives in its historical, common, and unreflected situation."[26]

This structure that human beings live is the structure of their own being, including the demands that they become what they are meant to be as these demands emerge from who they are. Dussel reiterates his position in *Para una de-strucción de la historia de la ética* that humanity does not arbitrarily construct this being and its demands, but, rather, finds being with its accompanying prescriptions imposed. Though one may through praxis become more than what one received as one's being at birth, one cannot cease to be that which one is; nor can one radically alter one's being. One's being constitutes an *a priori* of which one must inevitably take account and for which one must assume responsibility, not as the producer of being, but rather—to use Heidegger's term—as its shepherd. For Dussel, this character of being as importuning reverses the modern metaphysics of the subject whose goal and fundamental project rise willfully out of the subject it-

self. Dussel conceives being as a foundation that is not freely chosen but to which the human being opens through existential
comprehension. One is not free with respect to one's fundamental project, for one already finds oneself inevitably endowed with
such a project, which emanates from who one is and with which
one must come to terms.[27]

The being of the human person is essentially non-totalized,
open; that is, the human person is always able to be something
different, and therefore is, in Dussel's words, a being-able-to-be
(*poder-ser*). One experiences such possibilities emerging from the
life-situation into which one has been born, not which one has
chosen. One does not, in fact, choose to be a being faced with
possibilities, but is, rather, "thrown" into such a situation. One's
family, city, nation, and cultural group give one's fundamental
life-project a certain direction that one can follow, reject, or mod-
ify. In making choices regarding this fundamental project and
thereby realizing certain possibilities, one finds new horizons
opening up, new possibilities appearing, and the *poder-ser* dynami-
cally unfolding without reaching completion. This dynamic pro-
gression from horizon to horizon may be grasped through
existential dialectical comprehension, rather than through dialectical thinking. Dussel speaks of a "moral ontological conscience" that continually calls one to take up consciously and
responsibly one's fundamental project, that which "covers the
sense of what we pursue every day." Often this call of conscience
is necessary, since one can lose oneself in "the public impersonal-
ity of the *One* [*das Man*] and its idle rumors in which *one stops
listening* to one's authentic *self* in order to listen to the *one*" voice
of society calling for mindless conformity. Because this call to authenticity, experienced as a demand that one emerge from the
comfort and security of the herd, does not appear to be a product
of arbitrariness, Dussel can easily speak of it as the voice of being
(*la voz del Ser*) coming from without (*ad-viniente*), as he did in *Para
la de-strucción de la historia de la ética*. Here being, insofar as it is
being-able-to-be, is the ontological fundament of the ought-to-be.
Duty and obligation in Dussel as opposed to Kantian ethics, are
founded in the ontological structure of the human being who is
a being-able-to-be.[28]

Dussel explicitly reads Heidegger as converging with the natural law ethics of Aristotle and Thomas Aquinas, which, in Dussel's opinion, specifies moral commands that circumscribe and limit all the diverse projects undertaken by humanity: "The law, rules, or norms, as ex-igencies of being, will have as many modalities as the horizons of the being-able-to-be [*poder-ser*] are dia-lectically com-prehensible: the ultimate being-able-to-be, that of humanity as such, has been denominated natural law."[29]

It is questionable, though, whether Heidegger can be so easily conflated with natural law. I would suggest that Dussel would never be satisfied with the requirements flowing from Heidegger's fundamental ontology, since those requirements are actually ethically neutral. Heidegger insists, for instance, that every *Dasein* by its ontological structure must adopt *some* fundamental project calling for compliance to it, although this project remains indeterminate and varies from person to person. Since Dussel equates *Dasein*'s being with human nature as understood within the natural law tradition, it is probable that there are some fundamental projects that he would have to proscribe since they are contrary to human nature and therefore "unnatural." Thus, "Being destines us," in the sense that one's own being/nature provides indications that appear as specifically *moral* exigencies, norms, and laws; the structure of nature becomes here the source of moral obligation.

Remarkably, Dussel altered this entire philosophical framework, which had been guiding his entire ethical project from the earlier *Para la de-struccion de la historia de la ética* through the first two chapters of *Para una ética de la liberación latinoamericana*. It seems almost as if he never returned to revise these first two chapters after his switch from Heidegger to Levinas, since many of the above affirmations are not accompanied by any foreshadowing of the coming future changes. What motives prompted this critique of Heidegger and this reversal of a project that had been building for years?

In the sixth chapter on the method of ethics, Dussel makes a telling comment, after observing that fundamental ontological thought illuminates daily praxis by making explicit the suppositions of its praxis, fulfilling, as we saw earlier, a descriptive function:

The daily existential ethics, the communication of the existential interpretive totality of the *ethos*, is yet, as Sartre says, a "complicit" thinking. It is complicit in the sense that it communicates, that it knows how to express that which everyone lives, but only to corroborate it, to affirm it. It does not have a critical method which might permit one to overcome those suppositions and from the fundamental horizon of being re-found or de-stroy what is affirmed in everyday life. In this sense it is still a naïve ethics, since it presupposes this foundation implicitly without recognizing this supposition.[30]

In simply thematizing philosophically a prevailing *ethos*, in simply describing the ontological structures it presupposes, ontological ethics clarifies for humanity its finitude, its limits, its inevitable fall, the concealment of being effected by everyday life, and thus permits one to assume one's being more responsibly and authentically. But the function of such an ethics is purely clarificatory, such that, as Dussel concedes, "the normativity of ontology is making clearly evident [*clarividencia*], whereas the normativity of alterative or metaphysical ethics is much more." Ontological ethics lacks critical resources when faced with an immoral suppression of the Other as non-being; the examples of injustice that Dussel frequently criticizes—Hegel and the European/North American *conquistadores* of Latin America—can be seen as fulfilling equally well the norms of an ontological ethics by transcending conformist norms and responsibly taking up their past in directing themselves resolutely toward a freely embraced life-project. Heidegger's notion of authenticity entails no ethicity, since his major concern is not morality, but the *existential conditions of the possibility of moral good and evil*. Properly speaking, there is no such thing as ontological good or evil, only a tragically immobile fundamental structure, which one might approach through a kind of *gnosis*, discovering a fundament which is "thus as it is" and nothing more.[31]

This later Dussel interprets Heidegger's discussion of "authenticity" as a new version of *gnosis* in which one takes account of one's own being, one's most authentic being-able-to-be (*poder-ser*), in which the ontological-existential condition of the possibility of being free for the existential, authentic possibilities of one's unique destiny resides. An authentic person, freed from the forgetfulness of being that is typical of those too immersed in daily preoccupations, could conceivably join with other authentic persons to produce a closed society (without alterity) in which members live indifferent to the rest of people. Moral ontological conscience, for Heidegger, remains entrapped in this gnostic solipsism, since it is only a voice that interpellates one from oneself, in which the Other is reduced to the mere position of something intramundane, someone with whom one exists but who is without radical importance.[32]

Dussel permits no interaction between the Heideggerian existential of *Mitsein* and the Heideggerian emphasis on authenticity in a way that authenticity might be deprivatized, perhaps because he believes that, in spite of Heidegger's talk of being-with (*ser-con*), Heidegger always departs from the self, from *Dasein* (*ser-ahí*), as the center of the world. Dussel further criticizes Heidegger's notion of *Mitsein* in that the Other becomes simply that one with whom I am in my own world. It is always possible to include the Other in my world as a mediation or an instrument and to allow the Other to become distantly impersonal as *Mitsein* (the soldier for the general, the postal employee for the purchaser of stamps).[33]

The entire discussion of the Other undergoes a radical transformation in Dussel's passage from Heidegger to Levinas. First, the centripetal focus of Heidegger's *Mitsein*, in which the Other is comprehended as part of one's world, is radically reversed, the Other in Levinas becoming incom-prehensible precisely because he or she is exterior to one's world. For Dussel, the focus is placed, not on one's own liberty, but on the liberty of the Other, which cannot be submitted to rationalization and cannot be fitted into the being-able-to-be (*poder-ser*) and the being that approaches (*ser ad-viniente*) of one's own world. Instead of reconfirming Heidegger's notion of "anticipation" (*Vorlaufen*) as *my* living toward *my* death, the ontological limit-experience, Dussel looks forward to the joy of the liberation of the Other, the miserable one. Hope no longer aims at realizing a privatized project within the Totality, but focuses on the future, full realization of the Other beyond the Totality and one's own servicial responsibility to bring about that future: "Hope is, precisely, the moment of affirmation of the future of the Other, and it is here that the first negativity, the Alter-

ity of the Other, shines forth most mysteriously. *Her* project, that
of the Other, is a being-able-to-be; it is *her* being that approaches;
it is *her* future."[34] In brief, all the Heideggerian categories now
stand under a different index: they are oriented toward the
Other, who takes priority over oneself.[35]

In addition to these external criticisms of the limitations in Heidegger's view, Dussel also undertakes an internal critique. He
notes that in *Gelassenheit* the later Heidegger discovered a new
philosophical attitude: "openness before the mystery," "serenity
before things." Heidegger resists any effort to domesticate this
"openness" by safely subsuming it under familiar categories. This
later Heidegger was beset by the problem of how to think being
positively, and his search for transexistential categories led him to
poetic and mystical language. Heidegger's intent was to go beyond ontology as a totality, and beyond demonstrative philosophical science and dialectical or existential foundational ontology as
well. Dussel argues that ultimately Heidegger was trying to describe the face-to-face, the immediacy of the experience of the
Other, when he spoke of an "openness before the mystery" and
"serenity before things," the surpassing of his own ontological
horizon. The overcoming of modernity, of the ontology of the
subject, is not achieved in Heidegger's transcendence of the
human being/world dichotomy that lies at the base of subject–
object polarizations, as *Being and Time* attempted to show. Rather,
one must discover that the Totality of humanity and being must
open to a deeper fundament—the Other, who is trans-ontologi-
cal, meta-physical. The conversion to ontological thought is one
important step en route to the final overcoming of modernity's
metaphysics of the subject in the Other. Heidegger took that step,
but his own trajectory could reach its fulfillment only in Levinas.[36]

Dussel has, in effect, discovered a foundation deeper (*más abis-
mal*) than the ontological horizon: namely, the Other. This
deeper foundation constitutes the ethicity of the ontological itself, such that one's fundamental project is judged as evil if it is
not dedicated to the Other. The relationship with the Other now
provides the starting point and wider context within which Dussel
can situate Heidegger's ontology. Dussel thus places the categories of that ontology under a different index and submits them
to another criterion of judgment. This turn toward Levinas also

demands a reorientation of the relationships between the two branches of philosophy, ontology and ethics. Dussel concludes that ontology offers an introduction to ethics, and this explains his placing of the first two chapters on Heidegger's fundamental ontology before his discussion of meta-physical exteriority beginning in chapter 3 and extending to chapter 6. But this ordering of presentation (*ordo diciendi*) for pedagogical purposes does not correspond to the order of importance for ethics as first philosophy, because the face-to-face is prior to all else—it is the access to first truth (*acceso a la veritas prima*).[37]

This transition from Heidegger to Levinas provides the framework for Dussel's collection of essays entitled *América latina: Dependencia y liberación*. The book is divided into four parts: two sets of philosophical anthropological reflections, one ontological and one beyond the ontological; and two sets of theological reflections, one based on a universalist theology and one directed toward a theology of liberation. An example of the change can be seen in the theological essays. In the first section, which is based on a universalist theology, Dussel seems concerned with helping the institutional Catholic Church to survive paganization, secularization, and social change and to expand its influence in the face of these movements. He urges the Church to support social change and to integrate itself into society without fearing secularization. This concern for the institutional preservation of the Church all but disappears in the second theological section. Here Dussel urges atheism against the European God, and speculates on what it would have been like had the sixteenth-century European colonizers in Latin America understood the indigenous people from their own world (*desde su mundo*) and loved them instead of violently imposing Western capitalism and Christianity upon them. Here the question becomes, not self-expansion, but ruthless self-critique before the face of the Other. Dussel's own philosophical transformation from ontology to ethics suggests that he gradually became a philosopher who, as Levinas might describe it, came to fear murder (of the Other) more than death (of myself).[38]

Dussel's attempt to fuse Heidegger with the natural law tradition founders in his ethics when he recognizes that the mere thematization of a prevailing ethos and the description of the fundamental conditions of its possibility of good and evil can yield an account only of what *is* the case, not of what *ought to be* the case. All of Heidegger's categories could explain as well a fundamental project immorally intent on the destruction of the Other as one morally dedicated to the liberation of the Other. In a critique that could be elaborated (but not in this limited space) to extend to natural law, Dussel comes to see that an ethical viewpoint distinct from an ontological one is required in order to assess the morality of any fundamental project, the essential structure of which Heidegger's thought (and phenomenological eidetics) can illuminate. In a sense, Dussel completely reverses his conviction in *Para una de-strucción de la historia de la ética* that all ethics is but a branch of fundamental ontology. He also withdraws from his earlier position that had rejected all non-ontological ethics, such as Kant's, because they seem to float "in the air." Indeed, this recognition of the distinction between the 'is' and the 'ought' has been a part of modern philosophy since Hume. It underlies Kant's fundamental distinction between speculative and practical-ethical reason, with the priority being put on practical reason, and it accounts for Levinas's efforts to found ethics on "metaphysical" rather than ontological grounds and to establish ethics as first philosophy. Though Dussel's critique of Heidegger prompts him to turn to Levinas instead of Kant, there is a sense in which this change involves embracing a fundamental tenet of modern philosophy: namely, that the 'is' and the 'ought' are radically distinct. This metamorphosis further entails abandoning a motive for his earlier rejection of the metaphysics of the subject, that is, that its ethics seems ungrounded ontologically. The problem with the ethics of the metaphysics of the subject—which Dussel continues to oppose in his later ethics—rests, not on its independence from ontology, but, as will be seen, on the arbitrariness of the subject, which, according to the earlier Dussel but apparently not the later, can be constrained only by an ethics based on some kind of ontological grounding.

It is interesting that in his search for ethics Dussel should turn to Levinas, who could also be considered as engaging in a phenomenological project parallel to Heidegger's: namely, trying to recover what has been forgotten, bringing to light the unnoticed and structural features of the intersubjective relationship. But

Levinas's eidetic description reveals not just what *is* the case, but also an *ought*, in fact, the *ought* of all *oughts*, or, as Derrida has put it, the ethics of all ethics.[39] That Levinas's phenomenological description yields an obligation, contrary to Heidegger's phenomenology and in apparent contradiction to a traditional dichotomy upheld throughout modern philosophy, highlights the uniqueness of Levinas's philosophy. In contradistinction to Heidegger, Levinas surpasses Heidegger, in that he attends much more thoroughly to the relationship with the Other than Heidegger's account of *Mitsein* does, with the result that Levinas sees what Heidegger and the phenomenological tradition had never seen. In regard to the is/ought divide, on the one hand, Levinas gives no rational derivation of any specific obligation from a factual situation and in this sense conforms with the modern insight. The rational derivation of obligations must occur at a philosophical level different from that of Levinas's phenomenological description of the human relations preceding rationality. Indeed, at that "higher" philosophical level, one might turn to a philosophical position such as Kant's which refuses to derive obligations from facts, especially since the critical force of Kant's ethics against prevailing factual arrangements would correspond to the critical stance Levinasian "metaphysics" adopts toward all predominating ontologies and totalities. Levinas's description that yields obligation could also be seen as evading the criticism that it commits the naturalistic fallacy since it refers to a philosophical level prior to the level at which the 'is' and the 'ought' are theoretically dissected.

But if independence from ontology does not offer sufficient grounds for rejecting Kantian ethics and modernity's metaphysics of the subject, do Dussel's other grounds withstand critique? Following Scheler's and Sombart's critique of the bourgeois underpinnings of Kant's thought, Dussel, too, raises the question of individualism. In fairness to Kant, though, it must be insisted that his demand that a moral agent test maxims to see if they are universalizable, and not based on merely subjective inclinations, testifies to his desire for universally binding norms contrary to private, individualistic approaches to ethics. Indeed, recent criticism of Kant by critical theory has furthered this very purpose of Kant's by calling for a dialogical search for universals to replace Kant's own monological approach, uncritically wedded as it was to the philosophy of the subject begun by Descartes. The individualism of the origins of the modernist quest for rationally grounded universal norms does not undermine that quest, as critical theory has shown, but invites the development of a dialogical rationalism, an alternative that Dussel does not explore before rejecting modernity.[40]

Other criticisms of Kant that Dussel offers fall short of the mark. When he argues that Kant's formalism and *a priori* approach manifest Galileo's mathematicization of nature, he seems to overlook the fact that Kant's distinction between speculative and practical reason is meant to protect the domain of ethics from the reductionism and determinisms governing scientific domains. To make ethics depend on theology, anthropology, physics, or hyperphysics would leave it vulnerable to empirical contingencies and contribute to its complete relativization. Kant's effort to mark out the distinctive domain of ethics and the *a priori* structures of rationality—far from falling prey to Galileo's worldview—actually constitutes a powerful critique of it. Dussel's equation of *vernünftigen Glaubens* with *fe racional* through his translation (might not *fe* be better translated as *creyencia?*) fails to grasp the positive importance Kant attributes to practical reason, and reduces it to irrationalism in comparison with an omnipotent science—contrary to Kant's intentions. Finally, Dussel's equation of the "universal law of nature" in Kant with "natural law" confuses modernity's understanding of scientific law (stressing universalizability without metaphysical connotations) with medieval metaphysical structures. The "kingdom of ends" refers not to metaphysics but to transcendental structures presupposed before one ever takes up metaphysical questions.

Dussel's remaining, and perhaps deepest, objection to the modern philosophy of the subject is the arbitrary character of that subject. The first thing to note is that Kant would absolutely agree that the subject is arbitrary. Kant shows no illusions about the corruptness of human motivation when he admits that, because we can never, even by the strictest examination, completely plumb the depths of the secret incentives of action, it can never be proved that a single person has ever acted from pure motives. But this lack of experimental evidence that anyone can act from moral motives does not undermine the ethical demands of practical reason, which commands regardless of whatever is factually or experimentally the case. Practical reason commands that one strive to be a purely sincere friend, even though one has never experienced such a friend and even though one mistrusts that one's own and others' protestations that they are sincere could merely serve to cover over secret, uglier motives. Levinas would agree, for he holds that morality begins when freedom, instead of being justified by itself, feels itself to be arbitrary and violent.[41]

Perhaps, though, the question for Dussel is whether the subject is so arbitrary that it would not be able even to articulate the universal norms that Kant hoped practical reason could deliver. Dussel is well aware that totalized systems invent "moral" (as opposed to "ethical") principles that serve simply to protect themselves. He notes, for instance (and many similar instances will be seen later), how the Argentinian military in the 1980s had elevated obedience to superiors' orders to an absolute value, as a support for the "universal order that founds the juridical itself"—all this simply to vindicate the corrupt government's legitimacy. Dussel's justifiable suspicion of moral universals protecting and concealing power relationships leads him to Nietzsche. As he comments, no one in modernity has discovered and explained thematically the fundaments of modernity as Nietzsche has. In Dussel's view, Nietzsche saw the dominant virtues of the totality as hiding their true nature as nothing more than sublimated vices. Ideology, which Nietzsche grasped so clearly, is the ontic-conceptual formulation that justifies the established order and covers its reality. Marx, too, realized that acts of domination become fixed as custom, promulgated as law, and respected as if they belonged to nature itself, so thoroughly does the totality cover its domination. The ethical totality, ethically evil as it is, hides itself from itself by creating its own quiet moral consciousness. Violence is rationalized, sacralized, and "naturalized."

> Violence is consecrated like a virtue. The man does violence to the woman by closing her within the house and yet venerates her as "master of the home" (mystifying her alienation); the father does violence to his son by obliging his obedience to repressive authority and educating him in his own image ("the Same"); and brother does violence to brother by demanding that the brother love the

4ETHICAL HERMENEUTICS

State under pain of death for the sake of security and the ideal of the fatherland (the ancient fatherland now under the power of the brother who dominates).[42]

Sensitive to these dangers of universalization and mistrustful of objective, abstract, and universal conceptualization processes more suitable for entities than for human beings, Dussel insists that the Other is concretely unknowable in the proximity of the face-to-face. Before the Other, the universalizing intelligence finds itself perplexed and impelled to surrender its arms. The veneration of the Other's liberty is founded, not in reason or *logos*, in intuition or comprehension, but in the confidence that affirms the Other as prior, anterior to oneself. This mistrust of false universalization and rationality so often at the service of reigning powers no doubt prompts Dussel's repeated willingness to be classified as postmodern.[43]

But his very distinction between "ethics" and "morality"—that is, between a level of practical demands valid for every human being in every historical situation and a concrete level that remains delimited within a certain historical system (for example, Inca or capitalist European)—indicates at least a hope that authentic universals, beyond those pressed into service for oppression, are discoverable. The Other of Levinas and Dussel can be seen as aiding negatively in the continual criticism of false universalization and ideology detection and positively in the discovery of authentic universals. As Jürgen Habermas has remarked, so much of postmodern critique from Nietzsche to Foucault could be seen as an effort to refine the project of modernity, rendering it more self-critical and ultimately more rational, but, unfortunately, this critique is seen as ultimately destructive of any possibility of rationality and universalization.[44]

We have seen that in fashioning his own ethics Enrique Dussel sought out Martin Heidegger's fundamental ontology as a corrective to the modern metaphysics of the subject, which formed a single unity from Descartes's *cogito* to Nietzsche's will-to-power. But when Dussel discovered that he could neither derive norms from Heidegger's basically descriptive ontology nor sustain his synthesis of a Heideggerian ontological ethics with the natural law, he thus found himself gravitating toward Levinas's ethics, which gave him the objectivity and capacity for critique against the modern metaphysics of subject. Yet we have examined Dussel's reasons for rejecting Kantian ethics and basically found them wanting.

In opting for Levinas, Dussel has chosen to work at the lived experience prior to theory—a level parallel to Husserl's notion of the life-world, if our pinpointing of the level of Levinas's philosophy's in the first chapter is accurate. In a reflection he offers on moral theology, Dussel himself seems to admit that his work begins at that level.

> It is not possible to begin by defining—as moral theologies do—the morality of an action by its transcendental relation to a norm or law. On the contrary, the absolute morality of the action indicates its transcendental relation to the building of the kingdom in the historical processes of the liberation of actual material peoples "who are hungry." It is only subsequently, within this framework, that it becomes possible to situate all the problems of abstract moral subjectivity (within which all moral theologies start).[45]

Yet, the question arises whether it is possible also to work at the transcendental level, as Kant did, and to develop a theory of ethics there, correlative to and in constant tension with the level of lived experience that Levinas and Dussel describe so well. The possibility of a two-level ethical theory, at lived and transcendental levels, will occupy us in the last chapter. Through such a possible ethical theory, I will attempt to show how Dussel's philosophy of liberation can respond to and accommodate Karl-Otto Apel's transcendental pragmatics without losing the constant source of renewal and critique that Levinas's Other affords to any philosophy seeking to be fully rational.

NOTES

1. Enrique Dussel, "Liberación latinoamericana y filosofía," in *Praxis latinoamericana y filosofía de la liberación* (Bogotá: Editorial Nueva América, 1983), pp. 9–12. Enrique Dussel, "Supuestos histórico-filosóficos de la teología desde América Latina," in *La nueva frontera de la teología en América Latina*, ed. Gustavo Gutiérrez, Rosino Gibelli, and Raul Vidales (Salamanca: Ediciones Sigueme, 1977), pp. 176–77. En-

rique Dussel, *Hipótesis para una historia de la Iglesia en América Latina* (Barcelona: Editorial Estela, 1967), pp. 157, 160, 171. Enrique Dussel, "Hacia una historia de la Iglesia latinoamericana," *Stromata* [Argentina], 21 (1965), 501, 503. Enrique Dussel, "Hernando Arias de Ugarte, obispo de Quito y arzobispo de Santa Fe de Bogotá, Charcas, y Lima (1561–1638)," *XXXVI Congreso Internacional de Americanistas,* Seville 1966, p. 178. Enrique Dussel, "Situación problematica de la antropología filosófica," *Nordeste (Resistencia),* 7 (1965), 115–21, 126, 129. It should be noted that Dussel's rather traditional views here are actually liberal relative to conservative "integrists" who would have had Christianity seal itself up against the outer world.

2. Enrique Dussel, *El dualismo en la antropología de la cristiandad: Desde el origen del cristianismo hasta antes de la conquista de América* (Buenos Aires: Editorial Guadalupe, 1974), pp. 14–15. Enrique Dussel, *El humanismo semita: Estructuras intencionales radicales del pueblo de Israel y otros semitas* (Buenos Aires: Editorial Universitaria de Buenos Aires, 1969), pp. xi, 121. Enrique Dussel, *El humanismo helénico* (Buenos Aires: Editorial Universitaria de Buenos Aires, 1975), pp. ix, xii, 115.

3. *El humanismo semita*, pp. 41–42, 45, 100, 110–11, 117–18, 120, 163.

4. *El humanismo helénico*, pp. xviii, xix, xxiv, 3, 17–18, 32. Enrique Dussel, *Cultura latinoamericana e historia de la Iglesia* (Buenos Aires: Ediciones de la Facultad de Teología de la Pontificia Universidad Católica Argentina, 1968), p. 65.

5. *El dualismo en la antropología de la cristiandad,* pp. 17, 24, 62, 103–104, 160, 198, 231, 244.

6. Ibid., pp. 26, 62, 147, 231, 259, 263, 266, 269, 270.

7. Ibid., pp. 11, 26, 93, 104, 282–83, 287. Enrique Dussel and Antonio Blanch, "Fisionomía actual del catolicismo latinoamericano: Considerando su génesis histórica," *Fe cristiana y cambio social en América Latina* (Salamanca: Ediciones Sigueme, 1973), p. 345; Enrique Dussel, *Ethics and the Theology of Liberation,* trans. Bernard F. McWilliam, C.SS.R. (Maryknoll, N.Y.: Orbis Books, 1978), p. 134; Enrique Dussel, *Para una ética de la liberación latinoamericana. II. Eticidad y moralidad* (Buenos Aires: Siglo Vientiuno Argentina Editores, 1973), pp. 120–21; Dussel points out features of Semitic culture before introducing Levinas's ethical theory.

8. Enrique Dussel, *América Latina: Dependencia y liberación* (Buenos Aires: Fernando Garcia Cambiero, 1973), p. 146. *El dualismo en la antropología de la cristiandad,* p. 24. *El humanismo semita,* pp. 57, 59, 63, 167–70. Enrique Dussel and María Mercedes Esandi, *El catolicismo popular en la Argentina* (Buenos Aires: Editorial Bonum, 1970), p. 27. Secretariat for Catholic–Jewish Relations, NCCB; Adult Education Department, USCC;

Interfaith Affairs Department, ADL, "Within Context: Guidelines for the Catechetical Presentation of Jews and Judaism in the New Testament [1986]," in *In Our Time: The Flowering of Jewish–Catholic Dialogue*, ed. Eugene J. Fisher and Leon Klenicki (New York and Mahwah, N.J.: Paulist Press, 1990), pp. 62, 69. Eugene J. Fisher, "A New Maturity in Christian–Jewish Dialogue: An Annotated Bibliography, 1975–1989," *In Our Time*, p. 127; Rosemary Radford Ruether, *Faith and Fratricide: The Theological Roots of Anti-Semitism* (New York: Seabury, 1974), pp. 141–44, 233–39.

9. *El humanismo helénico*, p. 91.

10. Ibid., pp. xxii, 51, 91. *América Latina: Dependencia y liberación*, pp. 28–29, 32, 34, 56. *Cultura latinoamericana e historia de la Iglesia*, p. 45.

11. *El humanismo helénico*, p. xxii. Enrique Dussel, "Sobre el sentido de la traducción," *Actos del Primer Congreso de Estudios Clásicos* (Mendoza, Argentina: Universidad Nacional de Cuyo, 1972), p. 134. Dussel and Esandi, *El catolicismo popular en la Argentina*, pp. 19, 49, 164. *El dualismo en la antropología de la cristiandad*, pp. 26, 62, 147, 231, 259.

12. "Liberación latinoamericana y filosofía," p. 13. Enrique Dussel, *Método para una filosofía de la liberación: Superación analéctica de la dialéctica hegeliana*, 3rd ed. (Guadalajara: Editorial Universidad de Guadalajara, 1991), pp. 9, 13.

13. Enrique Dussel, *La dialéctica hegeliana: Supuestos y superación o del inicio originario del filosofar* (Mendoza, Argentina: Editorial Ser y Tiempo, 1972), pp. 154–55. *Para una ética de la liberación latinoamericana*, 2:171.

14. *La dialéctica hegeliana*, pp. 107, 111, 122. Enrique Dussel, *Para una ética de la liberación latinoamericana. I. Acceso al punto de partida de la ética* (Buenos Aires: Siglo Vientiuno Argentina Editores, 1973), pp. 115, 118; *Para una ética de la liberación latinoamericana*, 2:69, 73, 76, 132.

15. *Método para una filosofía de la liberación*, pp. 181–85, 186.

16. Enrique Dussel, *Para una de-strucción de la historia de la ética* (Mendoza, Argentina: Editores Ser y Tiempo, 1970), p. 200; see also pp. 164, 168, 191.

17. Ibid., pp. 195–96, 199, 223, 224.

18. Ibid., p. 311.

19. Ibid., pp. 232–38, 247, 293. *Para una ética de la liberación latinoamericana*, p. 68.

20. *Para una de-strucción de la historia de la ética*, pp. 236, 238, 242, 247, 249.

21. Ibid., p. 280; cf. pp. 275–80.

22. Ibid., pp. 312–18.

23. Ibid., pp. 236, 252, 255, 260–61, 264, 267, 268, 270–74.

24. *Para una ética de la liberación latinoamericana*, 2:129, 145, 162–63, 187.

48   ETHICAL HERMENEUTICS

25. Ibid., 1:35–37, 73–74; 2:133, 141–42.
26. Ibid., 1:38, 56; 2:135–38, 143–45, 151, 182.
27. Ibid., 1:45, 77.
28. Ibid., 1:47, 48, 54, 55, 56, 58–60, 63–64. *Para la de-strucción de la historia de la ética*, pp. 195, 223.
29. *Para una ética de la liberación latinoamericana*, 1:90–91. For other convergences between Aquinas and Heidegger (for example, between *Sorge* and intention, *boulesis* and *poder-ser*), see pp. 169 and 171.
30. Ibid., 2:190.
31. Ibid., 2:14–15, 19–20, 179, 184, 190–92.
32. Ibid., 2:21, 34, 56.
33. Ibid., 1:123. Enrique Dussel, "Del descubrimiento al desencubrimiento: Hacia un desagravio histórico," *Misiones Extranjeras*, 86 (1985), 107.
34. *Para una ética de la liberación latinoamericana*, 2:119.
35. Ibid., 1:123.
36. Ibid., 1:98–99, 119, 124–25; 2:153–55, 163, 213. Enrique Dussel, *Método para una filosofía de la liberación: Superación analéctica de la dialéctica hegeliana*, 2nd ed. (Salamanca: Ediciones Sigueme, 1974), p. 269. *La dialéctica hegeliana*, pp. 146–47.
37. *Para una ética de la liberación latinoamericana*, 2:26, 30–32, 187.
38. *América Latina: Dependencia y liberación*, pp. 171–72, 200–202.
39. Derrida, "Violence and Metaphysics," pp. 35–39.
40. Jürgen Habermas, *The Theory of Communicative Action*. I. *Reason and the Rationalization of Society*, trans. Thomas McCarthy (Boston: Beacon, 1984), pp. 390–91. Karl-Otto Apel, *Transformation der Philosophie*. II. *Das Apriori der Kommunikationsgemeinschaft* (Frankfurt am Main: Suhrkamp Verlag, 1973), pp. 414, 417; English translation: *Towards a Transformation of Philosophy*, trans. Glyn Adey and David Frisby (Londonand Boston: Routledge & Kegan Paul, 1980), pp. 269, 272. Karl-Otto Apel, *Diskurs und Verantwortung: Das Problem des Übergangs zur postkonventionellen Moral* (Frankfurt am Main: Suhrkamp Verlag, 1990), pp. 98–99, 113, 166. Thomas McCarthy, *The Critical Theory of Jürgen Habermas* (Cambridge, Mass.: The MIT Press, 1978), p. 326.
41. Immanuel Kant, *Grounding for the Metaphysics of Morals*, trans. James W. Ellington (Indianapolis, Ind.: Hackett, 1981), pp. 19–20. Levinas, *Totality and Infinity*, p. 84.
42. *Para una ética de la liberación latinoamericana*, 2:79.
43. Ibid., 2:35, 76–79, 81, 85, 93, 97, 102, 103, 173. Enrique Dussel, "Existen 'Dos Morales' en Argentina? Límites éticos de una orden oficial superior," *Iglesias*, 2 (1985), 14–15. *América latina: Dependencia y liberación*, p. 125.

44. Enrique Dussel, "Puede legitimarse 'una' ética ante la pluralidad histórica de las morales?" in *Praxis latinoamericana y filosofía de la liberación* (Bogotá: Editorial Nueva América, 1983), p. 119. Jürgen Habermas, *The Philosophical Discourse of Modernity*, trans. Frederick Lawrence (Cambridge, Mass: The MIT Press, 1987), pp. 97, 103, 120, 125, 127, 283, 292, 302, 341.

45. Enrique Dussel, "An Ethics of Liberation: Fundamental Hypotheses," *Concilium*, 192 (1984), 60.

3

Overcoming Levinas: Analectical Method and Ethical Hermeneutics

ANALECTICAL METHOD BEYOND LEVINAS:
LATIN AMERICAN MEDIATIONS AND THE ANALOGICAL
WORD OF THE OTHER

IN *América Latina: Dependencia y liberación, Para una ética de la liberación latinoamericana,* and *Método para una filosofía de la liberación,* after extensive discussions of the critics who moved beyond Hegel (Feuerbach, Marx, Kierkegaard, and Schelling), Dussel explains at length how his philosophy surpasses Levinas's. His introductory remarks indicate how his critique/development will proceed.[1]

> The real surpassing of this whole tradition, beyond Marcel and Buber, has been the philosophy of Levinas, still European and excessively equivocal. Our surpassing will consist in rethinking the discourse from Latin America and from ana-logy; this surpassing I formulated after a personal dialogue held with the philosopher in Paris and Louvain in January of 1972. . . .
>
> Nevertheless, Levinas always says that the Other is "absolutely other." Thus he tends toward equivocity [*equivocidad*]. For the other part, he has never thought that the Other could be an Indian, an African, an Asian.[2]

Dussel's criticism of Levinas's Eurocentrism—that he never thought that the Other could be an Indian, African, or Asian— seems to fault Levinas for working at the abstract level of the essence of the ethical intersubjective relationship without discussing concrete instantiations. This criticism seems unfair, particularly given Dussel's careful and laudatory recognition of the abstract level at which Marx pitches his analysis of economic systems, seeking out, for instance, the essential determinations of "production," whether in an Aztec, Incan, Egyptian, European, or Latin American context. But Levinas's abstract level could certainly accommodate Dussel's Latin American situation; for, as Dussel's own account of their conversation shows, Levinas, instead of resisting Dussel, "could only accept" (*no pudo menos que aceptar*) that he had never thought that the Other could be Indian, African, or Asian since he had been preoccupied with the sufferings inflicted by Stalin and Hitler. Dussel's self-described task of the "implementation of the mediations" of Levinas's description of the originary experience of the face-to-face in its erotic, pedagogic, and political dimensions—for all its creativity—involves a superpassing that preserves Levinas (*Aufhebung*, in Hegel's sense) and still depends upon him. Dussel himself admits that his conversation with Levinas turned up both a "similitude" between their thought and a "radical rupture."[3]

One can better appreciate this criticism of Levinas's Eurocentrism and Dussel's relationship to Levinas after considering the second mode of surpassing: namely, "from analogy," as developed in the three texts mentioned above. Before taking up a series of questions on analogy, Dussel sketches some principal features of his "ana-lectical" method: its opposition to a dia-lectical method proceeding from out of itself instead of from the Other beyond the Totality, its replacement of a Heideggerian ontological fundament by a prior ethical moment, and its inclusion of a constitutive practical, historical option to listen to, interpret, and serve the Other. This analectical method, beginning with the Other, discovers the analogical character of the word of the Other.[4]

Dussel begins his discussion of analogy by defining terms. *Logos*, at the root of analogy, signifies to "collect, reunite, express, define," whereas its Hebrew correspondent, *dabar*, means "speak, talk, dialogue, and reveal." *Logos* tends toward a univocity that subsumes and suppresses differences, whereas its Hebrew correspondent, *dabar*, entails ana-logy discoverable to one who assumes an attitude of trust and the obedience of a disciple (*ob-ediencia discipular*) toward the Other who is different. Dussel speaks here of *analogia verbi* or *analogia fidei*, different from (and yet related to) Thomistic discussions of analogy that focus on the analogy of expressive words (*analogia nominis*).[5]

There are even different, analogous kinds of analogy, or in Dussel's words, "the notion of analogy is itself analogical." Dussel explains one such type of analogy by citing Aristotle's *Metaphysics* to the effect that "Being is predicated in many ways, but always with respect to some origin." Following Aristotle, the philosophical tradition, including thinkers such as Kant, Hegel, or Heidegger, realized that Being is not predicated as a genus of its species. Rather, Being, which transcends every genus and is not even conceivable as the genus of genera, can better be understood as the horizon of the world or light of all that exists or the totality of meaning. Nevertheless, ultimately the content of the word "Being" is identical with itself, one and the same, and the many forms in which it expresses itself fail to escape the identical and univocal ontological totality. Face to face with the Other, however, one discovers that Being as the fundament of the totality is not the only manner of predicating Being. This Other above and beyond the totality, possesses Being in an ana-logical, distinct, and separated way from the way it is possessed within the Totality. Though there would seem to be a shared concept (Being) within this analogy as within the first kind, here one may apply any predicate to the Other at most tentatively, dependent upon the revelation of an Other "whose presence makes evident the absence that attracts and provokes" and who is still incomprehensible and transontological. Here metaphysical distinction replaces the ontological difference of the first type of analogy.[6]

According to Dussel, the revelatory word of the Other, although similar to the word employed by other users of the same language and therefore comprehensible in a derived and inadequate way, still does not lend itself so easily to interpretation because of the depth and incomprehensibility of its distinct origin: namely, the Other who speaks it. When a young man tells a young woman "I love you," the words carry with them pretensions to a truth as yet unverified (that the man really loves her) and an obligation and demand that the listener place faith in the speaker. The said ("I love you") refers radically to the saying (especially the presence of the revealer) beyond the said and beyond the listener's own ontological comprehension as a totality.[7]

Dussel amplifies on this reference of the revealed word to the revealer, since it touches on the essence of the human person, of historicity, and rationality. The word of the Other comes from beyond the mundane listener's existential comprehension of the world, and in order to understand that word, the listener must at first accept it only because the Other speaks it.

> It is the love-of-justice, transontological, that permits one to accept as true her [the Other's] unverified word. This act of historical rationality is the supremely rational act and manifests it [historical rationality] from the fullness of the human spirit: to be capable of working on the basis of a *believed* word is, precisely, a creative act that proceeds beyond the horizon of the whole and that advances *on the basis of the word* of the Other into the new.[8]

Inversely, to reduce the word of the Other to what has been already said, to make the Other's analogical word identical to (and therefore univocal with) one's own, is to deny the distinctiveness of the Other's word; it is to kill and assassinate the Other. To avoid such a univocal obliteration of the Other, one must commit oneself in humility and meekness to a pedagogic apprenticeship with the Other as master and to a following of the way that the Other's word traces, day in and day out. Philosophy, beginning from this analectic starting point, proceeds dialectically, borne forward by the word of the Other. When one actually hears this novel word of the Other, the result is that the prevailing Totality is placed in movement toward a correct interpretation of the word of the Other, finally achievable when the new Totality, the new fatherland, the new future legal order, is established.[9]

Dussel's insight here that the word of the Other means the same to all language users and yet carries with it a depth and incomprehensibility because of its distinctive origin, the Other, resembles Alfred Schutz's important differentiation between the objective and the subjective meanings of signs. In Schutz's view, signs have an objective meaning within a sign system when they can be intelligibly coordinated to what they designate within that system independently of whoever uses the sign or interprets it. At the same time, however, an aura surrounds the nucleus of objective meaning in that everyone using or interpreting a sign associates it with meanings that have their origin in the unique experiences in which that person learned to use the sign. This aura constitutes the subjective meaning. Schutz concludes: "Exactly what Goethe means by 'demonic' can only be deduced from a study of his works as a whole. Only a careful study of the history of French culture aided by linguistic tools can permit us to understanding the subjective meaning of the word 'civilization' in the mouth of a Frenchman."[10] Furthermore, since each person's stream of consciousness never completely overlaps another's, the meanings one gives to another's experience can never be precisely the same as the meanings that the Other gives to them, since one would have to be the other person in order to interpret them in exactly the same way. Dussel readily admits these difficulties of translation, for he recognizes that the passage from one world to another in an adequate, complete, perfect manner is impossible, insofar as one word carries in its train the totality of a world that is untranslatable and that needs to be uncovered if that word is to be understood. Within this understanding of language, every word usage becomes essentially analogical, meaning the same and yet not quite the same to conversants. By what Schutz calls the general thesis of the reciprocity of perspectives, commonsense individuals overleap these discrepancies in meaning by assuming that they would see things as the Other does if they were in the Other's place. Although this thesis might lead to an uncritical assimilation of the Other's meanings to one's own, it also underlies the confidence that the Other is rational and that one would act and think as the Other does if one were in the Other's position. Of course, such trust in the rationality of the Other becomes more difficult and more daring, the farther the Other's exteriority lies from one's Totality, and the more divergent the Other's history and social background from one's own, and the more the Other's belief and action system (and not just individual words) seem at odds with one's own.[11]

Dussel's emphasis on trust in the analogical word of the Other need not contradict Jürgen Habermas's conviction that one can understand another only if one is involved as a participant in assessing the validity claims of the Other through "rational interpretation." Such assessing involves no expectation that the Other will prove to be irrational; in fact, our assessments for the most part find the Other conforming to rational standards we would hold regarding consistency and basic empirical beliefs. Donald Davidson's principle of interpretive charity would have it that in order "to understand others, we must count them right in most matters." But there will come moments in which another's statements seem to contradict commonsense beliefs or logical principles, such as those of identity or noncontradiction. To use an example drawn from anthropology: the Nuer spoke of a sacrificial cucumber as an ox, or a human twin as a bird. Even here, though, anthropologists, almost as if driven by a conviction of the rationality of the Other, have attempted to provide contextual interpretations that might explain away seeming contradictions as part of ritual behavior or as metaphor. Because of this trust in the analogical world of the Other that, according to Dussel, constitutes the first moment in the encounter with the Other, interpreters can also decide that at the moment they are not in a position to judge the soundness of the reasons of the Other—and Habermas admits that such postponement of judgment would be a legitimate evaluative alternative for a rational interpreter. Still, if, after exhausting efforts to understand and after trustingly postponing final judgment, one finds oneself compelled to disagree with the Other's beliefs or practices, one could do so for the sake of the Other in complete consistency with the invitation to responsibility for the Other flowing from the initial moment of the face-to-face. Such judgment reveals the presence of the second moment in Levinas's account of intersubjectivity, the intervention of the Third who introduces comparison, measuring, and equality (as if "before a court of justice"). This second moment always occurs with reference to the originary moment, since, as Levinas puts it, "proximity is not from the first a judgment of a tribunal of justice, but first a responsibility for the other which turns into judgment only with the entry of the third party." Since these moments are not chronological moments, the standards of judgment (introduced by the Third) can penetrate to the assessing activity that takes place as one stands face to face with the Other, under obligation to be responsible for the Other. Even to recognize that the Other is different and that one ought to refuse any judgment of the Other because one does not as yet understand the Other would presuppose the presence of just such standards; to set in abeyance temporarily one's standards of judgment for the sake of the Other presupposes that they are there.[12]

The task of listening to the analogical word of the Other transforms philosophy itself. Philosophy becomes a pedagogics, the method of knowing how to believe the word of the Other and interpret it. Committed to the Other, the philosopher gains access to a new world and sets about destroying the obstacles that impede the revelation of the Other. In Latin America, philosophy becomes a cry, a clamor, an exhortation of those who have taught the philosopher: the people dominated by the ruling system centered in the North Atlantic community. Latin American philosophy itself appears as a new and analogical moment in the history of philosophy. On one hand, it is tied to and expounds the history of philosophy to which it belongs and to which it is therefore similar, but not with a similarity that might be confused with the identity and univocity of Hegelian history, in which each philosopher or people is valued as part of one, identical, unfolding historical process that began with Europe and is Europe's own process. On the other, if Latin American philosophy is completely distinct, the history of philosophy breaks down into a series of equivocal "philosophical biographies," in Jaspers's terms. For Dussel, though, we are left with neither Hegelian identity nor Jasperian equivocity, but with the analogy of a continuous history of philosophy, whose discontinuity is evidenced by the liberty of each philosopher and the distinctiveness of each people.[13]

It is fitting that Dussel should conclude his discussion of his overcoming of Levinas by reflecting on the analogical character of philosophy. For the critic who would describe Dussel's implementation of the mediations of Levinas's description of the originary face-to-face as only a continuation of Levinas, or as only an application of Levinas, reads philosophy as a univocal unfolding and overlooks the novelty of Dussel's thought. Is there perhaps in this refusal to recognize the analogical character of philosophy, in this tendency to reduce all philosophy to its historical predecessors and its European roots, a philosophical affront to the metaphysically distinct Other, the Other as Latin American philosopher? If the voice of the poor of Latin America speaks through Dussel and others as a philosophical mouthpiece, isn't something distinctive going on there, however much Dussel may utilize Levinasian categories?

Perhaps Dussel's most original surpassing of Levinas lies precisely in this notion of analogy, which does not tolerate the equi-

vocity of Levinas's totally Other and questions the univocity of the
critic who shields himself from the challenge of the novel by striv-
ing to show that there is nothing new under the sun.

ANALECTICAL METHOD AND THE UNMASKING
OF FALSE UNIVERSALISM

In Dussel's hands, the analectical method, which discloses the analogical word of the Other, develops further into a critique of
false universals that expands into a critique of philosophical-theo-
logical pretentiousness, science, and even the project of modernity—all this beyond Levinas's ethics, but also in its spirit. Such a
development is all the more remarkable when one samples Dussel's earlier works from 1965 to 1970 and finds an emphasis on
universalism almost at the expense of particularism. In the appen-
dix to *El humanismo semita*, he claims that the religious community
needs to free itself from any nationalistic particularism and that
only a *death to particularism* will permit Salvation to reach to the
ends of the earth. The poems of the Suffering Servant of Yahweh
express a universalism without frontiers, a centrifugal extrana-
tional universalism achieved by the *evacuation* of every particularism. In *El catolicismo popular en la Argentina*, Dussel discusses the
missionary universalism of the religion founded by Jesus that
ought to take the word of God (presumably given first as universal) and clothe it with cultural mediations. In theological articles,
Dussel urges that Christians abandon the methods and structures
of Christendom "in order to integrate themselves into the Universal Civilization of which Latin American is only a part and in
which it must participate each day more and more actively." In
Hipótesis para una historia de la Iglesia en América Latina, Dussel defends the *tabula rasa* methods of the Spanish missionaries who did
not build on religious practices of the Indians. Dussel argues both
that these missionaries sought to avoid syncretism and that these
indigenous cultures had not arrived at the evolutionary level of
the Roman, Hindu, or Chinese empires. Once Dussel underwent
his conversion to Levinas's thought, such "Catholocentric" and
"ethnocentric" judgments cease to appear, and he focuses his

efforts instead on an unmasking of false universalistic claims, such as these of his earliest period.[14]

Dussel's works after 1970 abound in criticism of such false universalizations. The pretended universality of North Atlantic culture camouflages an historical will-to-power evident from the first meeting of the Spanish *conquistadores* with the indigenous American cultures until the present. Dussel depicts starkly the original negation of the Amerindian culture in the name of this "universal" culture:

> Amerindia or Hispanoamerica is not so much a brute, mute being as a being *silenced* and *brutalized* in the presence of an ear habituated to hearing other music, other languages, other harmonies. The Indian is not a being in the rough, but rather one brutalized in the presence of a the unilateral consciousness of the conqueror, blind to Indian values. The Indian is the barbarian only for those who elevate their world into the only world possible.[15]

The Spanish king in the first law of *Bullarum* legitimates this oppression of America Indians in the name of the universal God: "God has entrusted to us in His infinite mercy and goodness the rule over such a great part of the world. . . . happily it has been given to us to lead the innumerable peoples and nations that inhabit America ('the West Indies') into the Catholic Church and to subject them to our rule."[16]

Just as the Spanish occupied the Indian kingdoms for the sublime motive of evangelization, the North Americans seized Texas, New Mexico, and California for another "rational" motive: manifest destiny. Sarmiento followed this pattern in the nineteenth century by elevating Latin American urban centers to a universal value over against the countryside: "The nineteenth century and the twelfth century live together: one in the cities, the other in the fields. . . . [We are speaking] of the struggle between European civilization and indigenous barbarism, between intelligence and matter, an unavoidable struggle in America."[17]

In the twentieth century, a pretended universal culture—of Coca-Cola and cowboy pants—destroys the cultural objects, customs, symbols, and meaning of life of peripheral peoples. Moreover, the doctrine of development (*doctrina del desarrollo*) universalizes the model of developed countries by insisting that underdeveloped countries lack elements of this model and need to imitate it, even though such a doctrine leads to the peripheral countries' losing control of their internal economies, transferring decisions to the center, and weaking their already unproductive commercial oligarchies—all because of basic inequalites in the terms of exchange. As Dussel remarks, every oppression has its ideology, and each commences when it situates the Other in non-being, reducing it to servitude as it pretends to pass on civilization.[18]

Throughout history, cultural systems of knowledge have involved the imposing of Eurocentric patterns of understanding on the rest of the world. For example, according to Aristotle the prevailing Greek social structures of slavery and the oppression of women take on an the physionomy of eternity and divine permanence. By imputing such economic and erotic depravity to nature itself, the ontology of the Totality, although presenting itself as light, fundament, and eternity, is nothing other than economically and erotically repressive. It is no wonder that Dussel describes philosophical ethics as concealing ideologies that naturalize or sacralize domination by dehistorifying the established order. Another instance of this cultural imperialism, Rousseau's pedagogy, rejecting feudal, noble, monarchic, or ecclasiastic modes of education, permits the bourgeois state to take over the education of the son since the family and popular culture have nothing to say or teach. For Rousseau, human nature is truly grasped only by the rising bourgeoisie, whose disdain of popular culture will lead to imperial and neocolonial extremes later. By stressing the unconditional character of the aseptic preceptor, the neocolonial state of the Center, by means of the enlightened and imperial culture, identifies itself as the universal culture, as human nature, without critical conscience. Freud, too, while adequately detecting the pedagogic domination of father over son, flowering under the sway of modern subjectivity, imputes this structure to a worldwide human nature, thereby invalidly universalizing a peculiar European experience. Historical accounts also substitute particularist perspectives for universal ones. Thus Alfred Weber's *History of Culture* pretends to present an account of universal culture, but it mentions Latin America in only four lines (regarding Spain's discovery of it), and Lortz's *History of the Church* never even mentions Latin America.[19]

Part of Dussel's struggle to unmask deceptive universals involves his criticism of Roman Catholic practices and teachings. The Church's liturgical year, for example, evidences the northern hemisphere's universalizing of its practices without regard for differences, thus ordering celebrations of the humble beginnings of the Son of God (Christmas) at a time when the earthly sun in Latin America is at its peak, and of the resurrection of Christ when all creation finds itself in an autumnal process of death. The fixing of the universal liturgy at the Council of Trent also undermined any efforts to include indigenous rituals at precisely the time when evangelization in Latin America might have been enhanced by such possibilities. Furthermore, the social doctrine of the Church, thought out in European context or in that of developed nations, does not correspond to the concrete situations of Latin Americans, since, for instance, it recommends that one overcome class war, but says little about overcoming the domination of one class by another. More recently, Dussel has criticized the Third World Synod of Roman Catholic bishops for failing to condemn injustice, and in his view the Latin American Episcopal Conference at Medellín found itself impelled to supplement the supposed universalism of this synod with mandates appropriate to Latin America. Christian doctrines afford a continual source for legitimating corruption, as in the case of the Pinochet-led military junta of Chile whose Declaration of Principles in 1973 styled the junta itself as the defender of the universally revered Christian concept of life against its Marxist opponents. According to Dussel, there is a constant danger of confusing Judeo-Christianity with a particular civilization, race, or a determinate nation or people. Hence, Dussel almost completely reverses his earlier Catholocentrism when he finally concludes that the role of Christianity is to demythogize the absolutized relative.[20]

Theological reflection, no less than Church practice, tends to cloak its particularity in universal garb. In his essay "Théologie de la 'Périphérie' et du 'Centre,'" Dussel chides the dogmatic slumber of a pretended theological universality which the particularity of the center has assumed. The center, the North Atlantic community, has been and still is able to impose itself on other countries because of the power of its economy, its technology, and even its libraries, publications, and theological administrative structures. It is still necessary, he believes, to envision "an international division of theological labor" in which theologians would humbly take up their partial, situated tasks, specific to a continent, and in which they could become cognizant of the determinations exercised on them instead of assimilating uncritically theologies inappropriate to their context. Dussel here merely follows the advice of Peruvian philosopher Augusto Salazar Bondy, who urges Latin Americans in his *Existe una filosofía de nuestra América?* to be vigilant and mistrustful in the extreme so as not to fall into alienating modes of reflection offered from outside Latin America. But such caution, far from undermining theology, will lead to a new vision of theology itself. Theology requires that one take the large way, that of "distinction," that of constructing a new "analogical" theology.

> Within the dialogues of the periphery have arisen differences among Africa, Asia, Latin America, and between the center and the periphery. Some bridges offering possible solutions have also arisen, first of all, for understanding the position of the Other, and then, for arriving at some method and some categories (a paradigm) which might be capable of opening to a future *mundial* theology. This new analogical totality will be built up in the twenty-first century beginning from affirmed and developed particularisms (among these, *as particulars*, Europe and the United States).[21]

Dussel's skepticism about universals is not, however, total, but, rather, heuristic and ethically oriented. In *Fundamentación de la ética y filosofía de la liberación*, Dussel observes that the philosophy of liberation inevitably maintains a continual suspicion of the nonfundamental character of every "real accord," and considers as possible domination every pretense to universalization following from such "consensus." For Dussel, though, this preference for suspicion is part of an inevitable and inescapable ethical exigency. Dussel finds Apel actually concurring with this suspicion, in that Apel defends the idea of a regulative principle of an ideal community of communication placing in question every real one—a questioning essential for the progress of interpretation.[22]
Because of this mistrust of the possibility of disguised oppres-

sion, Dussel at times makes disparaging remarks about the possi-bility of science. In *Para una ética de la liberación latinoamericana*, he states that the human sciences, and sciences in general, have questioned their own suppositions and have understood that there is no universality in science. To pretend to such universality is to calculate and conclude in favor of the dominator, the North Atlantic culture and civilization. Furthermore, even the axioms of science, including mathematical axioms, are neither universal nor eternal, but cultural. An axiom is accepted because it is wor-thy of being accepted as "cultural" evidence. Citing Cornelius de Pauw on how heat has damaged the brains of Africans and other false "scientific" demonstrations of the inferiority of blacks, Dus-sel concludes, against Althusser, that there is a grade of ideological contamination from which science can never free itself. In *Filo-sofía de la producción*, Dussel observes how scientists and technolo-gists, as if intent on hiding their particularity beneath a universalistic veil, prefer not to talk about a Latin American sci-ence, but rather about science and technology in general.[23]

In several of these contexts, though, Dussel indicates that his interpretation of science is not as arbitrary or relativistic as it might seem. For instance, the Latin American social scientists, questioning universality, really wonder whether the mere func-tionality of an economic system can satisfy the ethical criteria by which that system ought to be judged. In this view, although scien-tific conclusions might be autonomously valid, their *application* in a wider context depends on extra-scientific, ethico-political con-siderations. In addition to these considerations of the mission of science for society, Dussel also notes how prescientific ethico-po-litical commitments condition one's scientific "vocation" and the problems one chooses to address. In addition, such commitments determine what articles journals accept and what academic proj-ects receive financing. Although it is regrettably true that politics often plays a repressive role in academic settings, these practices do not undermine the validity of scientific claims to truth, but in fact could presuppose it as something they battle to suppress.[24]

In his essay "Historia y praxis (Ortopraxia y objectividad)," Dussel works out his most careful resolution of the tension be-tween the cultural determinants of science and its objectivity. Fol-lowing the later Husserl, he argues that everyday-life praxis and its interests provide for the constitution of objects, such that, for instance, it would have been impossible for the Pharaoh to recognize the legitimacy and consistency of the hope of exploited slaves: it was beyond the possible horizon of his capacity for object-constitution. The physical structure of the matter at hand and the practical, historical collectivity cannot be divorced from each other in the mutual roles they play in the building up an object. Of course, a methodic, disciplined scientific/transcendental subjectivity can supplant the empirical (pathological) subject producing the opinions of everyday life, and, as the later Husserl taught, one must never forget this subject-correlative character of scientific findings if one wishes to avoid forms of scientism and objectivism. According to Dussel's conception, recent philosophy of science has settled for a type of "abstract objectivity" that is achieved within the conditions of the elaboration of a discourse and in conformity with spelled out epistemologically required exigencies. Following Marx's *Capital* instead, Dussel opts for a "concrete objectivity" that, while it elaborates a rich totality of multiple determinations and relations, seeks correspondence with the real, validity, and the achievement of truth (as opposed to mere objectivity without truth). Not only does Dussel show himself highly unrelativistic at this point of the argument, but he insists that when a liberating praxis involves itself with what is exterior to the prevailing totality, it uncovers a rich mine of data, hypotheses, and reality neglected by those intellectuals of ruling hegemony whose prescientific constitutive processes have not even allowed such data to appear. Such praxis, elucidating a new horizon of knowability of daily and scientific objects, is intrinsic to theory itself and by no means extratheoretical. Dedication to the oppressed makes possible a greater degree of objectivity than is possible for the "new mandarins" of the system, as Chomsky describes them. Although scientific knowledge continues to be relative to disciplined subjective processes—and so is neither absolute (presuppositionless) Hegelian knowledge nor blind commonsense prejudice—there are degrees of objectivity possible that are enhanced, particularly when the scientist is exposed to the data of exteriority against which the prevailing system refuses to test itself.[25]

Here again, Dussel's analectical method leads him to question the universalizations in a domain where Levinas rarely ventured—science. Like Levinas, however, Dussel shows himself skeptical of any pretentious rationality that would legislate uncritically for all others. At the same time, Dussel's critique of science shows that the very Other who makes one doubtful about rationality holds the key for helping rationality to be more rational. In this, Dussel shows himself even more analogous to Levinas, who saw in the face of the Other, not the enemy of reason, but the positive invitation to discourse and the ultimate horizon (beyond even Husserl's life-world) that must be taken into account if rationality is to be truly rational.

Even the dialectical process itself can function as a type of oppressive universalization. Beyond the well-known and already discussed fact that for Hegel there is no exteriority, Dussel realizes that even a negative dialectics such as that of the Frankfurt School, Ernst Bloch, or Sartre ends up affirming the system it rebels against. If the Sandinistas risked their lives in Nicaragua simply because they wished to deny "Somocism," then Somocism would have become their central obsession, the focus of their energy, and thus embraced them within its tentacles even as they rebelled against it. But, in Dussel's view, the Sandinistas revolted before all and principally to affirm the Nicaraguan people, with their practices, values, memories, their "spaces" of liberty and dignity, their history, their accounts of liberation, their music, language, economy of self-subsistence and life outside the *Somocista* order, in the light of all of which they recognized Somocism as oppression. The Sandinistas negated the negation inflicted on the Nicaraguan people *from* (*desde*) the affirmation of the Nicaraguan people. As opposed to negative dialectics, authentic liberation springs neither from hatred nor from a desire for struggle in itself, but is moved by love and by appreciation for the value of the exterior culture.[26]

Bartholomé de las Casas exemplifies the authentic prophet, since he underwent tutelage at the hands of the oppressed and learned to admire the beauty, culture, and goodness of the indigenous, the new, the Other. Las Casas indeed appreciates the *pulchritudo prima* that Dussel claims is to be found in the face, carnality, and dark-skinned loveliness (*belleza criolla*) of the poor, the oppressed, the Other, giving the lie to aristocratic aesthetics that attributes only ugliness to the Other in order to make it easier to subjugate that Other. Unlike Gines de Sepúlveda or Fernandez de Oviedo, who saw the indigenous person as totalized within their system, Las Casas discovers the exteriority of indigenous persons in their positivity and out of his love begins a critique of their unjust totalization.[27]

Without falling into the later myth of the *bon sauvage*, he writes of them:

> God has raised all these universal and infinite peoples in their whole type as the most innocent people, without evils or duplicities, most obedient and faithful to their natural rulers and to the Christians whom they serve; and more than any other people on the face of the earth they are more humble, more patient, more pacific and tranquil, without bickering or harshness. They are, thus, the most delicate of people, thin, and tender in comportment, and less able to suffer labors, and they die more easily from any kind of sickness.[28]

Because Las Casas had transcended the ontological horizon of the system and come into contact with the Other as Other, it was love that fueled his protest:

> Then it was that they [the indigenous peoples] knew them [the Europeans] as wolves and tigers and the cruelest of lions who had been hungry for many days. And they have done nothing else these forty years to this part of the world until today, and even this very day, than [inflict] havoc, slaughters, distresses, afflictions, tortures and destructions by strange, new, and varied forms of cruelty that have never been seen, or read about, or heard of before.[29]

Although affirmation of the exteriority alone affords escape from the all-absorbing vortex of dialectics and negative dialectics, Dussel's analectic method, starting from the Other, never permits him to relax his restless doubting of universalizations and Eurocentric systems of knowledge, religious pratices, theology, and science. Such disbelief places the rational project of modernity in jeopardy for Dussel, who gladly exults in the epithet "postmodernist."

> Latin American philosophy is, then, a new moment in the history of human philosophy, an analogical moment that is born after Eu-

ropean, Russian, and North American modernity, but antedating the African and Asian postmodern philosophy which they will constitute with us in the next "mundial" [*mundial*] future: the philosophy of the poor, the philosophy of human-mundial liberation (not in univocal Hegelian sense, however, but in sense of an analogical humanity, where each person, each people or nation, each culture, can express its own [contribution] to the analogical universality which is neither abstract universality [totalitarianism of a particularism abusively universalized] nor the concrete universality [univocal consummation of domination]).[30]

Ironically, Dussel's own mistrust of oppressive universalization does not prevent him from engaging in similar behavior, as is evident in his repeated discussions of homosexuality. Dussel roots his opposition to homosexuality in the history of philosophy. In Plato's *Symposium* the celestial Aphrodite brings it about that males love males—the best type of eros—while the earthly Aphrodite inspires the heirs of the adrogynous one, men and women, to love each other with a heterosexual love that is to be despised because it is not a sexuality of those who are the same (*los mismos*). Homsexuality for Plato is the love of the same for the same, with all the exclusionary connotations that the word "same" carries for Dussel and Levinas. Dussel equates sex shops, drug orgies, and pornography with homosexuality as so many misguided efforts to overcome narcissistic, totalized eros, which can be overcome only through the marriage of the couple that procreates a son. When the Other is constituted as a mere sexual object, the act is one of homosexuality and alienation of the Other as a mere mediation of autoeroticism. The tension of erotic-dominating praxis is essentially homosexual and Oedipal, and negates the sex of the distinct Other, reduces the Other to the same, and portends the death of the family! Lesbianism becomes the sum of all perversions and the radical loss of a sense of reality, the final solipsism of the Cartesian or European ego. In speaking of the subjugation of exteriority to money, Dussel comments that "the fetish advances thus as the perfect phallus of perverse, homosexual, masturbative desire." It never seems to enter Dussel's imagination that committed, generous, generative, nonnarcissistic sexual relations are possible between homosexuals, so oblivious is he to his complicity with the heterosexual totality that inflicts enormous psychological and even physical violence throughout the world on those who are its Other. Other-oppressive aspects of Dussel's erotics, rightly criticized by Ofelia Schutte, may be traced to residual influences of his earlier natural law position (relinquished in his turn to Levinas) or even to his uncritical assimilation of *Totality and Infinity*'s patriarchal erotics, which Levinas abandoned by the time he wrote *Otherwise Than Being*. But pointing out how Dussel himself proffers false universalizations does not undermine his analectic method; it suggests, rather, how much more carefully and rigorously he needs to apply it.[31]

Analectical Method, Ethical Hermeneutics, and the Positive Assessment of Reason

Whereas the previous section highlights Dussel's critical, at times negative, stance toward universalization, science, and rationality in general and concluded with his saluting the banner of postmodernism, there is another side to his analectical method. Beginning with the Other, Dussel, in fact, develops what I would describe as an ethical hermeneutics that actually enhances and renews rationality. Viewed through this optic, Dussel will very much resemble Levinas the phenomenologist, who, as I argued in the first chapter, can only be characterized as antirational if he is misunderstood. This interpretation of Dussel can be corroborated, in that the later Dussel dubs himself, not postmodern, but "transmodern."

Following Heidegger's rooting of the theoretical attitude in a prior practical one (*Zuhandenheit* precedes *Vorhandenheit* which abstracts from it), Dussel recognizes that the act of knowledge is always inscribed, really and practically, in the total process of praxis, as an "internal" moment at praxis's service. The fundamental practical project of a society, group, or individual opens the horizon of possible constitution of the objects of knowledge, which need not preclude the attainment of scientific objectivity by means of a methodical, disciplined, or transcendental attitude, supervening upon that of the empirical, pathological, or daily subject. However, one first opens to the world, not through a theoretical attitude, but rather through a practical one that gives a

subsequent impulsion to theory. Thus, in Dussel's view, philosophy is a second act, to follow on the praxis of liberation; and
theology as a thematizing thought (*pensar temático*) succeeds prophetic commitment (*praxis existencial*). One ought not to define
the morality of an action by its transcendental relation to a norm
or law; rather, one ought to begin with the historical process of
the liberation of actual material peoples "who are hungry."
Within such a framework, one can situate all the problems of abstract moral subjectivity with which moral theologies often mistakenly begin. Dussel ties this practical option for the Other and the
poor in with his analectical method:

> What is proper to the ana-lectical method is that it is intrinsically
> ethical and not merely theoretical, as the ontic discourse of the
> sciences or the ontology of the dialectic is. That is to say, the accep-
> tance of the Other as Other signifies already an ethical option, a
> choice, and a moral commitment: it is necessary to deny the total-
> ity, to affirm oneself as finite, to be an atheist of the fundament as
> identity. "Every morning my ear is awakened so that I can hear as
> a disciple" (Isaiah 50:4). In this case, the philosopher, before being
> an intelligent person, is an ethically just person, someone who is
> good, who is a disciple. . . . The analectic method includes then a
> previous practical historical option.[32]

Immediately after Dussel points to this option for the poor in
his *Método para una filosofía de la liberación*, he begins to describe
what he calls the "ethos of liberation," a particular attitude assumed by one who opts for the poor. One must silence the dominating word, open oneself interrogatively to the provocation of
the poor one, and know how to remain in the "desert" with an
attentive ear. In the second volume of *Para una ética de la liberación
latinoamericana*, Dussel expounds more fully on this ethos. It involves a sacred fear, respect before the Other as other. It is neither
sympathy, which remains bound to the eros of the Same, nor the
love of friendship, which demands mutuality, but rather the habit
of creatively putting oneself forward without seeking reciprocity,
gratitude, or gratification. It consists in confidence in the Other,
faith in the Other's future and liberty, accrediting the truth of
the Other's word, denying any possibility that one can have total
comprehension of the Other. In this attitude, one affirms the exis-

tence of another culture in the supposedly "uncultured" or "illiterate."[33]

The polar opposite of this ethos of liberation is to be found in the Heideggerian/Nietzschean ethos of the hero, the exact inverse of the Jewish thinking of alterity. In the ethos of the hero, the perfection of humanity is achieved in arriving at what one is able to be, in realizing one's own most authentic possibilities. Such an ethos affirms the Totality as the uniquely valuable and, with a depreciation of the Other based on self-love, despises the Other. The heroic ethos mistrusts the Other as acting exclusively from cynicism, hypocrisy, convenience, and astuteness, and whatever sign of infidelity the Other gives only confirms this suspicion. Such lack of confidence in the Other eventually leads to a despairing solipsism, self-fixated upon an abstract, convenient, and dead past. Disordered pleasure is condemned, but the order of comfort is esteemed. This hero eliminates anyone who threatens his gluttony, luxury, inebriety, and regulated incontinence and adopts a stony insensibility in the face of the Other's misery. The hero undertakes arduous and fearful projects and exercises power over the weakest with pride and ambitious ostentation. Preeminent examples of this heroic ethos are Caesar in Gaul and Cortés and Pizarro in Amerindia. Their activities involved denying the Other as a Germanic barbarian or Indian and reifying them as an oppressed "thing" at the service of the dominant group.[34]

One who lives out of the ethos of liberation locates herself in the "hermeneutic position" of the oppressed and takes on their interests, thereby discovering previously unnoticed values and emphases and opening the horizon of the possible constitution of objects of knowledge often invisible to those ensconced within the Totality. Beginning with the poor (*desde el pobre*), the hero of liberation thereby discovers a whole new critical perspective, a new criterion of philosophical and historical interpretation, a new fundamental hermeneutics, typical of the Gramsci-type "organic intellectual." Dussel comments on this perspectival approach to hermeneutics in one of his theological writings:

> A beggar, for example, sees the color on the outside of the rich man's house from the outside, something the rich man on the inside doesn't see. We have a better view of the house of the center

because we live on the outside. We are not stronger, but weaker. But in this case weakness is an asset. Our theology engages in criticism of the theology of the center precisely because ours is a theology of the periphery. Therefore, it is a theology that will clearly propose critical points of support for Latin America but also for the Arab world, for Africa, India, China, and for the blacks and Chicanos of the United States—by far the greater part of humanity.[35]

In a Latin American context, these different perspectives of interpretation shape the meaning one gives to legality and justice, as when, for instance, the powerful accuse the heroes of liberation of being subversives and communists intent on destruction and deserving prison and torture, even as these heroes know that their praxis highlights the perversity and evil of prisons and torturers, the tribunals of justice and governors. Historical examples also illustrate Dussel's hermeneutical perspectivism: of Miguel Hidalgo, for instance, whose action was legal according to the "law of the poor," even though he was denounced by theological faculties and excommunicated by the Mexican bishops. Transvaluating Nietzsche's transvaluation of values, Dussel illustrates how the perspective of the ethos of liberation inverts the reigning "virtues" of the *conquistador* by giving priority to service of the poor and mercy toward the oppressed; the very meaning of "virtue" is understood differently, depending on one's perspective.[36]

Dussel, in fact, defines the philosophy of liberation as being, not a theoretical option, but rather a practical-political option for the poor, a moral commitment to the Other, open to a plurality of theoretical categorizations (for example, Frankfurt School, philosophy of language, Levinasian metaphysics, or Marxism) and even political options. Dussel insists, though, that this practical option for the Other is not be considered extra-theoretical, since, by displaying new horizons of knowability, it determines knowledge and plays a role in constituting theory. For instance, great politicians like Bolívar or Sandino achieved a greater degree of rightness (*rectitud*) and everyday-life (*cotidiana*) objectivity than those lacking any political knowledge or those protected from reality by their position in the dominant classes.[37]

While one commits oneself to the poor ethically merely in response to the face of the Other, not for the knowledge to be gained from the Other or for any ulteriorly sought advantages for oneself—otherwise one would be subjecting the Other to one's own Totality and not really committing oneself to the Other—in Dussel's view improved prospects of knowledge result as an unintended by-product from such a commitment. He speaks, for instance, of an increased understanding of Others resulting from commitment to them. Dussel even suggests that this process of understanding the Other through "deculturation" of oneself is achieved through a kind of secondary socialization at the hands of the Other—a socialization that could be accelerated if there were a "novitiate" set up to enable people to understand divergent cultures. In contrast, Cardinal Daniélou's 1972 universal condemnation of violence and his censuring of the priests of the Movement for the Third World for their involvement in politics involved a violation of the first rule of hermeneutics: "It is necessary to situate oneself correctly in the world in which an event occurs."[38]

The commitment to the Other heightens self-criticism, particularly for philosophical discourse bound to academic university settings and prone to ideologize, cover, and justify existing domination because of its isolation from real, concrete, historical contexts. To be critical and aware of one's own limitations, one must establish relationships with the historical, real practices of oppressed peoples. Dussel cites Noam Chomsky to the effect that "in the measure that power is made more accessible [to the intellectual], the inequalities of society recede from his/her vision." While Dussel recalls Marcuse's observation that intellectuals transform crimes against humanity into a rational enterprise, it is clear that the ethical commitment to the Other that enhances self-critique does not lead to despair over reason, but hope for its liberating power. Dussel repeats Marcuse's claim that "if nature is in itself a legitimate, rational object of science, it is not only the legitimate object of Reason as power, but also of Reason as liberty, not only as domination, but also *as liberation*." Self-critique takes its start when one understands that it is only in relation to the Other that one can even become aware that one is located within a Totality.[39]

In the Other, theory itself finds a source for its own renewal. Just as Thomas Kuhn has noted that scientific revolutions begin when "an existing paradigm has ceased to function adequately," so

> The objects situated in the sphere of exteriority . . . are no longer able to be treated by the paradigms that have risen to explain fact within the horizon of I [the interest-orientation of the Totality]. The intrasystemic explanation . . . is no longer considered as "objective" by the dominated subject. . . . The *loss of objectivity* of the historical explanation is confused, in the system that the praxis of liberation *leaves behind*, as if it were something "subjective," badly intended, reduced, not real, ideological at least for its real function of hiding E [the sphere of exteriority]; the sphere of exteriority discovered from liberating praxis is the origin of the crisis of the explanatory paradigm.[40]

The power of the Other to renew theory is further illustrated in the cases of Ernst Bloch and the early Frankfurt School who remain caught in the "evil infinite" of negative dialectics because they lack a positive, affirmative starting point in the Other. This point of aid would have given their theory, as it gives all theory, the capacity for novelty beginning from the perspective of what it totally Other, that is, from a perspective of real, total oppression.[41]

Although Dussel conceives empathic identification with the Other as expanding the limitations of reason confined within a self-enclosed totality because the condition of the possibility of the constitution of the objectivity of the object depends on the project and interests of knowers, his recognition of the sociohistorical conditioning of hermeneutic perspectives does not lead to epistemological relativism. He admits the existence of a physical structure of matter that is interrelated with historical collective practices—both of which constitute supports (*soportes*) of objectivity. Even dialectical explanation (including Marxist brands), in Dussel's opinion, must include correspondence with the real. He further distinguishes the empirical or pathological subjectivity, which holds those merely probable opinions accepted by most people, from a scientific or transcendental subjectivity, more methodic and disciplined, whose conclusions must comply with the exigencies of epistemological apparatuses. In each case "knowledge" is always correlative to a type of subjectivity, but a greater objectivity is to be found in the conclusions of science which must be proven valid according to reflectively established criteria and standards. There is, then, an autonomy of science, but it is relative to a transcendental or scientific subjectivity that has elaborated through history its exigencies and criteria. Finally, if one admits that interests can occlude from sight the issues and persons on the exteriority of the Totality, then one must also conclude that certain valid claims can be justified about that exteriority and its legitimate ethical claims and that the totality would either have to concur with the validity of those claims or persist in its ideological, irrational blindness to their truth.[42]

It should be pointed out that the servicial initiation of the relation with the Other does not preclude secondary rational, critical exchanges with the Other at the level of what Levinas might call the Third (although Dussel does not use this language) and on the Other's behalf. Every culture, in Dussel's view, grasps itself as the center of the world, and every stage in development tends to absolutize itself. For instance, the Neolithic urban revolution brought about the complication of political structures and new Amerindian modes of production, with the result that increasing injustice climaxed in the domination of brother by brother in the Incan and Aztec empires. Contrary to those critics who claim that he is naïvely populist, Dussel recognizes that "the people" are not free from inauthenticity, voices misgivings about popular religiosity, observes that the oppressed have often introjected the oppression they have received, and refrains from any uncritical endorsement of populist spontaneity. The prophet or the philosopher can aid the people, the collective Other outside the center of power, to become more productive, just as enlightened pedagogues strive to promote critical attitudes among those for whom they are responsible. Philosophers and prophets can discover and highlight the self-critical elements already to be found within cultures and popular art, such as the tango *Margot* written by Celedonio Flores in 1918 in Argentina about a young woman who foresakes her poor barrio to become a prostitute of a wealthy man of Buenos Aires. This critical approach to the Other can be reconciled with the primacy of place given to the Other in the first moment of encounter only through a communicative dialogue between philosopher and the Other and between prophet and people, but there is in Dussel no irrational worship of the Other.[43]

These indications of a prorational strain in Dussel's hermeneutics on behalf of the Other, or "ethical hermeneutics," as I have dubbed it, come to clearer expression in a series of more recent lectures Dussel delivered in Frankfurt on the five hundredth anniversary of Columbus's landing in America, entitled *1492: El encubrimiento del Otro—Hacia el origen del "Mito de la modernidad.".* In these lectures, Dussel sets his position off from postmodernism. Whereas postmodernism criticizes modern reason *as reason,* Dussel criticizes modern reason for concealing an irrational myth. In Dussel's view, Europe, prior to the conquest of the Americas, was isolated, after having failed in the Crusades to recover control over the Eastern Mediterranean. Islam extended across northern Africa through Iran to northern India. Only in 1492, and with the conquest of Mexico in particular, did Europe first experience "strongly" the European ego controlling another empire, subduing the Other, as servicial, colonized, dominated, exploited, and humiliated. Only then did Europe succeed in constituting other civilizations as its periphery. This "going out" of Western Europe from the narrow limits within which the Islamic world had confined it constitutes, in Dussel's opinion, the birth of modernity as a worldwide event, a "mundial" happening. Dussel believes that Germanic-centered scholarship, with little concern for Spain's significance in history, mistakenly designates the Renaissance or Reformation as the origin of modernity, even though those events were basically only intra-European occurrences.[44]

Europe, of course, interpreted the landing of Columbus in its own terms, calling the continent the "New World" and "America" in honor of Amerigo Vespucci. Dussel traces what he sees to be the European interpretation of the colonization of America. Europe considered its culture more developed than and superior to the cultures found there. If these other cultures could be made to "leave" their barbarity and underdevelopment through a civilizing process, this would constitute development (the fallacy of development, in Dussel's view). Europe's domination of other cultures was envisioned as a pedagogic action, a necessary violence, a just war, a civilizing and modernizing task, and the sufferings of these cultures were justified as the necessary costs of the civilizing process and the payment for a "culpable immaturity." The European conquest was thus perceived as not only innocent, but even meritorious. The conquered victims were "culpable" for their own conquest, for the violence exercised upon them, since they should have abandoned their barbarity voluntarily instead of obliging their conquerors to use force. Gines de Sepúlveda typifies this Eurocentric self-justification by applying Christ's parable urging his disciples to go out into the byways and *force* those who were not originally invited to attend the banquet to the indigenous peoples of America: "As regard these barbarians, let us say, violators [that is to say, culpable], blasphemers, and idolators, I maintain that we not only can invite them, but ought to compel them so that receiving the empire of the Christians they might hear the apostles who announce the Gospel."[45] Dussel sees Sepúlveda's recommendation as justifying the use of violence to include the Other in the "community of communication" and employing irrationality (war) to initiate argumentation, as opposed to Bartolomé de las Casas who demanded that Europe comport itself rationally from the beginning of the dialogue with the Other.[46]

Though Dussel admits that European modernity conceives itself as rational emancipator, it is also accompanied by an irrational "myth" by which it justifies its own violence against the rest of the world, its sacrifice of others on the altar of "development" and "civilization."

Modernity, in its rational nucleus, is emancipation of humanity from the state of cultural, civilizational immaturity. But as myth, in the mundial horizon, it immolates men and women of the peripheral colonial world (and the Amerindians were the first to suffer) as exploited victims, whose victimization is covered with an argument for sacrifice as the cost of modernization. This irrational myth is the horizon that the act of liberation must transcend (and so this act is rational, as deconstructing the myth and practico-political, as an action that surpasses capitalism and modernity in a transmodern type of ecological civilization, popular democracy, and economic justice).[47]

This myth was clearly evident at the beginning of modernity, when Europe "discovered" America, not as something that resisted Europe as distinct, as the Other, but as the material on which the same projected itself, eclipsing the Other.[48]

What is evident here is that Dussel envisions the philosophy of liberation as dissolving the myth accompanying the emancipative dimensions of rational modernity, as unmasking the false universals and misuses of reason that would justify North Atlantic violence against the rest of the world and clothe naked power motives in the garb of moral-pedagogic rhetoric. This Nietzschean-like project of Dussel's, born in an un-Nietzschean way from an ethical hermeneutics, which interprets the events of history and the structures of society from the perspective of the poor and outcast Other, is directed, not at discrediting rationality, but at making rational modernity more rational. Since Dussel's ethical hermeneutics enriches processes of rationalization, he exchanges his early self-characterization as postmodernist to "transmodernist," not as disdainful of reason as postmodernity and yet too suspicious to endorse wholeheartedly critical theory's project of rehabilitating modernity.

> We have attempted to outline the manner of analyzing the question in order to introduce the historical conditions of a theory of dialogue that does not fall (1) into the facile optimism of an abstract rationalist universalism (which can confuse universality with Eurocentrism and modernizing developmentalism) from which the actual "Frankfurt School" could derive, or (2) into the irrationality, incommunicability, or incommensurability of the discourse of the postmodernists. The Philosophy of Liberation affirms reason as a faculty capable of establishing a dialogue, an intersubjective discourse with the reason of the Other as an alterative reason. In our time, it is this reason that denies the irrational moment of the "sacrificial Myth of Modernity," in order to affirm (take up into a liberating project) the rational, emancipatory moment of the Enlightenment and of Modernity, but now a Trans-Modernity.[49]

Here Dussel's analectical method, which began with the analogical word of the Other, like our own word and yet bearing its own distinctive meaning, and ended with an analogical philosophy of liberation, indebted to Europe and yet distinct from it, comes to its full flowering. Dussel's transmodern philosophy of liberation owes itself to rational modernity and yet cannot be subsumed under it. Dussel also shows himself, like Levinas understood as a phenomenologist (more than a postmodernist), finding in the Other an Archimedian point from which to place reason in question and yet thereby make it all the more rational. But in an interesting way, for all his allegiance to Levinas, Dussel has not forsaken his earlier devotion to Heidegger. For his philosophy is an ethical hermeneutics that, beginning from a rootedness and embodiedness in the perspective of the Other, patiently acquired through a tutelage at the hands of the Other, undertakes an interpretation of history, the economy—in particular Marx's reading of the economy—religion, and theology. It is to the implementation of this hermeneutics of these diverse realms from an ethical perspective that we must now turn. It will be apparent that only in adopting the posture of an ethical hermeneutics, a synthesis of Levinas and Heidegger, can one truly understand history, religion, and the economy. Only from an ethical hermeneutics can one be fully rational.

NOTES

1. *América Latina: Dependencia y liberación*, pp. 113–25; *Para una ética de la liberación latinoamericana*, 2:161–74; *Método para una filosofía de la liberación*, 3rd ed., pp. 185–98.
2. *América Latina: Dependencia y liberación*, pp. 112–13; *Para una ética de la liberación latinoamericana*, 2:160–61; *Método para una filosofía de la liberación*, p. 185.
3. Enrique Dussel, *La producción teórica de Marx: Un comentario a Los Grundrisse* (Iztapalapa, Mexico: Siglo Veintiuno Editores, 1985), pp. 30–63, 362–64; Enrique Dussel and Daniel E. Guillot, *Liberación latinoamericana y Emmanuel Levinas* (Buenos Aires: Editorial Bonum, 1975), pp. 8–9.
4. *América Latina: Dependencia y liberación*, pp. 113–16; *Para una ética de la liberación latinoamericana*, 2:161–64; *Método para una filosofía de la liberación*, pp. 186–88.
5. *América Latina: Dependencia y liberación*, pp. 116, 127n32; *Para una ética de la liberación latinoamericana*, 2:164, 238n486; *Método para una filosofía de la liberación*, pp. 188–89, 201n32.
6. *América Latina: Dependencia y liberación*, pp. 116–18; *Para una ética de la liberación latinoamericana*, 2:164–67; *Método para una filosofía de la liberación*, pp. 189–91.
7. *América Latina: Dependencia y liberación*, pp. 118–19; *Para una ética de la liberación latinoamericana*, 2:167–68; *Método para una filosofía de la*

78   ETHICAL HERMENEUTICS

liberación, pp. 191–92. Dussel here clearly evidences influences from Levinas's *Otherwise Than Being.*

8. *América Latina: Dependencia y liberación*, p. 120; *Para una ética de la liberación latinoamericana*, 2:168; *Método para una filosofía de la liberación*, p. 193.

9. *América Latina: Dependencia y liberación*, pp. 119–22; *Para una ética de la liberación latinoamericana*, 2:168–71, *Método para una filosofía de la liberación*, pp. 192–95.

10. Alfred Schutz, *The Phenomenology of the Social World*, trans. George Walsh and Frederick Lehnert (Evanston, Ill.: Northwestern University Press, 1967), pp. 124–25; Dussel, "Sobre el sentido de la traducción," pp. 135–36.

11. "Sobre el sentido de la traducción," *Actos del Primer Congreso de Estudios Clásicos* (Mendoza: Universidad Nacional de Cuyo, 1972), 99, 123–25; Alfred Schutz, *Collected Papers. I. The Problem of Social Reality*, ed. Maurice Natanson (The Hague: Martinus Nijhoff, 1962), pp. 11–13.

12. Habermas, *Reason and the Rationalization of Society*, pp. 102–20; Steven Lukes, "Relativism in Its Place," in *Rationality and Relativism*, ed. Martin Hollis and Steven Lukes (Cambridge, Mass.: The MIT Press, 1982), pp. 262–71; Ernest Gellner,"Concepts and Society," in *Rationality*, ed. Bryan R, Wilson (London: Basil Blackwell, 1970), pp. 33–49; Levinas, *Otherwise Than Being*, pp. 157–62, 190–96.

13. *América Latina: Dependencia y liberación*, pp. 122–25; *Para una ética de la liberación latinoamericana*, 2:171–74; *Método para una filosofía de la liberación*, pp. 195–98.

14. *El humanismo semita*, pp. 168–70; Dussel and Esandi, *El catolicismo popular en la Argentina*, p. 30; "Hacía una historia de la Iglesia latinoamericana, 503; *Hipótesis para una historia de la Iglesia en América Latina*, p. 171.

15. *Cultura latinoamericana e historia de la Iglesia*, p. 93.

16. Enrique Dussel, *Los últimos 50 años, 1930–1985, en la historia de la Iglesia en América Latina* (Bogotá: Indo-American Press Service, 1986), p. 310.

17. *Para una ética de la liberación latinoamericana. III. Filosofía ética latinoamericana: De la erótica a la pedagógica de la liberación.* Mexico City: Editorial Edicol, 1977), p. 199.

18. Ibid., 1:154; 3:199, 205, 209; 4:61; Enrique Dussel, *Ética comunitaria* (Madrid: Ediciones Paulinas, 1986), p. 216.

19. *Para una ética de la liberación latinoamericana*, 2:73, 3:67, 91, 139, 149; *Cultura latinoamericana e historia de la Iglesia*, pp. 90–92.

20. *Para una ética de la liberación latinoamericana. V. Filosofía ética latinoamericana: Arqueológica latinoamericana—Una filosofía de la religion antifeti-*

chista (Bogotá: Universidad Santo Tomás, Centro de Ensenanza Desescolarizada, 1980), p. 109; ibid., 3: 219; *El catolicismo popular en la Argentina*, p. 60; *Ética comunitaria*, pp. 228–230; Enrique Dussel, *De Medellín a Puebla: Una década de sangre y esperanza (1968–1979)* (Mexico City: Editorial Edicol, 1979), p. 64; *Hipótesis para una historia de la Iglesia*, p. 30; *Ethics and the Theology of Liberation*, p. 146.

21. Enrique Dussel, "Théologie de la 'Peripherie' et du 'Centre': Rencontre ou confrontation?" *Concilium*, 191 (1984), 158; see also 152, 157; *Ethics and the Theology of Liberation*, p. 159; Augusto Salazar Bondy, *Existe una filosofía de nuestra América?* (Iztapalapa, Mexico: Siglo Veintiuno Editores, 1975), p. 132.

22. Enrique Dussel, "La introducción de la 'Tranformacion de la filosofía' de K.-O. Apel y la filosofía de la liberación: Reflexiones desde una perspectiva latinoamericana," in Karl-Otto Apel, Enrique Dussel, and Raul Betancourt-Fornet, *Fundamentación de la ética y filosofía de la liberación* (Iztalpalapa, Mexico: Siglo Veintiuno Editores, 1992), pp. 75–76.

23. *Para una ética de la liberación latinoamericana*, 2:187, 3:165, 216; Enrique Dussel, "Racismo, América Latina negra, y teología de la liberación," *Servir* [Mexico], 86 (1980), 187–88; Enrique Dussel, *Filosofía de la producción* (Bogotá: Editorial Nueva America, 1984), p. 98.

24. *Para una ética de la liberación latinoamericana*, 2:187, 3:164–65, 216–18.

25. Enrique Dussel, "Historia y praxis (Ortopraxia y objectividad)," *Praxis latinoamericana y filosofía de la liberación* (Bogotá: Editorial Nueva América, 1983), pp. 307–29.

26. *La dialéctica hegeliana*, pp. 82, 96, 107; Enrique Dussel, "Respondiendo algunas preguntas y objeciones sobre filosofía de la liberación," *Praxis latinoamericana y filosofía de la liberación* (Bogotá: Nueva América, 1983), pp. 95–96; *Para una ética de la liberación latinoamericana. IV. Filosofía ética latinoamericana: La política latinoamericana.* Bogotá: Universidad Santo Tomás, Centro de Enseñanza Desescolarizada, 1979), pp. 101–102. For Dussel, popular culture, exterior to the system of capital, can achieve liberation as a creative, analectic subject according to *Cultura latinoamericana y filosofía de la liberación*, pp. 29–30.

27. *Para una ética de la liberación latinoamericana*, 3:75–76, 178.

28. Ibid., 4:41.

29. Ibid.

30. Ibid., 2:173; see also 2:167–68, 3:173; *América Latina: Dependencia y liberación*, pp. 124–25; *Método para una filosofía de la liberación*, p. 197; "Théologie de la 'Périphérie' et du 'Centre,' " 157–58; *Praxis latinoamericana y filosofía de la liberación*, p. 88.

31. Enrique Dussel, "Fundamentación analéctica de la liberación," *Método para una filosofía de la liberación*, 2nd ed. (Salamanca: Ediciones Sigueme, 1974), p. 263; *Ethics and the Theology of Liberation*, p. 102; *Para una ética de la liberación latinoamericana*, 3:69, 72, 83, 101–102, 113, 117; 5:84; Ofelia Schutte, "Origins and Tendencies of the Philosophy of Liberation in Latin American Thought: A Critique of Dussel's Ethics," *The Philosophical Forum*, 22 (1991), 277, 284, 293; for a critique of heterosexual totalization within the *feminist* tradition, see Judith Butler, *Gender Trouble: Feminism and the Subversion of Identity* (New York and London: Routledge, 1990). Fortunately, in his recent *The Underside of Modernity: Apel, Ricoeur, Rorty, Taylor, and the Philosophy of Liberation*, ed. and trans. Eduardo Mendieta (Atlantic Highlands, N.J.: Humanities Press, 1996), pp. 9–10, Dussel has retracted this earlier position on homosexuality and several of the ethical positions for which Ofelia Schutte criticized him. *The Underside of Modernity* appeared after *Ethical Hermeneutics* had already been sent to press, so I was unable to take account of its many important discussions, including Dussel's engagement with Ricoeur, Rorty, and Taylor. By far, Dussel's most extensive philosophical encounter has been with Apel, and I have taken into account the essays in *Underside of Modernity* dealing with this encounter, because I had access to them before that book was published.

32. *Método para una filosofía de la liberación*, pp. 187–88; Enrique Dussel, "Una década argentina (1966–1976) y el origen de la 'Filosofía de la liberación,'" *Reflexão*, 38 (1987), 31. Enrique Dussel, "Retos actuales a la filosofía de la liberación en América Latina," *Libertação/Liberación*, 1 (1989), 13; "Historia y praxis (Ortopraxia y objetividad)," pp. 312–17, 322–26. *Filosofía de la producción*, pp. 26, 62; "An Ethics of Liberation: Fundamental Hypothesis," 60; Enrique Dussel, "Sentido teológico de lo acontecido desde 1962 en América Latina," *Organización Internacional de Universitarios Catolicos, Pax Romana*, Ref. doc. mind. No. 239, September 30, 1971, p. 7.

33. *Método para una filosofía de la liberación*, p. 188; *Para una ética de la liberación latinoamericana*, 2:114–17.

34. *Para una ética de la liberación latinoamericana*, 2:35, 72, 86.

35. *Ethics and the Theology of Liberation*, p. 166.

36. *Praxis latinoamericana y filosofía de la liberación*, pp. 71, 301; Enrique Dussel, "Ética de la liberación," *Iglesia Viva*, 102 (1982), 596; *De Medellín a Puebla*, p. 44; *Ethics and the Theology of Liberation*, p. 138.

37. *Praxis latinoamericana y filosofía de la liberación*, pp. 71–72, 324–25; "Una década argentina," 31; *Para una ética de la liberación latinoamericana*, 4:95; *Método para una filosofía de la liberación*, p. 187.

38. Enrique Dussel, *Teología de la liberación y ética: Caminos de liberación*

latinoamericana (Buenos Aires: Latinoamerica Libros, 1975), p. 167; Peter Berger and Thomas Luckmann, *The Social Construction of Reality: A Treatise in the Sociology of Knowledge* (Garden City, N.Y.: Doubleday Anchor, 1966), pp. 138–47; on "secondary socialization," see pp. 171–72. *De Medellín a Puebla*, p. 120.

39. *Praxis latinoamericana y filosofía de la liberación*, pp. 301, 311; *Para una ética de la liberación*, 2:175.

40. *Praxis latinoamericana y filosofía de la liberación*, p. 323.

41. *Para una ética de la liberación latinoamericana*, 2:102.

42. *Praxis latinoamericana y filosofía de la liberación*, pp. 313, 315–16, 322, 324–26.

43. Enrique Dussel, *A History of the Church in Latin America: Colonialism to Liberation (1492–1979)*, trans. and rev. Alan Neely (Grand Rapids, Mich.: William B. Eerdmans, 1981), p. 214. *Praxis latinoamericana y filosofía de la liberación*, p. 273. *América Latina: Dependencia y liberación*, p. 215; Enrique Dussel, "Cultura latinoamericana y filosofía de la liberación: Cultura popular revolucionaria mas allá del populismo y del dogmatismo," *Cristianismo y Sociedad* [Mexico], 80 (1984), 43–44; *Para una ética de la liberación latinoamericana*, 2:106, 109, 178; 3:126, 155, 188, 215, 221; 4:36, 38, 120–121; 5:108. *Teología de la liberación y ética*, pp. 149–58; *Hipótesis para una historia de la Iglesia*, p. 54.

44. Enrique Dussel, *1492: El encubrimiento del Otro—Hacía el origen del "Mito de la modernidad": Conferencias de Frankfurt, Octobre de 1992* (Madrid: Editorial Nueva Utopia, 1992), pp. 9–13, 41–47, 125–29. After this book had been submitted for publication, a translation of Dussel's book on 1492 appeared: *The Invention of the Americas, Eclipse of the "Other" and the Myth of Modernity*, trans. Michael D. Barber (New York: Continuum, 1995). In the footnotes that follow, references will be made to this Spanish edition.

45. Ibid., pp. 87–92.

46. Ibid.

47. Ibid., pp. 176–80.

48. Ibid., pp. 29–30, 41–47, 169–80.

49. Ibid., p. 203.

4

Ethical Hermeneutics: History, Economics, and Theology

THROUGHOUT HIS CAREER, Enrique Dussel has been preoccupied with historical issues. While he was attempting to recover the pre-history of Latin America through his anthropological works, he was also studying the history of the Catholic church with Lortz. He completed a doctorate in history at the Sorbonne, with a thesis published in 1970 as *Les évèques hispano-americains: Défenseurs et évan-gélisateurs de l'Indien, 1504–1620.* A later abridged Spanish edition, following this French version, documents some of the anti-indige-nous policies of Spain and the Church, itemizing the great but subsequently forgotten deeds of the first generation of bishops in Latin America, who distinguished themselves by their outspoken defense of indigenous people and suffered persecution, even martyrdom, at the hands of wealthy and powerful Spanish oppres-sors. These bishops exemplify one of Dussel's frequently used his-torical categories, namely, "Christianity" (*cristianismo*) in which Christians show themselves to be outside the state and critical of its oppressiveness, as they were in the case of early Christianity, as opposed to "Christendom" (*cristiandad*), in which the church aligns itself uncritically with the state and implements an inter-nally oppressive hierarchical structure. Dussel conceived these earlier historical works as a type of cultural psychoanalysis, a pre-condition for assuming responsibility for one's history in Heideg-gerian style and consciously directing it toward a new future.[1]

Scattered thoughout Dussel's writings are several examples of the erroneous interpretation of history. The king of Spain, for example, mistakenly interprets the conquest of the Americas as

God's blessing on Spain when he writes: "God has entrusted to us in His infinite mercy and goodness the rule over such a great part of the world. . . . happily it has been given to us to lead the innumerable peoples and nations which inhabit America ('the West Indies') into the Catholic Church and to subject them to our rule."[2] Indeed, the very idea of the "discovery of America" involves an historical interpretation that amounts to creation of an entity out of nothing since the Europeans endowed the entity "America" with meaning from their own resources, with no regard for the viewpoint of those already dwelling there. As we shall see, repeated misinterpretations of history surround the meeting of the Spanish and the indigenous peoples in what is now called America. Other distorted histories include Alfred Weber's *Kulturgeschichte als Kultursoziologie,* a purported history of the world, which contains only four lines on Latin America (and that on the conquest by Spain) and Lortz's *Geschichte der Kirche,* which never mentions Latin America. Dussel, as we have seen, also criticizes historians such as Étienne Gilson, G. Fraile, and Heinz Heimsoeth for jumping from the Greek philosophers and the New Testament to the Neoplatonists and Saint Augustine without exploring the role of the Apologists, who sought to integrate the Semitic ethical roots of Christianity into the ontological Hellenic worldview that Christianity faced. The stinging ethical demands of the Other— the origin of the notion of the person—were thereby clothed in equivocal cultural mediations through a process of acculturation to Hellenism. This domestication of the ethical demand of the Other reflected philosophically the ethical and religious compromises for which Christendom settled when Constantine removed the Church from its persecuted status and welcomed it into the establishment. These present-day historians who neglect the forgotten period of the apologists when Semitic-Christian ethical categories had not yet been co-opted by Hellenism, prove thereby how deeply submerged they are within the Christendom that has triumphed. All these inadequate historical hermeneutics reflect a centeredness of the interpreter in his or her own self and culture, a particularism impeding the authentic comprehension of the phenomena and calling for a demystification (*demitificación*) of history. Dussel pinpoints this hermeneutic deficiency in commenting on Cardinal Jean Daniélou's erroneous censuring of the

priests of the Movement for the Third World during the cardinal's visit to Argentina in 1972. "My professor in the Catholic
Institute of Paris had not completed the first rule of the hermeneutics upon which he insisted so much with us in his classes: It
is necessary to know how to situate oneself correctly in the world
in which an occurrence takes place."³

Dussel's writing of history, like his critique of mistaken readings
of history, rests on certain philosophical-methodological presuppositions that he himself elucidates. First of all, Dussel rejects any
positivistic methodology. "We are far from imagining, as a very
extended historicist positivism might propose, that the facts speak
for themselves, and that history only demonstrates only what the
documents manifest in a univocal manner."⁴ Instead of a positivistic view of history that might claim that facts are obviously available to an ahistorical, nonsituated, disembodied Cartesian type of
consciousness, Dussel follows Heidegger's fundamental ontology
and begins with humanity's historical incarnatedness; this inevitably results in interpretations dependent on one's historical background and language. Edmundo O'Gorman's *La invención de
América* neglects this historicity of interpretation by seeming to
postulate the "*ser americano*" as already having its meaning when
Columbus arrives, instead of seeing that this being lacks meaning
(for Columbus) until it has been subsumed under his historically
conditioned interpretive framework. Once one recognizes one's
historicity, one must acknowledge the divergent perspectives
from which interpreters embark and to which they will return
reflectively after constructing their interpretations, as they bring
the hermeneutic circle to completion. It is no wonder then, given
these perspectives, that the intrusive Spanish will interpret their
meeting with indigenous peoples in the Americas as "discovery/
conquest," and the oppressed will understand it as "despair/in-
trusion/servitude." Dussel concludes that there is no pure objectivity in history and that since the human person is always finite
and relative to his or her historical situation all history is situated.⁵

But perspectivism on Heideggerian bases need not result in relativism, since objects exist with their own reality, consistency, and
resistance prior to being subsumed under historical categories,
and, consequently, knowers are not enclosed within an absolute

idealism. Because of this possibility of objectivity, historians must strive to return to the originary events by softening (*ablandar*) traditionalist interpretations as they struggle to unearth the forgotten sense (*sentido olvidado*) of previous texts or authors. It is even possible that one employ a scientific historical method (for example, using only tested evidence and relying on historical-critical methods of reading texts) and yet uncritically proceed within (*desde*) the framework of the prevailing social order, as those do who write "aristocratic" histories, oblivious to the "documents" of the poor or oppressed. In such a situation, the way to ensure a greater self-criticism and objectivity in one's historical method is to seek out the viewpoint of the poor one, who is exterior to whatever is valued within the Totality.

> This, it seems, ought to be the essential criterion of our history. It would be a history that asks itself before whatever problem and before whatever description: What relation does this have with the poor? We, for example, studying the confrontation of Columbus with the Indian, ought to ask ourselves: What is the more significant, Columbus or the Indian? The Indian, as the poor one, is the one who ought to interest us more.[6]

While, ideally, the poor themselves would be able to write their own history to maximize objectivity, the historian committed to them can still surface previously ignored historical materials and must strive to avoid falling into any capricious periodification of history. It is not surprising, then, that Dussel can speak in one and the same breath of a history of the Church that proceeds scientifically/theologically and at the same time finds the meaning of an event given from its positive or negative relation to the poor or oppressed. Dussel's conclusions here that a greater historical objectivity can be achieved through exposure to exteriority coincide with the epistemology he articulates in "Historia y praxis" in *Praxis latinoamericana y filosofía de la liberación.*[7]

Dussel's most recent historical work, *1492: El encubrimiento del Otro—Hacia el origen del "Mito de la modernidad,"* a series of lectures delivered in Frankfurt in October of 1992, exemplify both his general ethical hermeneutical approach and his method for doing history. Dussel confesses from the outset that his philosophy of liberation begins with the affirmation of alterity, of the

Other who is oppressed, excluded, and denied access to communicative processes, instead of starting with communication theory
as the Frankfurt School does. He acknowledges, though, that he
is not opposed to the philosophy of liberation's developing later
a theory or philosophy of dialogue as an ancillary component.
This ethical starting point from exteriority governs his subsequent
hermeneutics—a conscientious effort to sketch the historically
conditioned worldviews and interpretations of both the Spanish
and the indigenous peoples from the time when the Spanish
landed on the island of Guanahaní, later named San Salvador
by the Spanish, on October 12, 1492, according to the Spanish
calendar, until the conquest of Mexico. In careful descriptions of
the two worldviews, each of which takes up about half the book,
Dussel puts his Heidegger at the service of his Levinas.[8]

In Dussel's opinion, the European worldview already operated
among the Spanish *conquistadores* before it ever found its philosophical expression in the *ego cogito* of Descartes and in horribly
Eurocentric passages from Kant and Hegel, whom Dussel cites
extensively. The *Yo-conquistador* forms the protohistory of the constitution of the *ego cogito*, the beginning of a solipsistic discourse
without the recognition of any equal partner beyond European
borders. "America" was discovered, not as something that resisted, as something distinct, as the Other, but as material on to
which "the Same" projected itself in a process of covering over
(*encubrimiento*) what was there. The relations between Europeans
and indigenous peoples quickly became violent, with a militarily
developed technology pitted against one militarily underdeveloped. Dussel recalls how Pedro Alvarado, during Cortés's absence
in order to battle Panfilo Narváez, invited the warrior nobility of
the Aztecs to a festival, without their weapons, only to surround
the party with Spaniards who closed off all exits and commenced
a slaughter, decapitating and dismembering all who were there.
After the military conquest, the Spaniards not only seized Indian
women for their often sadistic sexual pleasure, but proceeded to
subject the indigenous men to brutal labor, such as the mine in
Bolivia that Bishop Domingo de Santo Tomás described as a
"mouth of hell through which enter every year a great quantity
of people whom the greed of the Spaniards sacrifices to their
god" (that is, silver). The Other was denied as Other and alien-

ated in order to be incorporated into a dominating Totality, as a thing, as an instrument, as someone oppressed, as property of an *encomienda* (plantation), as meagerly paid labor, or as an African slave, working sugar fields. Dussel cites abundant evidence of the degrading attitudes the Spaniards held toward the indigenous people, whom they characterized as "irrational and bestial because of their idolatries, sacrifices, and infernal ceremonies" (Fernandez de Oviedo); as "stupid" (*rudos*), "children" (*niños*), "immature," "savage in a barbarian manner" (José de Acosta); as "violators of nature, blasphemers, and idolaters," whom it is permissible "to compel [with force] so that, being submitted to the power [*imperio*] of the Christians, they might hear the apostles who announce the Gospel," (Gines de Sepulveda); as people whose houses and commerce prove only "that they are not bears or monkeys totally lacking in reason" (Gines de Sepúlveda). The "Requirement" (*Requerimiento*), a text read by the Spaniards to the indigenous people before battle, indicated that the disasters about to befall the indigenous people after battle were their own fault, something due them for resisting the emancipation and modernization the conquest was bringing them.[9]

Midway through the book, Dussel shifts his focus to the point of view of the indigenous cultures "discovered" in 1492. Eschewing the notion that the development of civilization moved westward from the East (Europe) to the West (America)—as a more Eurocentric position might contend—Dussel traces the more ancient passage of civilization eastward from the West (Mesopotamia and Egypt) to the East (India, China, Mayan–Aztec–Inca civilizations). He discusses the rationalization present in mythological-ritual cultures, with their enormously complex codified systems, as explained by Claude Lévi-Strauss, and investigates the nomadic, agricultural, and urban levels of cultural development in the Americas. He comments, in particular, on the communitarian rationality and economic reciprocity typical of the agriculturally oriented Tupi-Guaraní who lived in the Amazon forests extending to what is now Paraguay.

Dussel's tour de force in the essay *1492: El encubrimiento del Otro* consists in his interpretation of Moctezuma, whose position as a member of Aztec wise men (*tlamatini*) and whose cosmogony and parousiac expectations Dussel thoroughly describes before considering Moctezuma's reactions to Cortés. Unfortunately, because they have failed to grasp his "rationality," historians have depicted Moctezuma as vacillating, contradictory, and scarcely comprehensible. As a learned *tlamatini*, Moctezuma, when faced with the Spanish, considered three possible interpretations: namely, that Cortés was either (*a*) a mere human being, or (*b*) a face of the supreme god (Ometeotl), who was about to put an end to the Aztec world and usher in the dreaded era of the Sixth Sun, or (*c*) the returning god Quetzalcoatl, who would have been appeased had Moctezuma alone simply resigned his throne. Moctezuma tested the third and least threatening option first by offering his throne to Cortés—an action considered highly irrational unless one avoids projecting upon him Eurocentric expectations. Tragically, the second option became reality—the Aztec world was destroyed—Moctezuma discovered too late that the first option was true: Cortés was only human, for he seemed to require reinforcements after subduing Narváez's rebellion and after Alvarado's murderous slaughter of the Aztec elites. Here Dussel's history appears preeminently an ethical hermeneutics, selecting as the starting point for its interpretation of history the viewpoint of the vanquished and discredited (even to this day) emperor of the oppressed indigenous peoples of Mexico. Dussel seems to have lost his earlier interest in understanding *his* own history as a Heideggerian hero in pursuit of authenticity through cultural psychoanalysis; here he undertakes instead a Levinasian retrieval of the history of the defeated and forgotten Other.[10]

But not only is Dussel's ethical-hermeneutical history interested in recovering the forgotten viewpoint of the oppressed Other; by redefining the origin of modernity it also aims at correcting a major false periodification of history. Habermas and others situate the beginning of modernity in the Renaissance and Reformation, but in Dussel's view this explanation is not only excessively German, consigning significant Spanish-Hispanic occurrences to the periphery of Europe, but also entirely intra-European, as if the origin of modernity had nothing to do with the rest of the world. To establish the true beginning of modernity, Dussel points out that Europe had never considered itself the center of history since it had been ringed around by Islam, which extended from the Atlantic to the Pacific. Only in 1492 did it first constitute other nations on its periphery, only then did it first break out of the limits within which the world of Islam had confined it. The year 1492 constitutes the beginning of the experience of the European ego, expressed subsequently in the history of philosophy from the *ego cogito* to Nietzsche's will-to-power, by constituting other subjects and peoples as objects, instruments that it could utilize for its European, civilizing, modernizing purposes. On one hand, Dussel admits that modernity contains a rational nucleus, involving the rational emancipation of humanity from the state of cultural immaturity through a critical process, and hence Descartes's self-reflective turn to the *ego cogito* perhaps deserves greater admiration than Dussel often allows. On the other hand, modernity is accompanied by an irrational sacrificial myth, evident in the conquest, to the effect that the colonial and economic victimization of the peripheral Third World is justified as the price of modernization. That Europe considers modernity to begin with the culturally admirable and self-flattering intra-European events of the Renaissance and Reformation conceals the other face of modernity, its irrationality, violence, and exploitativeness. Dussel's locating the origin of modernity in the world event of the conquest of the Americas is itself a work of ethical hermeneutics, interpreting history so that Europe is held responsible for its past victims and made aware of the present and future danger that it might hide its exploitation of the poor and oppressed beneath its uncritical conviction that it is bringing modernization and rationalization (cultural or economic) to other peoples.[11]

The essay *1492: El encubrimiento del Otro* manifests the several ingredients of the methodology for historiography under the impetus of an ethical hermeneutics. No positivistic presupposition that the facts speak for themselves is to be found here, since Dussel's study illustrates how differently the facts were interpreted by the *conquistadores* and the indigenous peoples. Indeed, Dussel's entire whole way of proceeding, which, like his redefinition of the origin of modernity, is so different from previous histories, depends on his unique perspective: that of an historian whose view is shaped by the Latin American starting point and the philosophical premisses of his ethical hermeneutics. At the same time, however, Dussel does not lapse into any relativism here; he is convinced both that the Spanish never fully grasped the viewpoint of the indigenous peoples, which was reducible to Spanish interpretations, and that his account of modernity's origin is superior to the prevailing one. In fact, one can discover true history only by casting off the shackles of traditional interpretations and straining back toward the things themselves, as Dussel does when he refounds modernity, illuminates the forgotten cultural achievements of the Mayan–Aztec–Inca worlds, and displays the "deep" rationality of Moctezuma's vacillation. Although Dussel's history is enhanced by his extensive familiarity with historical sources, Spanish, ecclesial, and Aztec, and the most recent anthropological findings, one can also clearly see that the writing of history can attain greater objectivity by searching out the viewpoint of the defeated, discredited, and forgotten and approaching the course of history through their eyes.

Economics (Marx)

Dussel has produced an ethical hermeneutics of capitalism through an in-depth study of Karl Marx's later pre-*Capital* manuscripts in the Marxist-Leninist Institute of Berlin. He began that study in the late 1970s and ended it with the publication of the final book in his trilogy on Marx, *El último Marx (1863–1882) y la liberación latinoamericana,* in 1990 (the earlier volumes were *La producción téorica de Marx: Un comentario a los Grundrisse* and *Hacia un Marx desconocido: Un comentario de los manuscritos de 61–63.*[12]

It is somewhat ironic that Dussel should have undertaken such a serious study of Marx, since his earlier works are peppered with facile dismissals of Marx for which his critics have assailed him. For instance, the earlier Dussel states that Marx forgets the Other; that Marxist humanism is not reconcilable with Christian humanism; that Marx's opposition to any notion of "creation" indicates that he has no room for alterity; that Marx's theory is an ontological totality without exteriority; that, although Marx is an atheist, he really is a *"panontista,"* religiously affirming a totality; and that Marx is really not atheistic enough since his failure to affirm God leaves his system with no possibility of critique from without.[13]

Nevertheless, after his extensive investigation, Dussel himself

admits that in the past he rejected the mechanistic mass-material-
ism (*masismo mecanista*) that Marxists, without knowing the real
Marx, put forth as Marx's thought. Paraphrasing Marx's own dedication to Hegel when Hegel was a "dead dog" and commenting
on his own conversion to Marx after the fall of Eurocommunism,
Dussel notes: "Years ago everyone was a Marxist and I was opposed to Marx, and now they have declared Marx a dead dog and
I present myself as a disciple of that great master." Dussel's retrieval of Marx, then, involves giving expression to the viewpoint
of an Other excluded for a long time from his own personal philosophical totality and at present excluded from the totality of the
philosophical enterprise itself. Dussel recovers a philosophical
Other who in turn dedicated his entire life to the recovery of
the Other of capitalism—the living laborer as the origin of the
production of wealth.[14]

For an appreciation of what is novel in Dussel's interpretation
of Marx, it is necessary to review briefly the contents of his trilogy
on Marx. In *La producción teórica de Marx*, Dussel discusses the
1857 manuscripts of the *Grundrisse*. The method of Marx, who was
always aware of the levels of his reflection, begins with the real
concrete, abstracts (in the sense of separating and distinguishing)
the simple components of capitalism, "ascends" to a (re)con-
struction of the concrete totality, and, finally, descends to explain
the concrete world, such as that of bourgeois society. Marx begins
the *Grundrisse* manuscripts with a discussion of money, then proceeds immediately to money's presuppositions: the production
process that begins when the propertied "capitalist confronts
what is not capital, exteriority, the Other (as someone, as living
subject): the worker as capacity and creative subjectivity of value"
and contracts for this worker's labor. The capitalist purchases the
worker's capacity to work for a full day by paying the worker a
wage sufficient to sustain a person for a day. Whatever the amount
of value the worker produces beyond what is necessary for his or
her reimbursement belongs to the capitalist as surplus value. The
capitalist tries to increase absolute surplus value by increasing the
length of the worker's day, but when the worker reaches his physical limits, the capitalist augments productivity (for example, with
machines) so that workers can produce more quickly the sum
value needed for their sustenance and increase the capitalist's

surplus value relative to that sum value (relative surplus value). By increasing the productivity of the worker, the capitalist can increase the total amount of surplus value, but the percentage increase of surplus value in relation to the increasing productivity will decline. Likewise, as productivity increases, larger outlays will be needed for raw materials and machinery, and the rate of profit relative to total outlay decreases. Similarly, the declining amount of worker time invested in products relative to the larger number of products being produced diminishes the value of those products. Capitalism's increasing productivity paradoxically devalues its products, and frenetic efforts in search of a greater, compensatory productivity result finally in overproduction and consequent crises. In the *Grundrisse* manuscripts, Marx goes on to consider how surplus value, produced as it is by workers who erroneously believe that the wages received from the capitalist adequately compensate them for the value they produce, forms the basis from which profit and interest derive, depending on how competition and other circulation factors intersect with the primary sphere of production.[15]

Dussel's second study, *Hacia un Marx desconocido*, comments on the manuscripts of 1861–1863. Beginning with Marx's 1859 *Contribution to a Critique of Political Economy* regarding merchandise and money at the more superficial level of circulation, Dussel follows the pattern of the first book and immediately turns to the manuscript accounts of production, the capitalist/worker relationship, the distinction (explicit here for the first time in Marx) between variable (labor) and constant capital (machinery and raw materials), and absolute and relative surplus value. Once again, Dussel shows how Marx is intent on denying that the surplus value derives from the sale of a good above its value in the sphere of circulation; rather, Marx insists, surplus value originates from the laborer's creation of it in the sphere of production. Marx interprets machinery as conserving value, not producing it, thereby ensuring that only labor counts as the origin of new value. Maintaining the sequence of Marx's own manuscripts, Dussel shows how Marx critically confronts diverse categorial systems in such a way that he wins sufficient epistemic security to continue, later on, his own more systematic investigations. In opposition to mercantilists such as J. Steuart, Marx argues that merchandise is sold, not *above* its value on the market, but *at* its value, including the surplus value created by workers never compensated for it. Against physiocrats, Marx insists that value springs, not from agricultural holdings, but rather from labor that works the land. Adam Smith, in Marx's view, mistakenly conceives surplus value as profit realized in the sale of goods. Marx reiterates that the source of value is found, not in circulation, but in production through labor. Supply and demand may drop the price of a good, but that reduction merely diminishes the amount of profit a capitalist will realize from the surplus value the object contains from the time it leaves the sphere of production and the workers' hands. As Marx notes in reference to Rodbertus, because of competition and the leveling of prices to an average price, merchandise sells above or below its value, and thus a transfer of surplus value is effected from one piece of merchandise to another. Supply and demand in the sphere of circulation thus distributes the surplus value already instituted in the sphere of production. In his confrontation with Ricardo, Marx sharpens his concepts beyond what he offers in the *Grundrisse* by distinguishing the value of the market from that which is derived from production and produced by living labor and that is the basis for every price derived from it. For instance, Marx notes that, on the "price side," one begins with the price of cost (*precio de costo*), that is, the cost (variable and constant capital), of making the product as that product enters the market. Once on that market, the product will accrue a greater price, the price of production (*precio de producción*) since the average profit on the market for that good must be added to the price of cost. However, one needs to ground these prices in the "value side" of the merchandise. That value includes not only variable and constant capital (found in the price of the cost), but also the surplus value created by living labor in the production sphere. As a result, whatever the average profit may be, ingredient in the final price of production and determined by competition in differing contexts, that profit emanates from the surplus value. Ricardo equates the price of cost with the value of the merchandise and traces the origin of profit to selling merchandise above its price. All these distinctions, of course, are aimed at not letting us forget that profit in capitalism originates in the surplus value created by exploited labor.[16]

Dussel's final book on Marx, *El último Marx (1863–1882) y la liberación latinoamericana*, presents the third and fourth redactions of *Capital* (the *Grundrisse* and the 1861–1863 manuscripts composing the earlier redactions). In the third redaction, which includes manuscripts from the period from 1863 to 1865, Dussel restates Marx's opinion that although the price of cost (constant and variable capital) and surplus value constitute the value of merchandise (*mercancia*), it is possible to sell merchandise below its value in the market and still make a profit since the capitalist will lose some of, but not all, the surplus value. In these manuscripts, Marx also explains not only that competition does not create value but merely levels, distributes, and transfers surplus value, but also that interest and rent as well derive from surplus value and thus trace their origin to living labor. The fourth redaction of *Capital*, which includes Marx's edited and unedited writings from 1866 to 1882, begins, as is usual with Marx, with the appearance of money before he turns to production. In a lucid discussion, Dussel shows how the rate of surplus value more clearly manifests worker exploitation than the rate of profit. For instance, if a total advanced capital of 500 obtains 90 in profit, the rate of profit is 18 percent, but the rate of surplus value (surplus value/variable capital) could be 100 percent if the variable capital were 90 (and assuming that all surplus value became profit and that constant capital were 410). Dussel's third book in the trilogy concludes that after publishing *Capital*, Marx, through an interchange with Russian revolutionaries, came to hope that Russia could bypass capitalism in its route to socialism. Marx thereby abandons his earlier unilateral and rigid philosophy of history (in texts of 1848) as a lineal succession of economics systems passing developmentally and mechanistically through capitalism to socialism.[17]

On the basis of his expositions of Marx's thought in these three volumes, Dussel proceeds to offer a highly original interpretation of Marx. He claims, first of all, that his careful work with Marx's manuscripts has enabled him to appreciate the archeology of Marx's categories as they developed and, more important, the philosophical dimensions of Marx's work in a way that the superficial, nonphilosophical character of the pared-down texts of *Capital* does not permit. Though he frequently acknowledges that Marx lacks an *explicit* philosophy, Dussel insists that one must not rely, as Louis Althusser does, only on Marx's explicit formulations of what he was doing. In fact, a philosophical structure so pervades the entire discourse of Marx's work that Dussel asserts that those who interpret Marx only as an economist—and often a mechanistic one at that—never understand that Marx is blending ontology and economics and producing both an ontology of the economy and an ontological economics, neither pure philosophy nor pure economics. For Dussel, the anthropological, ethical, and metaphysical sense of Marx's texts has been overlooked by most Marxists, such as Althusser, who construes the later Marx as having abandoned his earlier philosophy, even though, as Dussel points out, Manuscript VII of 1878 shows Marx to be more Hegelian than ever.[18]

In the second chapter of Book I of *Capital*, in texts that lack his usual pathos, Marx describes the meeting of the propertied capitalist with propertyless labor, in which the capitalist purchases the "capacity of labor" or the "force of labor." In Dussel's view, this terminology obscures important distinctions between the capacity to work, which precedes the use or consumption of labor, the force that is employed in the process of labor, and "living labor," that is, the subjectivity (person and corporality of the laborer) which itself is without value which contains the "capacity" and the "force." Intent on delineating Marx's implicit discourse and retrieving a meaning that *Capital* itself blurs, Dussel returns to the most important philosophical text of the *Grundrisse*, which describes "living labor" and, according to Dussel, provides the key for deciphering Marx.

The dissociation between property and labor presents itself as the necessary law of this interchange between capital and labor. Labor, posited as *non-capital* [*Nicht-Kapital*], insofar as it is, is: (1) *Labor non-objectified*, conceived *negatively* (even in the case of an objective being, the non-objective in objective form). As such, it is first non-matter [*Nicht-Rohstoff*], non-instrument of labor, non-product in raw form: labor dissociated from all the means of labor and objects of labor, from all its objectivity; *living* [*lebendige*] labor, existing as abstraction from those aspects of its real reality [*realen Wirklichkeit*] (equally non-value); this total dispossession, this nudity from every objectivity, this purely subjective existence of labor. Labor as *absolute poverty* [*absolute Armut*]: poverty not as lack, but as full exclusion from objective wealth . . . (2) *Labor non-objectified*, non-value, conceived *positively*, or negativity related to itself: it is the nonobjectified existence—that is, nonobjective or, rather, subjective—of labor itself. Labor not as object, but as activity, not as self-*value*, but as the *living* fount of value. . . . There is not an absolute contradiction in affirming, then, that labor is, on one hand, *absolute poverty as an object*, and, on the other, the *universal possibility* of wealth as subject and activity.[19]

Dussel depicts living labor as "exteriority," in the nonspatial sense in which Levinas utilizes the term—that is, labor as one dispossessed of wealth in history and thus forced to sell one's capacity to work; as the nothing (*Nichts*) without value in relation to the entire capitalist system; as virtually a *pauper*, whom, when no longer needed, the capitalist can dispense with and cast into the industrial reserve army; as one perceived in the contract with the capitalist only as a thing capable of producing goods. Dussel shows how Marx, following Feuerbach, emphasizes the corporality of the subjectivity of the laborer, that is, the laborer possesses hands, feed, stomach, brain, eyes, and feels the sting of human need. Alienation occurs when this living labor is hired and incorporated into capital, now as a determination of capital, as "unexteriorized." Once incorporated into the capitalist system, labor exercises a positive, creative activity, by working on raw materials and bringing forth surplus value for the capitalist "from nothing." Just as Schelling attributes truly creative power to the Absolute Creator outside of the Hegelian system, so Marx assigns this power to the one who is originally nothing for the system of capitalism.[20]

Dussel argues that in identifying with oppressed labor Marx is thoroughly consistent with his earlier 1844 demand that one needs "new eyes" in order to know "the unemployed and the laboring person." Marx not only asserts that those works upholding the point of view of the proletariat recognize that labor is everything (*Die Arbeit ist alles*), but he struggles throughout his own works to defend the interests of impoverished labor by linking all value in capitalism back to its origin in living labor. If "totality" is the fundamental category for the analysis of capital as already given (*ya-dado*), only from the category of exteriority, from the reality of living labor beyond capital, can one expect to understand the origin of capital and to criticize it. The point of view of living labor—for whom Marx felt himself ethically responsible—has become here the hermeneutic perspective from which to approach the totality of the capitalist system. Marx's economics is none other than an ethical hermeneutics of the economy itself. Dussel, furthermore, taking this concept of living labor as the hermeneutic key for understanding all of Marx, feels entitled to associate his reading of Marx and capitalism with his own ethics. Hence, Dussel comments, "To criticize ontology, being (capital), from a practical and utopian exteriority . . . is what we have denominated the 'analectic transcendentality.' "[21]

One needs to understand that Marx's theoretical maneuvers, described in Dussel's trilogy, reflect his response to the ethical demand of the Other, living labor. Marx's unflinching convictions that surplus value comes into existence as the result of the unpaid labor—what he repeatedly calls a "robbery"—of workers in the sphere of production, and that profit comes from there, not from selling a good beyond its value in the marketplace, depend on his ethical commitment to labor. Only against this ethical foundation is it possible to understand such features of Marx's theory as his efforts to prove that supply and demand do not create value, that prices are based on prior value from the sphere of production, that production takes priority over circulation, that rent and interest do not contradict the law of value, and that the rate of profit conceals the degree of worker exploitation evident only in the rate of surplus value. As Dussel puts it, "When the price of production is determined from the market and competition [and the value side neglected], the door is closed to anthropology and ethics." Although Marx may have rejected the hypocrisy of most superstructural moral codes, it is clear that he is conscientiously aware of the ethical demands present (and often denied in capitalism) at the infrastructural level at which the worker faces capital.[22]

Dussel's novel interpretation of Marx configures the Marx-Hegel relationship in new and different ways. According to Dussel, capital, imitating the pattern of Hegel's *Logic*, self-dirempts into productive or circulating capital. Capital is the subject that includes the totality of all its determinations and modes of manifestation, such as value, money, merchandise, and so on. Of all

Marx's works, Book II of *Capital*, in treating of the movement, process, and circulation of value, comes most to resemble Hegel's *Logic*. But while Marx relies on Hegel to describe capital as given (*ya dado*), he also emphasizes that one must distinguish categories such as "productive force" (*fuerza productiva*), "productive process" (*proceso productivo*), "mode of production" (*modo de producción*), and "salaried labor" (*trabajo asalariado*)—all of which are "intratotalized" (*intratotalizadas*) categories—from "living labor" (*trabajo vivo*) and "capacity to work" (*capacidad de trabajo*), which indicate the perennial presence of exteriority outside of capital. To confuse such terms, to unify them as the previous Marxist tradition did, is to lose the whole sense of exteriority, which Dussel contends is the category par excellence for Marx. "Living labor," which always stands beyond capital, as Non-Being and yet origin of capital, is Marx's starting point; Hegel begins with Being which initiates everything and determines itself as the Same. In Dussel's terminology, "The transfundamentality, the transontologicality [the 'metaphysical' or ethical par excellence, as we shall see], of 'living labor' would indicate the absolute rupture of Marx from Hegel. The opposition of Marx and Hegel is located here." Marx's definition of *trabajo vivo* in terms of Schelling's creative fount of Being suggests that Marx might be better read through the prism, not of Hegel, but of Schelling, whose lectures on Hegel, Marx attended. At the same time as Marx denies Hegel, however, he includes him insofar as capital, once created, moves as the foundation of the alienation of "living labor" subsumed within it. Dussel preserves the tension between totality and exteriority in Marx's thought when he describes its basic components— applicable even to socialist systems in a way that the more specific *Capital* is not—in terms of the "rational nucleus" (*nucleo racional*) which contains all Marx's fundamental abstract philosophical concepts, including Hegelian distinctions between essence and appearance and non-being as the origin of being, and the "generative matrix" (*matriz generativa*) that treats "living labor" more concretely. Although the focus on exteriority distinguishes Marx from Hegel, Marx never abandons Hegel, whose notion of totality undergirds his portrayal of capitalism, against which exteriority stands in often mute protest. Those who wish to cling to the previous readings, which considered Hegel as the whole and Marx as the part, Hegel as an idealist and Marx as a materialist, Hegel as a philosopher and Marx as an economist, will have to come to terms with Dussel's novel grasp of Marx and his relation to Hegel.[23]

Dussel's original interpretation of Marx from "exteriority" enables him to correct the hermeneutical errors of others. Since the capitalist has no notion of the essence of capital, surplus value exists only in the form of profit. The agents of capitalist production live in an enchanted world, and even their own relationships appear reified to them. The capitalist as interested practically only in the rate of profit (total profit in proportion to total outlay) "obscures" and "mystifies" from the beginning the origin of surplus value. The value of merchandise can be viewed from two different hermeneutical perspectives: that of labor (subjective, more fundamental, productive) or that of capital (empirical, phenomenal, superficial, circulative). Faithful to his ethical hermeneutical starting point, Dussel comments on bourgeois economists:

> The incomprehension of the *absolute* position (the only real absolute in the totality of Marx's thinking and the ethical rule of all his judgments of value) of living labor, the actuality of the corporality of the laborer, or, in another way, the person and subjectivity itself of the laborer—this incomprehension will lead the bourgeois economy (and its philosophies as philosophies of "domination") to commit necessary hermeneutical errors.[24]

Adam Smith derives the value of merchandise from the sum of salary, profit, and rent, completely overlooking labor's role in producing surplus value. Both Smith and Hegel, who read Smith, accept capitalism as natural, with wealth and poverty flowing from nature itself, rather than as being caused historically through human responsibility and, therefore, always with the possibility of being changed. Physiocrats, such as Quesnay, hold that surplus value emerges from nature, not from coercive human relationships, not from the worker who produces value by working nature, which of itself has no value, and turning his product over to a landowner. The capitalists and their theoreticians are not the only ones who fall into hermeneutical errors, since even workers themselves are convinced that the value produced by living labor is equal to the salary. "All labor appears [pure fetishist appearance] as paid labor" since the salary paid erases any trace of the distinction between necessary labor and surplus labor and conceals the fact that living labor, itself beyond value because it is the creator of all value, is the "substance" of salary.[25]

Dussel argues that the Marxist theoretical tradition itself has erred hermeneutically by interpreting Marx in terms of the totality of capitalism rather than on the basis of exteriority, insofar as it has not sufficiently distinguished *trabajo vivo* (creative and subsumable exteriority) from other categories, such as *fuerza de trabajo*, that is, living labor subsumed under capital—a mistake fostered at times by Marx's own carelessness. Dussel bluntly describes the options regarding the Marxist tradition when he observes that "either I am mistaken, and then Lukács, Kosik, and so many others are right, or they are wrong and therefore the *whole Marx* ought to be interpreted in a different way." In Dussel's opinion, Georg Lukács begins with totality as the key to the reading of Marx and therefore ends up downplaying the importance of surplus value. Karl Korsch, while recognizing the importance of philosophy for Marx, never clarifies Marx's philosophical approach. Herbert Marcuse reinterprets Hegel but, like Karl Kosik, remains confined in the notion of totality. Since Louis Althusser, following Engels, depicts Marx as being "scientific" and thereby denies the philosophical dimensions of Marx's work, he would have no use for either the Hegelian concept of totality or the Levinasian category of exteriority. Dussel rounds out his critique of neo-Marxist thinkers with an attack on Jürgen Habermas. Habermas, whose Marx-interpretation privileges Schelling's *Weltalter* over the *Philosophy of Mythology* and the *Philosophy of Revelation*, effectively reduces economics to politics, overlooks the importance of economics for liberation in advanced countries, and abandons the labor theory of value by envisioning science, technology, and machinery as other founts (*fuentes*) of value. For Dussel, Habermas shows his unfamiliarity with Marx's thought by reducing Marx's theory of action to merely instrumental, teleological (cognitive-instrumental) action instead of seeing the practical interpersonal aspects of Marx's thought (as Dussel does in his discussion of exterior living labor face to face with the capitalist) and by relying in his *Zur Rekonstruktion des historischen Material-*

ismus on such notions as the "superstructure" that Marx mentions in the *Contribution* of 1859, but never again in the thousands of pages of the four redactions that Dussel has poured over. In brief, Habermas reconstructs Marx but never on the basis of Marx's own interests, but always in terms of his own hope to enrich Marx with Habermasian additions.[26]

As Dussel realized in his nonpositivist approach to history, every critique in the domain of economics is always undertaken from a particular point of view and Marx's perspective of critique is that of living labor. Bourgeois economic theory, by shielding itself from that perspective, ends up delivering an *apologia* for capitalism, a covering over (*encubrimiento*) of its reality. Bourgeois economics consists, in Marx's view,in "*false* subterfuges that furnish the *appearance* of a *scientific explanation.*" Bourgeois economists, confined within the bourgeois interpretive "horizon," engage in a "sublime spiritualization" of the capitalist economy by viewing the social relationships at the root of capitalism as natural, eternal, capitalistic production relationships. Bourgeois science is actually the equivalent of a "fetishism," in "not focusing on the fundamental form of capital, the production developed on the appropriation of another's labor" and in "mystifying" the origin of surplus value. Classical economy is a pseudo-science insofar it has not adequately developed its concepts and has fallen into contradictions. Marx's practical commitments in London and his struggles on behalf of the European proletariat, which led Dussel to consider him to be the ethical hermeneuticist of capital, constitute "the epistemic condition of the opening of a new practical-theoretical horizon" that depends on subjective liberty, that liberates the theoretic process itself, and, finally, leads to the discovery of truth. Engaging in science (*Wissenschaft*), as it is defined in the tradition of German idealism, Marx attempted to move beyond the "forms of manifestation" to penetrate to their "hidden fundament" (*transfondo oculto*). "Science," in that German tradition, implies criticizing appearances on the basis of an underlying essence, seeking out mutual connections, passing from the superficial and visible to the "hidden mystery," and thinking back to the essence from the phenomena. To be sure, the laws discovered by such a process refer to Hegel's return to the identity of the essence that directs the movements of existing things, instead of some kind of naturalist, empiricist, or scientific proposition. Reflecting this notion of science, Marx remarks in his manuscripts that if "value in general were a source fundamentally different than that of *labor* . . . every rational fundament of political economy would disappear." In Dussel's view, while certain concrete phenomenal claims can be falsified, the rationality of Marx's thought lies in his effort to provide the systemic underpinnings of those phenomena: "In truth, the 'rationality' of Marx's discourse does not consist in the fact that what it affirms cannot be subsequently falsified or its impossibility shown. What is important to 'science' is the intent to show coherently the totality of the development of the concept of capital by means of the constitution of the categories rationally, that is, with systemic fundamentality."[27]

The role of Marx's thought in relation to capitalism resembles the role that Dussel's ethical hermeneutics plays in relation to history. Dussel's ethical hermeneutics provides an overarching interpretive framework for the writing of history, a privileging of the perspective of history's forgotten Other, that ought not to contradict provable facts, that could engender new, overlooked verifiable claims, and that cannot be undermined by proved empirical claims since it provides, at another level, the interpretive context for those claims. Similarly, Marx's economics becomes in Dussel's hands an overarching interpretive framework for economics, privileging the perspective of capitalism's forgotten Other, here living labor, through a categorial system that revolves around the notion of surplus value. This systemic framework also ought not to contradict empirical facts, can generate new claims, and cannot be discredited by particular empirical facts since it establishes an interpretive context for them on a different plane.

Dussel's reading of Marx enables him to offer an explanation of the reality of Latin America. Though Dussel argues that Marx's philosophical rational nucleus and generative matrix apply even to socialist systems in a way that *Capital* does not, he also claims that *Capital* is applicable to Latin American capitalism, "peripheral" as it is for "central" capitalism. The mere fact that Marx himself never exposited the problem of the competition between capitals at a world level does not show that it is not a perfectly Marxist question. In the sixteenth and seventeenth centuries, massive sums of silver and gold taken by Spain from Latin America and transferred to Holland and England supplied a superaccumulation (*sobreacumulación*) necessary for the rapid growth of central capitalism, while peripheral capitalism, based on the *encomienda*, mining, and slavery in sugar factories, generated a very weak accumulation (*minusacumulación*). From these highly discrepant origins, Dussel advances nine theses about the differences between central and peripheral capital:

(1) that central capital benefited from a slow dissolution of pre-bourgeois modes of appropriation;
(2) that proximity to this process permitted primitive accumulation;
(3) that central capital profited from an expansive politic relying on navigational and military technology;
(4) that internal capital, the importation of metals, and slave trade made a superaccumulation possible;
(5) that central capital expanded to a world market rather than remaining regional;
(6) that central capital self-determined its own production and circulation;
(7) that central capital ingested the industrial revolution first;
(8) that central capital has transferred its earning of surplus value from absolute to relative surplus value; and
(9) that increasing salaries in central capital have created vast internal markets.

In a better developed capitalist system, in which workers simply cannot work any harder and thus the possibility of gaining more absolute surplus value has yielded to the pursuit of relative surplus value, a greater amount of constant capital (raw materials and machinery) is introduced. The result is that, even though the mass of surplus value or profit might rise, the proportion of that surplus value or profit to the capital outlay declines. In addition, the increase in the mass of products has the effect of lowering the value of products since the labor establishing value is distributed among more goods. In the less developed system, on the other hand, still in pursuit of absolute surplus value, lower salaries afford a greater possibility of extracting more surplus value and thus eventually more profit relative to the total outlay (until the less developed economy reaches the organic composition of the developed economy). The result is that the products have less value in the more developed setting (and more value in the less developed one), since, as Marx summarizes the above analysis, "*the 'greater' the organic composition, the 'less' the value of the product.*" When these goods are now brought to the international market to enter into competition—and Dussel refers to competition as the "theoretical place of dependence"—the products of the periphery that have more (average) value meet products of the center with less (average) value, as the price of all goods merges toward a common average price (the international price of production with its constant and variable capital and the average medium profit). The result is that the merchandise of less value (from the developed capital) obtains a price better than it would have achieved within its own national market; and the merchandise of greater value (from less developed capital) fetches a price lower than it would have within its local market. The less developed capital can still make a profit if the price of its production (constant and variable capital) is lower than the price of production (constant and variable capital and the average medium profit). Since this profit, taken out of the price of production, actually derives from the surplus value created by variable capital, the less-developed capital, drawing a smaller price in the international competition than it would have drawn in its regional market, effectively transfers surplus value to developed capital. Less-developed capital, in order to compensate for this transfer of surplus value, resorts to superexploitation of labor, paying lower salaries, demanding more work, etc. The developed capital, which already would be gaining profit through its surplus value, gains all the more because of the higher price it sells for in the international competition. Transnational corporations straddle this competition between regional capitals since they import massive organic capital into the peripheral economy and thus produce goods of less value than local peripheral competitors. Though they produce the same quantity of goods as their central competitors, their payment of lower salaries to peripheral labor enables them to realize greater surplus value than their competitors, who must pay wages appropriate to the center.[28]

Moreover, Dussel's interpretation of Marx prevents many of the tragedies inflicted on humanity in the name of Marx. Dussel's

Marx is not a collectivist proposing the subsumption of the individual within some undifferentiated mass; rather, Marx affirms individuality, not the defensive, self-protective individuality of the existentialist, but the indivividuality of the Other, neglected by the system. Dussel's Marx, as can be seen in his writings on Russia after *Capital*, does not lay out a universal philosophy of history in which socialism will emerge mechanistically out of capitalism, a developmental process in which Latin America would first have to become like Europe or the United States before it could arrive at socialism. Dussel's Marx, who focuses on the Other of the system, also would not allow that class would be rigidly maintained as the only intepretive category for liberation, as Trotsky and Stalin did, since there are other ways of being Other than admittedly atrocious forms of economic alienation. Dussel cites Che Guevara and the Sandinista revolution as examples of efforts not to pit "the people" against the proletariat, since liberation includes economic and cultural dimensions and cannot be reduced to economism or naïve populism. Even socialism, whether of the Stalinist or Althusserian brand, can never enclose itself in dogmatism, but must be submitted continually to exteriority's critique. Following Gramsci's opposition to *economismo*, Dussel argues that his interpretation of Marx would be open to diverse nationalist strains of socialism such as Sandanista Marxism or the type recommended by Mariátegui in Peru. Trotsky and Stalin insisted on international socialism without attending to the interests of the nations on the periphery of capitalism, and such internationalism easily became a totality immunized against critique from without, such as Otto Bauer's: namely that revolution be national and colonial also. Dussel affords us a more humane Marx and opens the way for a more humane socialism that might engage in ethical hermeneutics, by attempting to see the world through the eyes even of those it itself excludes.[29]

Religion/Theology

Dussel presents numerous examples in which religious/theological traditions have offered ideological support for oppression. For instance, according to Dussel, while Vitoria justified warfare against the indigenous of Latin America so that faith could be preached to them and Rubio offered theological justification of their subjugation, the Council of Trent never mentioned the massive elimination of indigenous populations in the Americas occurring long before and during its extended sessions. Similarly, in Cuzco in 1776 the indigenous leader Tupac Amaru led a rebellion against indigenous slave labor, only to be condemned by Bishop Moscos of Cuzco as a "rebel against God, religion, and the law." Moreover, on June 20, 1886, the Vatican's Holy Office officially denied that slavery was contrary to natural law, and Jesuit J. P. Gury wrote a compendium of moral theology justifying slavery. Numerous other illustrations are scattered throughout Dussel's works.[30]

For Dussel, Marx's criticism of capitalism constitutes a rejection of such false religion, since Marx undertakes a hermeneutics from the point of view of exteriority, an ethical hermeneutics in the tradition of the Hebrew prophets. For Marx, as Dussel explains him, capital, by appearing to create value by itself in its products, circulation, and the interest it yields, even as it exploits labor, the true creator of value, resembles idolatry, which attributes to fetishes mystic powers of their own, even as it remains oblivous to the true creator. Furthermore, in capitalism, the products of human labor, endowed with fictitious autonomous power, consume the blood of human victims, as Moloch did. Marx's living labor, confined to the exteriority in spite of its awesome power to create all the value inherent in the capitalist system, resembles the God of the prophets, the Creator, banished to exteriority by a system of idolatry that ironically presupposes that true God for its very existence. As Dussel expresses it in *El último Marx*, "the offspring subsumes labor itself; the 'effect' dominates its creative 'origin.'" Dussel, though, argues that Marx is not atheistic enough, in that his destruction of idols still lacks a positive affirmation of the God who is Other, in order that the postcapitalist system might not deprive itself of the exteriority requisite for self-critique.[31]

One of Dussel's own pieces that best exemplifies an ethical-hermeneutical theology is an article entitled "Sobre el 'Documento de Consulta' para Puebla," published in *Puebla '78: Temores y esperanzas*. In that article, Dussel criticizes a document drawn up in Bogotá in 1977 in preparation for the meeting of the Latin

American bishops in Puebla with Pope John Paul II in 1979. Dussel attacks this document, which claims to open "new directions"—other than those opened in the radical 1968 council at Medellín—for arguing that the poor, "although deprived of everything" (*aún cuando desprovistos de todo*) can still live with strength because of "faith, as a word which nourishes" (*la fe, como palabra que alimenta*). Beginning from the concrete sufferings of the poor, Dussel objects, "Since when is it affirmed, and on what basis, that the word of God can replace material nourishment, proteins, and calories?" Such affirmations, in Dussel's opinion, explain why Christianity has been criticized as leading to a castrating, passive, tragic, ahistorical resignation among Latin American peoples.[32]

Ideological elements appear as well in that the document's emphasis on evangelization of "the Latin American culture" amounts to a "culturalist" vision, the equivalent of political populism, that all too easily overlooks the vast differences between imperial-oligarchic culture and that of dominated masses. Instead of urging the founding of a new society, the document settles for the struggle to obtain for the poor a "worthy position" (*un puesto digno*) within civil society as it stands at present. For Dussel, though, "evangelization" is not so much to incarnate oneself within a culture as to incarnate oneself among the poor of the society, in order not to exalt or sacralize the dominant culture, but to place it in question. Since the document is eager to conciliate the irreconcilable, to evade every conflict, to cover over ruptures, it is no wonder that it recommends a third way (*tercerismo*) between right and the left that would have no real historical significance for Latin America. One cannot imagine a text more abstract, universal, and vacuous than the document's assertion that God intervenes "in humanity" (*en el hombre*), since "humanity" could include the Herods and Pilates of this world and thus really refers to no one at all.[33]

The commitment to constructing theology from the perspective of the poor Other leads Dussel to question the document's Christology, Mariology, and ecclesiology. To the document's comment that Jesus's "death was caused by the evil [*maldad*] of human beings," Dussel responds that responsibility cannot be attributed to the "evil of human beings in general, but rather of

those responsible, the powerful, the governing classes, and the
rich; the poor, the humiliated, and the exploited who identified
with Jesus were not culpable." The document's Christology is
faulty. "This emptying of the conflict of Christology conceals the
struggle of Jesus against the sin of the rich and the oppressor.
It hides the fact that, by preaching eschatological hope and by
mobilizing the people, the powerful become disquieted."[34]

Mary is presented as one who impelled people toward unity
instead of being "the marvelous mother who knew how to edu-
cate her son not to tremble before conflict and to face death
head-on, even if he would be confused with being a zealot." The
document, which allots only fifteen lines to the widespread, popular "base communities" in Latin America, envisions the Church
as the institution that overcomes antagonisms via hierarchic authority. No importance is given to the Church living with the
poor, the marginal, the indigenous, or the blacks.[35]

The danger of false universalization comes to the fore most
clearly in the document's definition of poverty. At first, poverty is
defined as "being affected by real situations of lack and priva-
tion," but this definition is expanded to "lacking participation in
the services of society" and, finally, to "being weak in some other
dimension of existence, such as the sick or the one who is lonely."
To these definitions, Dussel responds:

> There can be poor people, according to the "social objective con-
> dition of privation" (which are, without doubt, those to whom Jesus
> refers when he says in Matthew "I was hungry . . ."), who, since they
> do not possess the richness of the Christian attitude ("enriched by
> the persistent heritage of evangelization"), are proud, lost, or sin-
> ful. On the other hand, there can be rich people in a "social objec-
> tive condition" who are religiously poor because of their attitude.
> In this manner, we have arrived at a total inversion: now there are
> poor who are rich and rich who are poor.[36]

Here, in its very effort to move to a more universal definition of
"poverty," the document effectively conceals the suffering of the
physically poor, making it equal to everyone else's pain. The document blunts the demand of the poor Other by constructing a
theology that will continue to hide from sight this Other's distinctive suffering. Only an ethical hermeneutical approach to a reli-

gious tradition and its texts can prevent theology from becoming the ideology of the status quo.[37] We have seen how Dussel gradually moved beyond his traditional education and his espousal of Heidegger to Levinas, and we have seen how that change transformed his own thinking into an ethical hermeneutics. In this chapter, we have shown how these philosophical presuppositions played themselves out in his approach to history, economics, and religion. It now remains for us to face the criticisms coming from different quarters to the effect that this admirable philosophical attempt on Dussel's part is ultimately nothing more than irrationalism.

NOTES

1. *El humanismo helénico*, pp. 51, 91; *History and the Theology of Liberation: A Latin American Perspective*, trans. John Drury (Maryknoll, N.Y.: Orbis Books, 1976), pp. 57–60; *El catolicismo popular en la Argentina*, p. 49; "Supuestos histórico-filosóficos de la teología desde América Latina," p. 177; "Liberación latinoamericana y filosofía," p. 10; *Les évêques hispano-américains: Défenseurs et évangélisateurs de l'Indien, 1504–1620* (Wiesbaden: Franz Steiner Verlag, 1970); Enrique Dussel, *El episcopado latinoamericano y la liberación de los pobres, 1504–1620* (Mexico City: Centro de Reflexión Teológica, 1979), pp. 30, 46, 51, 53, 70–71, 139, 221, 280, 287, 292, 313–14, 318, 339, 350, 359–60 (Bishop Antonio de Valdivieso, for instance, was murdered in Nicaragua for defending indigenous peoples); Enrique Dussel, "Die Ausbreitung der Christenheit und ihre heutige Krise," *Consilium*, 164 (1981), 307–16; "Auf dem Weg zur Geschichte der ganzen Kirche—Neue Horizonte," *Theologische Zeitschrift*, 38 (1982), 398. Some other explicitly historical works by Dussel include: *A History of the Church in Latin America: Colonialism to Liberation (1492–1979)*; *History and the Theology of Liberation*; *Cultura latinoamericana e historia de la Iglesia*; *Hipótesis para una historia de la Iglesia en América Latina*; *Hipótesis para una historia de la teología en América Latina* (Chapinero, Bogotá: Indo-American Press Service, 1986); *De Medellín a Puebla*; *Desintegración de la cristiandad colonial y liberación: Perspectiva latinoamericana* (Salamanca: Ediciones Sigueme, 1978); "Supuestos histórico-filosóficos de la teología desde América Latina"; "Hipotésis para una historia de la filosofía en América Latina," in *Perspectivas de la filosofía. III. Simposio de filosofía contemporánea* (Iztapalapa, Mexico: Universidad Autónoma Metropolitana, 1990), pp. 229–69; "Del descubrimiento al desencubrimiento: Hacia un desagravio historico," *Missiones Extranjeros*, 86 (1985), 113.

110 ETHICAL HERMENEUTICS

2. Book 1, title 1, law 1 of Bullarum, Port., cited in "Die Ausbreitung der Christenheit and ihre heutige Krise," 310.

3. *De Medellín a Puebla*, p. 120; "Del descubrimiento al desencubrimiento," 106; *Cultura latinoamericana e historia de la Iglesia*, pp. 80–81; *El dualismo en la antropología de la cristiandad*, pp. 147–48, 160; *América Latina: Dependencia y liberación*, p. 59.

4. "Criterios generales y periodificación de una historia de la Iglesia en América Latina," *Cristianismo y Sociedad* [Mexico], 82 (1984), 7.

5. "Del descubrimiento al desencubrimiento," 107, 109; "Reflexiones sobre la metodología para una historia de la Iglesia en América Latina," p. 99.

6. "Reflexiones sobre la metodología para una historia de la Iglesia en América Latina," p. 103.

7. "Del descubrimiento al desencubrimiento," 107; Dussel and Esandi, *El catolicismo popular en la Argentina*, p. 19; "Sobre el sentido de la traducción," pp. 133–34; *El dualismo en la antropología de la cristiandad*, pp. 259, 261; *Cultura latinoamericana e historia de la Iglesia*, pp. 92–95; "Reflexiones sobre la metodología para una historia de la Iglesia en América Latina," pp. 101, 103; "Criterios generales y periodificación de una historia de la Iglesia en America Latina," 17–18; "Auf dem Weg zur Geschichte der ganzen Kirche," 368–69; "Historia y praxis (Ortopraxia y objectividad)," pp. 307–29; see above, chap. 3, pp. 71–72; *América Latina: Dependencia y liberación*, p. 57.

8. *1492: El encubrimiento del Otro*, pp. 41–61.

9. Ibid., pp. 17–30, 41–47, 49–99.

10. Ibid., pp. 101–203.

11. Ibid., 17–47, 125–129, 205–213.

12. Enrique Dussel, "Hermeneutica y liberación." Dialogue with Paul Ricoeur, April 1991, p. 27.

13. Horacio Cerutti Guldberg, *Filosofía de la liberación latinoamericana* (Mexico City: Fondo de Cultura Económica, 1983), pp. 215, 255, 262; Schutte, "Origins and Tendendies of the Philosophy of Liberation in Latin American Thought," 276, 283, 287, 289; Dussel, *History and the Theology of Liberation*, p. 118; *América Latina: Dependencia y liberación*, p. 156; *Para una ética de la liberación latinoamericana*, 2:47; *Método para una filosofía de la liberación*, 3rd ed., p. 144; *Teología de la liberación y ética*, p. 132; *Ethics and the Theology of Liberation*, p. 17; Dussel and Guilolot, *Liberación latinoamericana y Emmanuel Levinas*, p. 41.

14. *La producción teórica de Marx*, p. 272; "Sobre la actualidad de Carlos Marx," in *Dando razón de nuestra esperanza: Los cristianos latinoamericanos frente a la crisis del socialismo y la derrota sandinista* (Managua, Nicaragua: Ediciones Nicarao, 1992), p. 111.

15. *La producción teórica de Marx,* pp. 31, 39, 40–42, 46, 51, 52–53, 57–58, 67, 71–75, 89, 97, 109, 110–11, 115–16, 121, 123, 137, 139–140, 147, 154, 164, 168–69, 170, 172, 177, 188, 189, 193, 197–98, 201, 203, 205, 208, 210, 305, 218, 220, 255, 255–56, 260–61, 264, 282, 293, 299, 301, 302, 307, 315, 316, 322–25, 328, 331, 333; Enrique Dussel, *El último Marx (1863–1882) y la liberación latinoamericana: Un comentario a la tercera y a la cuarta redacción de "El Capital* (Mexico: Siglo Veintiuno Editores, 1990), pp. 408, 409, 414–15.

16. Enrique Dussel, *Hacía un Marx desconocido: Un comentario de manuscritos del 61–63* (Iztapalapa, Mexico: Siglo Veintiuno Editores, 1988), pp. 52, 61, 66–67, 69, 76, 82, 87, 90–92, 93, 103, 105, 106, 107, 108, 112, 117, 119, 121, 123, 125, 128, 130–32, 145, 148, 158, 163, 167, 172, 176, 190, 193, 194, 200, 213, 240, 241, 244, 246, 248, 260, 305–306; *El último Marx,* pp. 73–76.

17. Enrique Dussel, *El último Marx (1863–1882), pp. 73–75, 81–82, 104, 113–16, 117, 119, 124, 127, 129, 140–42, 147, 238, 242, 243, 244, 253, 254, 255, 260, 261.*

18. *La producción teórica de Marx,* pp. 19–20, 271–72, 347–48; *Hacia un Marx desconocido,* pp. 24, 305; *El último Marx,* pp. 51, 141, 210–11, 212–13, 214, 231, 317, 344, 360, 437, 442, 448–49.

19. *La producción teórica de Marx,* pp. 138–39

20. *El último Marx,* pp, 138, 143, 333, 344, 351, 366, 373, 381; *La producción teórica de Marx,* pp. 6, 138–39, 336–43.

21. *La producción teórica de Marx,* pp. 155, 323, 359, 365–66; *Hacia un Marx desconocido,* pp. 55, 58, 231, 285.

22. *Hacia un Marx desconocido,* pp. 87, 113, 160, 194; *El último Marx,* pp. 68, 77, 78, 138, 147–48, 430.

23. *La producción teórica de Marx,* pp. 347, 361–64; *Hacia un Marx desconocido,* pp. 74–75, 365; *El último Marx,* pp. 333, 336, 340, 342–44, 348–49, 351, 353, 356–59, 360–62, 377, 401.

24. *Hacia un Marx desconocido,* p. 64.

25. Ibid., pp. 64, 117, 123, 132, 307; *El último Marx,* pp. 64, 66, 68, 138, 143, 165, 119, 395–96.

26. *El último Marx,* pp. 299–300, 303–304, 305–307, 312–13, 325, 317, 318, 320–31; *Hacía un Marx desconocido,* pp. 75, 294.

27. *El último Marx,* p. 119; *La producción teórica de Marx,* pp. 164, 365–66; *Hacia un Marx desconocido,* pp. 136, 174, 209, 225, 227, 243, 253, 286–87, 289, 293, 298–99; *El último Marx,* pp. 361, 376, 384, 424–25, 427–28.

28. *La producción teórica de Marx,* pp. 378, 379–84, 388–89, 392, 396, 398; *Hacia un Marx desconocido,* pp. 90, 330, 334, 339, 347–48, 355; *El último Marx,* pp. 348–84, 405.

29. *La producción teórica de Marx,* pp. 355–56, 368, 406; *Hacia un Marx desconocido,* pp. 75, 297; *El último Marx,* pp. 134, 253–55, 261, 265, 272, 274, 278, 280–81, 285, 288, 290, 368.

30. *History of the Church in Latin America,* pp. 309–10, 318; *América Latina: Dependencia y liberación,* pp. 197, 199; *Para una ética de la liberación latinoamericana,* 5:28–29; "Racismo, América Latina negra, y teología de la liberación," *Servir* [Mexico], 86 (1980), 195–96.

31. *La producción teórica de Marx,* pp. 115–17, 302, 315, 322, 345, 347, 365, 368; *Hacia un Marx desconocido,* pp. 55, 64, 75, 113, 194, 228, 245, 285, 305, 365, 369; *El último Marx,* pp. 51, 71, 165, 181, 333, 361, 365–66, 368, 370, 376, 384; Enrique Dussel, "El concepto de fetichismo en el pensamiento de Marx: Elementos para una teoría general marxista de la religión." *Cristianismo y Sociedad* [Mexico], 85 (1985), 41–43, 46, 51–52, 54–55, 57; *Ethics and the Theology of Liberation,* p. 17.

32. "Sobre el 'Documento de Consulta' para Puebla." In *Puebla '78: Temores y esperanzas,* ed. Clodovin Boff (Mexico City: Centro Reflexión Teológica, 1978), pp. 82, 83–84.

33. Ibid., pp. 86–87, 89, 91, 92.

34. Ibid., pp. 93–94.

35. Ibid., pp. 94, 99–100.

36. Ibid., pp. 96–97.

37. Ibid.

5

Rationality in Dussel:
The American Critics

ENRIQUE DUSSEL'S PHILOSOPHY of liberation has come under fire recently from different quarters. Horacio Cerutti Guldberg's *Filosofía de la liberación latinoamericana* (1983) and a related article by Ofelia Schutte in *The Philosophical Forum* (1991) have strongly attacked Dussel. Karl-Otto Apel, with whom Dussel has been in dialogue over the past several years, also raises pertinent objections. In this chapter, I will focus on the criticisms of Cerutti and Schutte, demonstrate how they converge on the problem of rationality in his thought, and discuss their validity.[1]

CERUTTI AND SCHUTTE ON DUSSEL

Horacio Cerutti Guldberg, whom Dussel himself originally classified among the first generation of the philosophy of liberation in Argentina, disputed first of all this very classification.[2] In Cerutti's view, only Dussel's own ideological leanings would have led him to include people of such different ages and ideological positions under a single generation. Ironically, however, in his *Filosofía de la liberación latinoamericana*, Cerutti later willingly identified himself with the philosophy of liberation as a part of its problematizing subsector, despite his earlier disclaimers.[3]

In Cerutti's view, the protagonists of the philosophy of liberation project an ethicist's self-image of moral superiority. Schutte would explain such an attitude by Dussel's tendency to set himself as the errorless, guiltless, blameless Other over against an evil, oppressive system. Any philosopher identifying with the Others of that system becomes uncritically deified as "ethically correct," capable of exercising a new authoritarianism legitimated in the name of "God," "liberation," and "exteriority."[4]

These self-righteous personality traits, which Schutte and Cerutti ascribe to Dussel, reflect, in their view, a deeper, erroneous philosophical approach. Dussel characterizes his philosophy as a first philosophy, a privileged first *logos*, a self-sufficient and fundamental knowledge like Heidegger's fundamental ontology, the ultimate criterion of reference and criticism, superior to the sciences and immune to their critique. Paradoxically, Schutte notes that Dussel offers no rational demonstration for this foundation for all other rationality.

> It is true that he [Dussel] has also claimed that there is no reason for him to give arguments for the foundations of his theory, since the foundation is beyond proof, anyway. I would point out, however, that whether one believes one's ideas are the manifestation of the divine on earth on account of so-called rationally demonstrated "proofs" (which may yield "certitude") or whether one holds the same belief because of some emotional or mystical conviction (as Dussel's theory seems to exemplify), the results are quite similar in terms of the pretense or claim to represent the voice of the divine in human affairs.[5]

Unsurprisingly, Cerutti's final verdict is that the philosophy of liberation opts for irrationality; it is a truly barbarian philosophy, but not in Dussel's sense, which is aligned with those excluded by power centers, as in the days of the Greeks.[6]

To deal adequately with questions about the rationality of Dussel's work, it would be necessary to take deeper account of his philosophical origins. The idea of a "foundation" not justified by "rational demonstration," or of an ethical "first philosophy" suggests Dussel's use of such sources as the phenomenologies of Husserl and Levinas, even though, as we have seen, Dussel developed them. It is important to note that neither Schutte nor Cerutti ever discusses these origins at length. Their lack of familiarity with this line of thought is suggested by several of Schutte's references to Dussel's mysticism, and by Cerutti's comment that in Marcuse's *Un ensayo sobre la liberación* (1969) the language of the Other acquired its first formulation, even though Levinas's *Totality and Infinity* had been published eight years earlier. Only a careful consideration of Dussel's sources and his use of them will enable us to assess the rationality of his own thought.[7]

Both Cerutti and Schutte relate this philosophical irrationalism to Dussel's and others' underlying religious commitments. Cerutti accuses Dussel of fideistically requiring religious faith as a prerequisite for philosophizing. Just as the Argentinian "Priests for the Third World" opposed Marxism as not yet purified of enlightenment rationalism and thus inexorably inclined to intellectualism and scientism, so Dussel's "populist sector" of the philosophy of liberation emphasized—in contrast to Marxist proclivities toward the urban proletariat—the role of *campesinos* in the process of revolution and supported Peronist populism because of its support for popular religiosity. Juan Carlos Scannone, an ally of Dussel's, uncritically utilized concepts of Ignatius Loyola's spiritual discernment to choose between Marxist and pastoral strategies. In addition, the philosophers of liberation resisted ideological or political confrontation by offering explanations of Christian morality or personal allusions. Similarly, Schutte finds Dussel longing for pre-Cartesian understandings of philosophy and duplicating Church teaching almost to the letter, theoretically condemning even divorce. In Schutte's opinion, the Other is used symbolically throughout Dussel's work as a "God-substitute."[8]

According to Cerutti, it is precisely these religious leanings that prompted Dussel and other liberationists to present the philosophy of liberation as an alternative to atheistic Marxism, to prefer analyses based on the category of the *pueblo* to class analysis, to substitute exaggerated populist rhetoric for careful philosophical analysis, and, finally, to support the return of Juan Perón, even though Peronism would eventually unleash fascist forces and result in so many tortures, disappearances, and deaths.[9]

In Cerutti's view, Dussel's foundationalist approach leads him to adopt an attitude of superiority over science and to close himself to science's findings. Dussel seems to assume that he knows in the abstract what the sciences will say in the concrete. Unlike liberation theologians such as Gutiérrez and Assman, Dussel tends to ontologize the findings of the social sciences on dependence theory because he is unaware of the limits of social scientific findings, neglects the multicausal character of dependence, and overlooks in a folkloric manner existing interdependencies. Schutte believes that since Dussel derives fundamental principles from faith rather than scientific knowledge, his thought will always be incompatible with Marxism. Dussel also shows himself opposed to Freudian and feminist thought. Cerutti finds Dussel's boast that Latin American philosophy begins with the philosophy of liberation negating all preceding Latin American thought. Philosophers of liberation denounce all European rationality, too, as imperial, academic justification of oppression.[10]

The original sacrifice of rationality appears in subservience to the Other, which can lead one to adhere "always to the other's authority on pain of being considered morally inept."[11] Paradoxically, the Others to whom one is to be subservient are portrayed as weak and needing help and hence incapable of thinking on their own. The result is that the expert, who began in subservience to the Other, assumes the role of representing and speaking for the Other, who ends up subordinate to that expert. The philosopher's near heteronomy before the Other leads to an eventual megalomaniac self-aggrandizement.[12]

Cerutti's and Schutte's criticisms, although predominantly negative in tone, flow from an underlying affirmation of the rational character of philosophy that, in their view, Dussel's philosophy threatens. For Cerutti, philosophy ought to avoid dogmatism and give an account of its own praxis. Taking part in philosophy demands that one not be partisan, but open oneself to the maximal possible criticism. Schutte, too, envisions philosophy as critical thinking, intent on testing the validity of its claims. To argue that claims possess clarity, truth, or correctness simply because they *originate* from an epiphany of the Other's face is to commit the genetic fallacy that the origin of a claim proves its validity.[13]

ASSESSING THE CRITICISMS

While Dussel's at times ostentatious self-expression may account for some of Schutte's and Cerutti's reaction to him, there is a constant danger of becoming self-righteous at precisely the point where, after listening to the Other, one is commanded to command others, as Levinas puts it. But for Levinas this commanding of others arises out of a context in which one first of all places oneself vulnerably before the exploited Other and then undertakes prophetic discourse to Others, including the exploitative Other, for whom and to whom one is also responsible. Levinas recognizes that the pervasive presence of the Other purifies even prophets of their arrogance, since he no sooner grants the need for commanding in *Totality and Infinity* than he immediately, in the next section, reasserts the asymmetry of the interpersonal. On the basis of these Levinasian underpinnings, two conclusions seem warranted regarding Dussel's imputed self-righteousness. On one hand, to the extent that Dussel transforms vulnerability before the Other into an instrument of dogmatic self-assertion, he betrays his own starting point and contradicts his Levinasian origins. On the other, one must be wary of the charge of self-righteousness and focus more on the contents of a prophetic discourse since throughout history people have attempted to silence authentic prophets by charging them with arrogance and self-righteousness.[14]

Whatever Dussel's personality traits may be, Schutte's and Cerutti's deeper critique is that such traits flow from an erroneous underlying philosophical approach: namely, that Dussel claims to produce a first philosophy, a fundament that the sciences and other forms of knowledge cannot shake. Here again, a more careful understanding of Dussel's Levinasian roots can meet the criticism. There is no doubt that Levinas conceives ethics as first philosophy—he has even entitled an essay to that effect—even though the explicit characterization of his philosophy as first philosophy diminishes in the later works. Ethics must be first philosophy for Levinas, because every cognitional domain pursued, every theme discussed, and every truth sought is situated in relationship with the Other as interlocutor, who arises behind even the theme in which he or she is presented and who continually issues inescapable ethical demands. The reference to an interlocutor breaks through the text that discourse claims to weave in thematizing and enveloping all things in such a way that even the discourse intent on totalizing being belies the very claim to totalize. Yet this "foundation" does not warrant self-righteousness or the sense that one is privileged over others, ultimate, self-sufficient, or exempt from critical scrutiny. For Levinas, on the contrary, theory of any sort requires an "unnatural" movement, a restraint of one's drives and impulsive movements—in brief, the attitude of a being that has learned to distrust itself by submitting to questioning from another. The ethical relation, as both origin and ally of the quest for truth, accomplishes the very intention that animates the movement unto truth. It is a strange foundation that Levinas provides since it affords no consolation or security and, unlike traditional foundationalist epistemologies which lull people into uncritically forgetting the arbitrariness of freedom and to which Schutte's and Cerutti's criticisms more aptly pertain, continually undermines any pretense to surety. For Levinas, on the contrary, "the essence of reason consists not in securing for man a foundation and powers, but in calling him in question and in inviting him to justice."[14]

Schutte's lack of familiarity with the Levinasian bases of Dussel's thought—fostered at times by Dussel's own effort to distance himself from Levinas—could also explain Schutte's complaint that Dussel seems to offer no rational demonstration or arguments for his viewpoint. But even if Dussel fully articulated all his Levinasian presuppositions, Levinas presents phenomenological descriptions for the judgment of autonomous knowers who ought to assent to such descriptions only if they, as Husserl expressed it, "see that it is so." Though such descriptions do not consist in rational demonstrations or arguments in the usual sense, they appeal to what Herbert Spiegelberg called "critical self-evidence," arrived at after careful and unbiased inspection and scrutiny and providing unobstructed cognitive accessibility in which the self-evident object or state of affairs "shines forth." Descriptions can be revised or even abandoned in the light of further evidence disclosed during the course of one's experience or through discourse with others. In such phenomenology, there is no appeal to self-evidence, in the naïve sense of a feeling of comfortable self-assurance, as it is understood especially by Anglo-American critics of self-evidence. Such phenomenological descriptions involve neither emotional nor mystical conviction and claim no divine guarantees. Furthermore, phenomenological insight is not offset by the fact that a statistical study might indicate that a majority of the population does not recognize it.[16]

It is not only the phenomenological nature of the Other's givenness that might make Dussel's foundations seem unprovable; it is also the foundational locus of the Other with reference to every type of demonstration. Levinas contends, for example, that every process of rational demonstration and discursive argumentation presupposes the Other whom Levinas describes and to whom justifications are presented. Even to try to prove to an Other the validity of Levinas's descriptions of the Other would presuppose what one is trying to prove. "The interlocutor cannot be deduced, for the relationship between him and me is presupposed by every proof."[17]

In addition, Dussel's Levinasian basis does not license attitudes of superiority toward the claims of any scientists, who constitute the Other of philosophy and deserve a fair hearing. It is difficult to see how any scientific findings could invalidate that demand for respect and responsibility from the Other that any presentation of scientific findings always presupposes. If Dussel neglects the multicausal character of dependence or of the existing interdependencies out of haughtiness toward social scientists—and I will discuss this issue in greater depth in the next chapter—then the fault lies, not in his philosophical presuppositions, but in his infidelity to them. Finally, Dussel's frequent and sometimes exaggerated claims of having overcome all preceding Latin American thought and all European rationality reflect more Levinas's assertion that his discovery of the ethical dimension subtending all discourse goes beyond earlier ontological and epistemological positions that have neglected what they presuppose and thereby tended to reduce the Other to the same. As I have argued above, Levinas's ethics is not to be construed as antirational; rather, in Levinas, European rationality achieves a summit of self-critique, becoming aware of the taken-for-granted horizons that invite rational discourse into being in the first place and renew rationality continually.[18]

In Dussel and Levinas, service of the Other does not demand that one sacrifice rationality and adhere "always to the other's authority on pain of being considered morally inept," as Schutte suggests. Dussel engages in no irrational worship of the Other, as mentioned above. Abundant textual evidence exists that Dussel believes that every culture, including the former Inca and Aztec empires, is prone to a mistaken self-absolutization. Moreover, he repeatedly admits that "the people" are not free from inauthenticity, voices frequent misgivings about popular religiosity, observes that the oppressed have often introjected the oppression they have received, and refrains from any uncritical endorsement of populist spontaneity. Prophets and pedagogues are obliged to foster those self-critical elements, often already to be found within their cultures and popular modes of expression, such as the narrative underlying the Argentinian tango.[19]

It is important to emphasize that Levinas's texts do not enjoin any blind servility or a forfeiture of personal autonomy that would be highly offensive not only to Schutte and Cerutti, but also to the entire modern mentality, including outlooks profoundly influenced by Kant, such as Karl-Otto Apel's. As the first chapter makes clear, Levinas acknowledges his debt to phenomenology, which depends entirely on the capacity of the free, critical agent to place in question all that the naïve natural attitude bequeaths. For this reason, Levinas insists on beginning, not with logical relations in which the I and the Other are reversible and undifferentiated, but with an I facing the Other. Hence, the I must be conceived first and foremost as separate, as atheist, that is, as independent of God, of any pantheism or emanationism, of any "participation" in being, free with regard to every system that might swallow him or her up. Just as sensation challenged the Parmenidean monism derived from logic, so, for Levinas, one's identity is established through sensible enjoyment—the joy of breathing, looking, eating, working, egoism—a happiness in which the I identifies itself in ignorance of the Other or the Totality and not in a dialectical opposition in which the I would be only one moment of the Hegelian-type whole it resists. If, as Levinas argues, one can surpass oneself and become preoccupied with the Other only at the apogee of enjoyment, and if one can be hospitable only if one already dwells in one's own home, then this trajectory in Levinas's works points toward the fact that only a full self can undertake service of the Other. On the basis of enjoyment, the I discovers its own interiority, its capacity to decide the meaning of its own life, in the face of death or the imperialism of the later historiographer's false interpretations. Interiority is "the refusal to be transformed into a pure loss figuring in an alien accounting system." Because of this interiority, one finds scandalous the control that violence can exercise over even the will that heroically resists it. It is to this separate, independent I, accomplished in its own autonomy, that the Other appears, as inescapably present to the I as its own body or its own history, in relation to which it must also take up its free choices.[20]

Indeed, Levinas's descriptions of ethical relationships presuppose this development of autonomy. If he is describing prescriptive rather than denotative statements, as Lyotard explains, then it can certainly be the case that some prescriptives emerging from the Other are not justifiable. At such a later justificatory moment—assumed in relation to the prior experience of the Other's prescriptions—one can and ought to turn to principles of consistency, equality, and impartiality introduced at the level of the Third, provided such norms are tested against the face-to-face so that they do not disguise oppression. Because of the autonomy and self-critical character of *both* parties, discourse occurs between two points that do not constitute a system, a cosmos, or totality—which would be the case if the Other suppressed the I. Discourse involves risk, as Levinas observes: "This discourse is therefore not the unfolding of a prefabricated internal logic, but the constitution of truth in a struggle between thinkers, with all the risks of freedom. The relationship of language implies transcendence, radical separation, the strangeness of interlocutors, the revelation of the other to me."[21]

Finally, the Other's call to infinite responsibility confirms the subjectivity in its apologetic position, but "apology" is precisely the word Levinas uses to describe those defending themselves before mistaken historical verdicts. It implies a defense of one's own position, which, although undertaken because of a sense of responsibility to the Other, could well be legitimate over against the Other. Apology is the opposite of blind concurrence with the Other.[22]

In fact, the intervention of the Other upon one's self augments one's autonomy by summoning one beyond the straight line of justice and the universal objective law which applies to all indifferently.

> Judgment no longer alienates the subjectivity, for it does not make it enter into and dissolve in the order of an objective morality, but leaves it a dimension whereby it deepens in itself. To utter "I," to affirm the irreducible singularity in which the apology is pursued,

means to possess a privileged place with regard to responsibilities for which no one can replace me and from which no one can release me. To be unable to shirk: this is the I. The personal character of apology is maintained in this election by which the I is accomplished qua I. The accomplishing of the I qua I and morality constitute one sole and same process in being: morality comes to birth not in equality, but in the fact that infinite exigencies, that of serving the poor, the stranger, the widow, and the orphan converge at one point of the universe. Thus through morality alone are I and the others produced in the universe. The alienable subjectivity of need and will, which claims to be already and henceforth in possession of itself, but which death makes a mockery of, is transfigured by the election which invests it, turning it toward the resources of its own interiority. These resources are infinite—in the incessant overflowing of duty accomplished, by ever broader responsibilities.[23]

Levinas's thought here gives the lie to the commonsense view articulated by someone like Ayn Rand that altruism reduces one to subservient feebleness. In addition, examples like that of Bishop Oscar Romero, the timid cleric turned by the sufferings of the poor into undaunted critic of the Salvadoran military who later assassinated him, support Levinas over Rand. In fact, those who consistently espouse positions like Rand's and who, because of what Levinas calls their allergy to the Other, consistently fear that the Other will exploit an "I" committed to Levinas's ethics must examine whether they may have unwittingly absorbed as their philosophical starting point the spontaneity of freedom whose value, Levinas says, is often exempted from further discussion. Though such a beginning is the target of Levinas's critique, his attempt to place the self and its critical powers at the service of the Other do not eviscerate that self or its powers. For to be a mindless puppet of the Other is in the end completely detrimental to the Other's own good.[24]

Contrary to Cerutti, Dussel does not require religious faith as a prerequisite for philosophizing, although Dussel's failure to discuss his Levinasian bases and the difference between an appeal to phenomenological intuition and a demonstration or organization might make it appear that religion or mysticism is substituting for philosophy. Furthermore, Dussel opposes vulgar Marxism not only because it denies the religious beliefs of those it seeks to liberate, but also because it overlooks their cultural and national characteristics. Ultimately, to subjugate the Other to a theoretical system centered in the category of class is but another form of totalization, contrary to Marx's own intentions as Dussel displays them in his trilogy on Marx.

However, I do agree with Schutte that Dussel's ethics in particular tends to reduplicate Church teaching and does not adequately take account of the implications of a theory of exteriority for women and homosexuals. Such errors do not undermine an ethics at the service of alterity, but require that that ethics be more rigorously applied. Furthermore, in regard to the charge that Dussel seeks a pre-Cartesian position, I have argued that he began with a natural law theory, attempted to integrate it with Heideggerian ontology, and abandoned the entire ontological project to embrace Levinas's ethics. Though many of his comments, particularly in the ethics, still reflect those natural law tendencies, the turn to Levinas involves an entrance into the modern (and even postmodern) philosophical arena.[25]

In his essay "Una década Argentina (1966–1976) y el origen de la 'Filosofía de la Liberación,' " Dussel himself has responded extensively to the objection that he supported Peronism in spite of its eventual fascist consequences. In that essay Dussel describes how, given the complex and ambiguous situation of Argentina in the early 1970s, he opted, in conjunction with the university youth with whom he worked, to situate himself within the populist anti-military movement in favor of Perón's return, and yet with criticism and creativity. Dussel claims that he considered the "true word" to proceed from the poor and the pueblo, not from a leader mandating that his word was the only word, as Perón did. In effect, Dussel also accuses Schutte and Cerutti of committing the genetic fallacy, since one ought not to confuse the concrete, historical conditions of the origin of the philosophy of liberation with the constitution of its categories or the growing structure of its discourse which applies to other sectors of Latin America, Asia, and Africa. Dussel's ultimate proof that he was a dangerous critic from within the people, that he was never allied with the populist party, is that his house was bombed and one of his students killed because he was perceived as "poisoning the minds of the young with his Marxist doctrine."[26]

It is evident that Dussel's philosophy, properly understood in its relationship to Levinas and, as we shall see later, Levinas's philosophy properly understood as phenomenology at a pretranscendental level, upholds the same standards of rationality as Cerutti and Schutte fear Dussel is abolishing. Dussel's philosophy, properly understood, can give an adequate account of itself and need not take refuge in uncritical dogmatism. In exposure to the Other and the Other's question, one opens oneself to the greatest possible criticism—in fulfillment of what Cerutti considers to be the task of philosophy. Surely, too, Dussel could agree with Schutte that philosophy involves critical thinking, testing the validity of claims, presenting phenomenological descriptions for scrutiny, and not holding that claims are justified merely because they emerge from the Other. It is the Other who invites self-criticism and the Other who asks that one justify one's positions and prove validity. One's responsibility for the Other, which precedes whatever stance one adopts, in no way precludes differing with the Other or criticizing the Other for the Other's sake. The nature of apology and the daring, risky character of discourse, which does not unfold like a prefabricated internal logic, do not demand a mindless conformity with the Other, and it is always possible that radical disagreement with the Other springs from the deepest love for that Other.

NOTES

1. Counterpositions to Dussel's such as those of Ricoeur, Rorty, and Taylor are not considered in this chapter and the next because the volume in which these counter positions are considered, *The Underside of Modernity*, appeared after this book had gone to press.

2. Enrique Dussel, "La filosofía de la liberación en Argentina: Irrupción de una nueva generación filosófica," *Praxis latinoamerica y filosofía de la liberación* (Bogotá: Editorial Nueva America, 1983), pp. 54–56. Cerutti, *Filosofía de la liberación latinoamericana*, pp. 31–37.

3. Cerutti, *Filosofía de la liberación latinoamericana*, p. 223.

4. Ibid., pp. 27, 56, 282; Schutte, "Origins and Tendencies of the Philosophy of Liberation in Latin American Thought,", 281–82.

THE AMERICAN CRITICS

125

5. Schutte, "Origins and Tendencies of the Philosophy of Liberation in Latin American Thought," 289, 293. In Schutte's view, Dussel never criticizes the phenomenological method which he utilizes either; see 290.

6. Cerutti, *Filosofía de la liberación latinoamericana*, pp. 40, 46, 50, 235–39, 271.

7. Ibid., p. 160.

8. Ibid., pp. 66–67, 153, 192, 201, 213, 278–79; Schutte, "Origins and Tendencies of the Philosophy of Liberation in Latin American Thought," 275, 277.

9. Cerutti, *Filosofía de la liberación latinoamericana*, pp. 12, 17, 21, 25, 55, 136–37, 157, 187–90, 194, 205, 213, 252; for Dussel's own comments on populism, see his "Una década argentina (1966–1976) y el Origen de la 'Filosofía de la Liberación.'"

10. Cerutti, *Filosofía de la liberación latinoamericana*, pp. 79–80, 86, 117, 119, 131, 202, 208–10, 216, 235, 236, 238, 239, 244, 271, 283, 288; Schutte, "Origins and Tendencies," 271, 278–79, 284; Leopoldo Zea, "Dependencia y liberación en la filosofía latinoamericana," *Dianoia*, 20 (1974), 180.

11. Schutte, "Origins and Tendencies of the Philosophy of Liberation in Latin American Thought," 280.

12. Ibid., 280, 283, 288; Cerutti, *Filosofía de la liberación latinoamericana*, pp. 257–58.

13. Cerutti, *Filosofía de la liberación latinoamericana*, pp. 292, 308; Schutte, "Origins and Tendencies of the Philosophy of Liberation in Latin American Thought," 291.

14. *Totality and Infinity*, pp. 213–15.

15. Levinas, "Ethics as First Philosophy," in *The Levinas Reader*, ed. Sean Hand (Oxford and Cambridge, Mass.: Basil Blackwell, 1992), pp. 75–87; cf. also,"Martin Buber and the Theory of Knowledge," in ibid., pp. 61, 66–69; "God and Philosophy," in ibid., p. 169; *Totality and Infinity*, pp. 28, 42–48, 65–66, 69, 72–73, 82–101, 201–12, 218–19, 302–303; *Otherwise Than Being*, pp. 16, 20, 160, 170.

16. Husserl, *Ideas*, pp. 74–76; Herbert Spiegelberg, *Doing Phenomenology: Essays on and in Phenomenology* (The Hague: Martinus Nijhoff, 1975), pp. 80–129, 154–55.

17. *Totality and Infinity*, pp. 43–48, 92.

18. Ibid., pp. 42–48.

19. *History of the Church in Latin America*, p. 214; "Hipótesis para elaborar un marco teórico de la historia del pensamiento latinoamericano," in *Praxis latinoamericana y filosofía de la liberación* (Bogotá: Editorial Nueva América, 1983), p. 273; *América Latina: Dependencia y*

liberación, p. 215; "Cultura latinoamericana y filosofía de la liberación,"
43–44; *Para una ética de la liberación latinoamericana*, 2:106, 109, 178;
3:126, 155, 188, 215, 221; 4:36, 38, 120–21; 5:108; *Teología de la liberación
y ética*, pp. 149–58; *Hipótesis para una historia de la Iglesia*, p. 154.

20. *Totality and Infinity*, pp. 28–29, 36, 54–63, 76, 110, 172–74,
229–38; "Time and the Other," in *The Levinas Reader*, ed. Sean Hand
(Oxford and Cambridge, Mass.: Basil Blackwell, 1992), p. 53; *Otherwise
Than Being*, p. 111. Chronologically, enjoyment or the establishment of
one's identity could never occur before the presence of the Other,
which is as present to the I as its own body, as *Otherwise than Being* continually points out. The chronology of the philosophical account, which
cannot take up everything at once, can, like Descartes's *Meditations*, discuss the *cogito* before the appearance of the idea of the Infinite. These
two temporal orders do not undermine the existence of the autonomous I before the Other whose demand reaches the I before the I
chooses it. See *Totality and Infinity*, pp. 54–55.

21. *Totality and Infinity*, p. 73.

22. Lyotard, "Levinas's Logic," pp. 125–26, 130, 144, 145, 152; *Totality and Infinity*, pp. 53–61, 73, 96, 212–14; *Otherwise Than Being*, pp. 120,
159, 190, 193, 196–97.

23. *Totality and Infinity*, pp. 245–46.

24. Ibid., pp. 82–90; *Otherwise Than Being*, pp. 116–17; Ayn Rand, *For
the New Intellectual: The Philosophy of Ayn Rand* (New York: Random
House, 1961), pp. 33, 38, 40, 63.

25. See above, chap. 2, pp. 28–45; chap. 3, pp. 66–67. As has been
mentioned, Dussel retracts his earlier position on women and homosexuals in *Underside of Modernity*, pp. 9–10.

26. "Una década argentina (1966–1976) y el origen de la 'Filosofía
de la liberación,'" 29–33, 35.

6

Rationality in Dussel: The Critique of Karl-Otto Apel

For many years, Enrique Dussel has been meeting with Karl-Otto Apel in a "North-South Dialogue" in which they and several other philosophers and theologians exchange papers. Here I will briefly summarize Apel's philosophical position and address what I see as the two central issues between Apel and Dussel: namely, whether the philosophy of liberation can be accommodated within Apel's transcendental pragmatics and whether Dussel's appropriation of Marx is anachronistic and mistaken, as Apel claims.

Karl-Otto Apel's Transcendental Pragmatics

Although Apel's philosophical vocation derived from his witnessing the destruction of moral consciousness that occurred during the Nazi era, developing a philosophy restorative of such consciousness required criticism of several philosophical alternatives. In the first place, Apel opposes logical positivism, which, in his view, illegitimately reduces the notion of meaning to verification, universally applies natural scientific method without first reflecting on its appropriateness for the problems considered, ignores how its emphasis on protocol statements depends upon an option for one language game and life form among many, and conceals its own metaphysics in trying to do away with the metaphysics of others. Apel's critique of positivism relies on a richer appreciation of the variety of language uses beyond the positivist focus solely on semantics and syntactics. This recognition of diverse language uses was ushered in by Charles Morris's recovery of the pragmatic dimensions of language, the supercession of the earlier Wittgenstein by the later, and the increasing linguistic awareness in phenomenology as it developed from Husserl to Heidegger. Once one is plunged into this richer pragmatic dimension of hermeneutics and communal language games, one no longer need philosophize on the basis of the relationship of isolated subject to a material object, that is, on the basis of the methodological solipsism that pervades the philosophical tradition. One must, instead, conceive of nonobjectifiable co-subjects in relationship. In a sense, positivism's metaphysical presuppositions never permit it even to envision this dimension, which can be described only through a reconstructive, nonempiricist methodology. Even within Apel's critique of positivism, one detects the outlines of his own transcendental pragmatics—"pragmatics" because it reincorporates the intersubjective and use dimensions of language neglected by a positivism focused solely on semantics and syntactics, and "transcendental" because it constantly and self-reflectively brings to light unacknowledged positivist suppositions. In so doing, Apel expands the idea of rationality, since the rationality by which positivism absolutizes scientific rationality does not fall under science itself.[1]

Following Peirce, who, unlike other pragmatists, did not sacrifice the regulative ideal of truth to his concern for cognition's function in real life, Apel does not find the turn to the hermeneutic-pragmatic dimension sufficient for a philosophy intent on reinstating moral consciousness. Apel sees Wittgenstein as evading the question of the bindingness of his own claims by stating that he does not present a general doctrine, but only therapeutically dissolves the webs that a linguistically naïve philosophy has woven for itself. By refusing to engage in any reflexive self-justification of his own philosophy, which includes an entirely new insight into the essence of speech, Wittgenstein falls prey to what Apel calls *Logosvergessenheit* ("forgetfulness of reason"). Similarly, Gadamer and Heidegger raise universal validity claims—for instance, that all truth-claims are a function of temporal being and history—on the basis of which they claim to undermine all claims to universal validity. This ignoring of the self-undermining of their own claims, another form of *Logosvergessenheit*, constitutes a central strategy of the philosophy of postmodernism and neopragmatism following the lead of Gadamer and Heidegger. For example, Gadamer, in Apel's view, leaves unanswered the question about the conditions of the possibility of the general validity of his own propositions, abandoning the ancient and modern idea of a universal science in favor of concrete immersion in what is "valid for us now." Without a critical mediation between a transcendental ethic and an historical hermeneutic, there is a danger of the relativistic reduction of the normative to the authority of a given tradition. Arnold Gehlen's authoritarian social theory—that the contemporary lack of meaning-orientation and stabilization of behavior can be remedied by compliance with what benefits positive functioning institutions (what Apel calls elsewhere "Eichmann ethics") reflects precisely this relinquishing of the central mission of philosophy as defender of the meta-institution of speech and the rational conversation of all humanity, in which what is taken for granted and unquestioned can always be problematized. Once again, by requiring them to recognize the status of their own philosophical position, which claims a validity not to be undermined simply because it has an historical genesis, Apel wields a transcendental method against the historicist/relativist tendencies in postmodernism. Although the pragmatic dimensions of Apel's theory surfaces in his critique of positivism, it is the transcendental aspects that gain importance in the criticism of hermeneutical philosophy.[2]

The inescapable character of these transcendental aspects becomes evident in Apel's discussion of Popper's belief that the choice between his own "critical rationalism," which is similar to Apel's view, and irrationalism depends on an "act of faith," an "irrational moral decision." While conceding that anyone can will what they want, Apel argues that, whatever one's choice, a choice for rationality is capable of being rationally grounded, and the opposing choice can be shown to be irrational (in Apel's terms, "performatively self-contradictory"). In Apel's view, the skeptic who argues against rationality already partakes in certain transcendental presuppositions in favor of rationality.

> In truth the presupposed *problem situation* does not exist, that is, the situation that we would stand *in front of* the question whether we should be rational, logical, or moral and at the same time that we could already offer arguments—or at least pose the question of why [be rational, logical, or moral].

130   ETHICAL HERMENEUTICS

Affirmatively expressed: Whoever seriously poses this why-question has already thereby entered upon the field of argumentative discourse. That is to say, through *reflection upon the meaning of his own action* he can realize that he has already necessarily recognized the rules, or norms, of rational, cooperative argumentation and therewith also the ethical norms of a communication community.[3]

Apel asserts further that the skeptic who refuses even to argue is doomed to become irrelevant for the discussion, and that even if the skeptic merely *acts* in a meaningful manner, he or she presupposes such transcendental rules of cooperative argumentation, for, as Wittgenstein has shown, no language game is possible on the basis of permanent lying and therefore no meaningful action would be either.[4]

But what precisely are these transcendental presuppositions of argumentation itself? Apel agrees with Habermas that every thinkable empirical examination of hypotheses presupposes the presence of the four validity claims of human communication acts (claims to factual truth, moral rightness, veracity, and comprehensibility), the hope for the consensual resolution of disputed claims, and the primacy of communicative rationality over merely instrumental/strategic rationality. Furthermore, on the ethical plane, in every authentic argument participants implicitly, reciprocally, and respectfully recognize each other as an autonomous subject of logical argumentation, as one not to be coerced by force, and entitled to assent freely only to arguments found convincing. Where this does not occur, where force other than the force of the better argument is employed, the communicative situation is experienced as falling short of the anticipation of an ideal communication community, which one might not have previously recognized as having been contrafactually anticipated in that very discourse and which one realizes is also anticipated in preferable noncoercive communicative settings. Since anyone who seriously argues presupposes these necessary conditions of argumentation, the conditions constitute a philosophically ultimate grounding point that one cannot evade (*nicht hintergehbar*) or contest without committing a performative self-contradiction. Thus, one arguing that there are not four validity claims could not avoid implicitly raising such claims in the argument, or one would act self-contradictorily in seeking consensual agreement that consensual resolution is not involved in argumentation, or one who argues for strategic rationality in discourse acts communicatively and not strategically in that very discourse (or if strategically, then parasitically within a communicative framework), or one arguing in favor of violence contradicts the nonviolent framework of the very argument he employs. These suppositions of argument are such that even the effort to falsify them must make use of them, and, as such, they form the transcendental meaning-conditions of the principle of falsification itself. Furthermore, while any particular validity claim is revisable, those conditions which make particular validity claims and their abrogation possible are not empirically examinable, falsifiable, or fallible.[5]

Important philosophical implications follow from this transcendental pragmatics. Not only does Apel battle methodological solipsism by making the structure of communication itself and the ideal communication community transcendental, but even private processes of thinking, doubting, questioning, self-criticism, and self-understanding presuppose the norms of straightforward communication under the conditions of a reciprocal recognition between communication partners. Furthermore, Apel's discovery of the transcendental communitarian conditions of all speech, including speech among scientists, indicates that science itself unfolds within the already ethical framework of discourse itself. Apel thereby reverses the centuries-old presumption, shared by Max Weber and Anglo-American ethics, that science has driven ethics from the field of rationality and left it to merely private, arbitrary choice. In further dialogue with Weber, Apel distinguishes between a first level of discourse ethics (A), in which the formal procedural principle of argumentative consensus formation is philosophically established, and a second level (B) of fallible application in which the interests of all affected and the knowledge of experts must be brought to bear. At the second level, one realizes that application conditions for discourse are not in place, and one may resort to a Weberian ethics of responsibility (as opposed to a Kantian conviction ethics) and may be forced to employ strategic action, even violence, to bring about one's *telos*, the realization of unconstrained discourse in which each participant's deontological rights are upheld.[6]

Transcendental pragmatics mandates that discourse be characterized by universal openness to considering and acknowledging, when justified, all possible claims of all possible discourse-members regarding all possible human needs. This openness, based on Apel's postconventional, universal-principle ethics, contrasts with the conventional ethics of someone like Aristotle, who prohibited killing, lying, cheating, and the violation of rights only with reference to fellow members of the polis, but not in regard to barbarians. In Apel's view, the restlessness of communicative rationality that cannot refrain from entertaining questions calls for what Peirce described as the self-surrender of egoistic self-interest in favor of the "transsubjectivity" of the argumentative representation of interests. To reach valid solutions, one cannot exclude from discourse potential members whose rights are equal to those of actual participants, whether those potential members are geographically distant or belong to future generations. The ethics of the ideal communication community, constantly challenging restrictive real communication communities, requires the institutionalization of repression-free consultation. For Apel, the quality of argumentation must correspond to this inclusiveness, in the sense that participants should not seek victory in argumentation as if it were a competitive sport, but, rather, allow the "arguments to struggle for victory and see which prove themselves stronger." Apel agrees with Rawls that discourse entails altruistic "role taking" in order that the other be adequately heard. A final consequence of Apel's view that transcendental pragmatic conditions govern every discourse is that there cannot be a wholly other kind of reason that would relativize these conditions of rationality, since one would have to argue for the validity of that other type of rationality and in that argument one would presuppose and make use of the very conditions one is trying to relativize. Though such an appeal to an "other reason" may express a legitimate demand for philosophical caution or modesty, this reason could never be used to falsify the necessary presuppositions of argumentation without a performative self-contradiction.[7]

Can Transcendental Pragmatics Replace the Philosophy of Liberation?

In recent meetings of the North-South Dialogue, Apel has recognized a rapprochement between his transcendental pragmatics and Dussel's philosophy of liberation. He agrees with Dussel's emphasis on the importance of the "interpellation" of the poor "Third World" "Other," but he believes that this interpellation in no way threatens his transcendental-pragmatic standpoint. Rather, in Apel's view, this Other's protest actually pertains to part B of discourse ethics, which must determine what ought to be done when the application-conditions of the ethics of an ideal communication community, grounded in part A, are not in place. Part A, in fact, demands that members of the privileged communication community must represent the interests of all *affected* by their decision, even if they are not at present participants, and part B further requires that relations be so established that no adult, mentally sound human being be excluded from discourse because of structural forces. In Apel's opinion, Dussel basically agrees that the situation of the exclusion of the Other could be handled (*behandelt*) as a theme of part B of discourse ethics. If Apel is correct, then transcendental pragmatics would be able to replace the philosophy of liberation effectively, since its nonnaturalistic concept of self-critical rationality could achieve the very solidarity and openness to the Other the philosophy of liberation calls for.[8]

It is interesting to notice that Apel does not identify Dussel as an anarchistic postmodernist in favor of irrationality. Apel is correct in so doing since Dussel himself, as I have pointed out, describes himself as a transmodernist who cannot rest content with the skepticism and relativism that often characterize forms of postmodernism. Similarly, my entire first chapter attempted to present Levinas as a prorational phenomenologist, exploring neglected horizons in the tradition of Husserl and articulating the preconditions of rationality itself—the face of the Other— inviting discourse, and placing in question all discourses on the verge of congealing into totalities. This Levinas, although usually associated with contemporary French postmodernists, cannot be construed as antirational or opposed to the rationalist leanings of transcendental pragmatics. Secondly, Apel, although clearly in the Kantian philosophical tradition, never complains about Dussel's heteronomy to the Other, as Schutte and Cerutti do. Apel's silence here is again accurate since, as I have shown in chapter 5, this understanding of Dussel and Levinas is not warranted.[9]

But it is doubtful whether the philosophy of liberation can be so easily accommodated within Apel's system. Apel's incorporation of Dussel in Part B overlooks their basic differences. First of all, Apel, in reaction to the traditional subject-object paradigm of philosophy and related functionalist–behaviorist objectifications of communication partners, conceives human relations as taking place between nonobjectifiable co-subjects reciprocally and respectfully recognizing each other as equal partners in a discourse. For Levinas and Dussel, such a view, though legitimate at the level of the Third, portrays relationships as reversible in terms of formal logic, in the mode of an "alongside of," from an extrinsic third-person perspective. Although Apel's reconstructive transcendental methodology makes an important advance over previous theories in bringing to light the co-subject one faces in discourse, Levinas and Dussel penetrate more deeply into the way that Other appears to an autonomous, phenomenologically self-reflective I prior to the question of reciprocation. Their phenomenological descriptions from the perspective of the I facing the Other disclose an Other commanding one ethically "from a height," not as one's equal, not as identical or interchangeable with one.[10]

The theories of both Apel and the philosophy of liberation target the skeptic, with Apel contending that the skeptic who argues need only become aware of the presuppositions she is already making use of, and the nonarguing skeptic, though consigned to irrelevance, would uncover transcendental presuppositions if he would simply attend to his own meaningful acting. Rather than adopting a maieutic, Socratic method of alerting a subject to his or her own (albeit communal) presuppositions, as Apel does, Levinas locates the challenge to the skeptic outside the skeptic, in exteriority, in the irrecusable face that opens the primordial discourse not even a proto-Nietzschean like Thrasymachus could avoid. In contrast to Descartes's idea of the Infinite, which we cannot account for out of our own resources, Socrates's method represents the primacy of the same determined "to receive nothing of the Other but what is in me, as though from all eternity I was in possession of what comes to me from the outside." Similarly, for Dussel, the Other, beyond every totality and before the commencement of argumentation, stands in a relationship that haunts even the cynic who bases his own morality of "national security" on the irrational impulse of power, governs with strategic reason alone, and refuses the rational discourse he regards as totally ineffective against his power. Here the philosophy of liberation, through illuminating the Other's inescapable ethical demand from the exteriority in spite of even the cynic's interior resolve not to pay heed, seems to afford a more comprehensive and primordial context within which discourse ethics might take its place.[11]

These diverse treatments of the skeptic/cynic demonstrate that, although both Apel and the philosophy of liberation assert the dynamism of rationality, they localize the source of that dynamism differently. Apel finds it within the demands for self-consistency essential to self-critical rationality, and Levinas and Dussel detect it in the Other preceding, evoking, and questioning rationality. These diverse understandings of the source of rationality's dynamism reflect fundamental differences in methodology. Dussel and Levinas opt for an intuitive-descriptive method that depicts the way the Other comes to appearance, and although one might posit the Other as an essential constituent of the ideal unlimited speech community, as Dussel has suggested, this intuitive-descriptive methodology will always be needed to revivify the height of the Other's demand and to prevent the face-to-face from collapsing into an "alongside of." Apel, in contrast, employs a transcendental method, continually searching for the presupposed but unreflected-upon presuppositions of argumentation itself. From this perspective, he can lay claim to the terrain on which the philosophy of liberation labors, since pretensions to validity are expressed in every face-to-face relationship and in Dussel's and Levinas's second-level, reflective account of such face-to-face relationships. Whenever one raises claims to validity, even if these must be adjudicated through compared intuitions as in the case of Dussel's and Levinas's phenomenologies, one is already implicitly partaking of the presuppositions that transcendental pragmatics articulates. These respective methodologies carry with them limitations, since transcendental pragmatics will inevitably level the "curvature of space" upward to the Other that a descriptive phenomenological method can disclose. Similarly, if

Lyotard's reconstruction of Levinas's prescriptive (as opposed to denotative) intent is correct, then an intuitive-descriptive methodology lacks the resources to justify ethical norms or to provide them with any transcendental foundation, as Apel's transcendental pragmatics has done. A phenomenological description of the conditions within which rationality arises cannot fulfill the task of providing a rational grounding of ethics, and there is no evidence that Levinas has ever conceived his philosophy in this role.[12]

Despite all these differences, there is a possible bridge between the philosophy of liberation and transcendental pragmatics in Levinas's discussion of the Third. The proximity of the third party modifies the asymmetrical demands of the face-to-face, and a series of questions arisess regarding comparison, coexistence, contemporaneousness, assembling, order, thematization, and the intelligibility of a system. The metaphysical relationship of the I with the Other moves into a form of the We, aspires to a State, institutions, and laws, which are the source of universality. Philosophy, too, undergoes transformation, searching for principles of unification and limiting the infinite demands experienced in the anarchic face-to-face. The self, Other-centered in the dyadic moment, is now called upon to concern itself with itself, to limit itself in trying to live up to its unlimited responsibility for the Other, although this self-restriction still ought to be motivated "in the name of this unlimited responsibility." In effect, at the level of the Third, a transition has taken place from the attitude of one facing another to the attitude of one extrinsically regarding the parties to a relationship as equal and interchangeable—to what Levinas might call a third-person point of view in the mode of "alongside of." At this level of the Third, one adopts a philosophical posture that, as Lyotard puts it, deploys a denotative metalanguage at one remove from the immediate prescription of the Other. At this level, though, it would seem that Apel's (and Kant's) norm that human relations ought to involve "nonobjectifiable co-subjects reciprocally and respectfully recognizing each other as equal partners to a discourse" converges with the experience of the prescriptive in the face-to-face better than other theoretical accounts.[13]

But for Levinas and Dussel, these norms of equality and reciprocity depend on the preoriginary moment of the face-to-face. "Equality is produced where the other commands the same and reveals himself to the same in responsibility; otherwise it is but an abstract idea and word. It cannot be detached from the welcoming of the face, of which it is a moment."[14] In a manner reminiscent of Husserlian constitution, Levinas attempts to dig beneath the abstract idea and word "equality" to uncover the motivations and interpersonal dynamics that lead from the face-to-face to the egalitarian society and that have eventuated in the build-up of the concept "equality." In a highly condensed passage of *Totality and Infinity*, Levinas observes how the poor one or the stranger, who had been above me in the dyadic relation, becomes my equal when the Third enters. At that point, I become conscious that the Other whom I serve also serves as Other, the Third, and that we are both equally servants. Even the Other's mastery of me is seen to be at the service of an Other (the Third). I realize that, as equal to the Other, I also possess mastery, but my mastery, like the Other's, is also mastery for the sake of Others. Equality need not originate from frustrated aspirations to dominate the Other, as Glaucon suggests in Book II of the *Republic*, rather, it bears the traces of an original reverence for the Other beyond solipsistic egoism, an original inequality of service demanded by the Other, from which, paradoxically, equality, as a toning down of exigencies, derives. One does not begin jealously guarding one's equality with the Other and occasionally undertake altruistic forays toward the Other, as traditional philosophical wisdom might have it; one experiences the Other's infinite demand first, before the idea of equality ever intervenes to restrain it. Once again, Levinas situates the theoretical activity of norm derivation with reference to the ethical relationship, just as throughout *Totality and Infinity* that relationship had formed the matrix within which the search for truth (epistemology), theology, and language emerges.[15]

What purpose can Levinas have for separating out these strata of experience, that of the face-to-face and that of the Third, with their accompanying notions of reciprocity and equality, such that equality becomes a "moment" of the face? After all, these strata are so inextricably interwoven in everyday experience that non-phenomenological common sense might balk at the idea that the Other's unlimited imperative takes precedence over duties to the

self. By distinguishing the stratum of the face-to-face prior to the
Third, Levinas obtains a fulcrum for the critique of institutions
such as the state, the economy, philosophy, or even Apel's reciprocal discourse—all of which develop in tandem with the appearance of the Third. Such institutions, in Levinas's view, are "at
every moment on the point of having their center of gravitation
in themselves and weighing on their own account." One can
come to think of them as impersonal totalities governed by anony-
mous human forces. In such a situation, reciprocity may degener-
ate into a mere compromise between conflicting strategic
interests, and any sense of reponsibility for those who are too
powerless to affect those interests may vanish. Levinas, however,
would protest in the name of the face of the Other, never elimi-
nated by the appearance of the Third.

> But the contemporaneousness of the multiple is tied about the dia-
> chrony of the two: justice remains justice only in a society where
> there is no distinction between those close and those far off, but in
> which there also remains the impossibility of passing by the closest.
> The equality of all is borne by my inequality, the surplus of my
> duties over my rights. The forgetting of self moves justice. It is then
> unimportant to know if the egalitarian and just state in which man
> is fulfilled (and which is to be set up, and especially maintained)
> proceeds from a war of all against all, or from the irreducible re-
> sponsibility of the one for all, and if it can do without friendships
> and faces.[16]

Not only does this command of the Other in the face-to-face
stand as an inexhaustible challenge to institutions generated at
the level of the Third to respond to those beyond their totalities,
but it also calls for a significant transformation of human motivation in at least two respects. Apel himself repeatedly and correctly
notes that even though one begins with discourse-ethical principles, one cannot presume that others are so directed; hence, one
even has a duty to mistrust others. Nevertheless, for Apel one
must tentatively and cautiously work to replace strategic interaction with discursive-consensual conflict resolution. Insofar as Levi-
nasian-Dusselian ethics employs the norms of equality and
reciprocity established at the level of the Third, and insofar as it
recognizes that capitulation to another need not be for that Oth-

er's good, it might share Apel's hesitancy. However, the face of the Other inspires one to take appropriate risks, to place oneself in danger for the Other, and thus to hasten this replacement of strategic relations with discursive ones. Dussel has masterfully described how liberation begins when the oppressor trusts in the world of the Other, at first inadequately comprehensible. A philosophy such as Dussel's or Levinas's, which is interested in the liberation of the poor, will tend to emphasize the risks that need to be taken on behalf of the Other, more than the healthy corrective that a Weberian ethics of responsibility affords an ethics of conviction.[17]

Furthermore, the truly heroic figures in human emancipation display a striking willingness to surpass reciprocity and to allow themselves to be held hostage in order that others' rights be upheld. Martin Luther King, Jr., for instance, endured firehosing, pelting with rocks and spittle, the constant threat of character assassination, and even death itself so that the rights of other African Americans would be respected. Unlike Western existentialists preoccupied with their own deaths, Mahatma Gandhi and Oscar Romero were so obsessed with the murder of Others that they did not protect themselves against their own deaths. To attend truly to the call of the Other motivates toward this extreme opposite of strategic rationality such that, in Levinas's terms, one comes to fear murder more than death.[18]

In summary, Levinas's level of the Third corresponds to the level at which Apel's transcendental pragmatics unfolds, with Levinas's phenomenological descriptions of the face-to-face constituting the Third's originary matrix and presupposition. Further, if my earlier interpretation was accurate—namely, that Levinas's philosophy of the face-to-face parallels the later Husserl's exploration of the horizons of theory itself, illuminating the ethical relationship as the context within which all theory arises, including Apel's transcendental theory—then could it not be said that Levinas's work must be understood as occurring at a "pretranscendental level," exploring essential ethical dimensions on a plane analogous to that of the Husserlian life-world? Apel, on the other hand, in his reaction to positivistic-scientistic portrayals of language and intersubjectivity, recovers the pragmatic dimensions of speech, the historical-linguistic-hermeneutic context for theory itself, forgotten by an abstract science no longer mindful of its own pretheoretical (life-world?) origins, which Heidegger and Wittgenstein have thoroughly explored. However, since Apel finds within these pretheoretical relationships only relative, socio-historically conditioned moral belief systems instead of the *essential* ethical features that Levinas's descriptive phenomenology turns up, he has recourse to a transcendental level to investigate the transcendental presuppositions implicit in all speech, whether in everyday life or science. Indeed, the development of Apel's entire system, as I have depicted it, revolves around the projects of countering positivism by restoring to philosophy a linguistic, hermeneutic life-world, and yet overcoming relativist-historicist tendencies through a species of transcendental reflection on the conditions of the possibility of speech itself.[19]

My suggestion would be that the philosophy of liberation and transcendental pragmatics can be located at different levels within a common architectonic. Just as the Husserlian phenomenological system extended from the life-world to the transcendental ego, so it is reasonable to posit a similar structure in the domain of ethics. At the pretranscendental level, the philosophy of liberation marks out rationality's beginning in the ethical demand of the Other, which extends even to the cynic who refuses discourse and ceaselessly renews all theory and thus rationality itself. At the transcendental level, Apel, who has made the linguistic turn and so cannot be satisfied with Husserl's solitary transcendental ego, reflects on reflection itself and its own intersubjective presuppositions, particularly the presuppositions of speech and argumentation. Whether reflecting on forgotten horizons prior to the origin of theory itself or on the operative but not admitted presuppositions within every ongoing theory, both levels belong on a common continuum, because they are the work of a single reason, authentically owning up to what it usually bypasses or ignores and thereby rendering itself all the more rational. Indeed, the statements of this paragraph itself are of a unavoidable transcendental quality, reflecting on reason's own unexplored horizons in the philosophy of liberation and reflecting on reflection's own often unacknowledged presuppositions in transcendental pragmatics and demarcating their distinctive positions on a common architectonic continuum.

These two points of view belong on a common scale for many other reasons. Both levels focus on intersubjectivity in contrast to the solipsism characteristic of the previous philosophies of consciousness. Whether we speak of the conviction of the philosophy of liberation that Levinas's ethical metaphysics precedes ontology and all other theory, or whether we recall that, for Apel, far from its driving ethics off the field of rationality, science itself unfolds within the already ethical framework of discourse itself, it is clear that both viewpoints espouse a first philosophy that is ethical in character. Whether we consider the authenticity of transcendental pragmatic rationality that would forbid the exclusion from discourse of any possible claims from any possible discourse partners regarding any possible human needs, or we look to Levinas's Other jeopardizing every closed totality, both viewpoints demand the demolition of barriers of exclusion. Whether we pay heed to the way transcendental pragmatics's conditions of argumentation render fallibilism possible and necessary, or take note of the Other in whose presence every claim becomes contestable and every discourse unpredictable, it is clear that in both perspectives reason shows itself as vulnerable and self-critical. In addition, it would seem that Apel's transcendentally developed notion of ethical rationality, equally supportive of human solidarity and equally resistant to the strategization of rationality, lives from the forgotten experience of the face-to-face that Levinas discloses. Finally, when transcendental pragmatics and the philosophy of liberation alike compete to include the other as a useful subsidiary of itself, one is reminded of the way in which Husserl's phenomenology could be legitimately undertaken from the starting point of either the life-world as the origin of theory or the transcendental ego as implicit in the life-world and in every reflective endeavor. Instead of competitively trying to subsume each other, would it not be better if the philosophy of liberation and transcendental pragmatics could conceive of themselves as two irreducible but complementary pursuits within a common ethical enterprise, in which each is particularly suited to the other for the many reasons mentioned above? Within such a philosophical division of labor, would not the hostile polarity between modernity and postmodernity be overcome as well?[20]

But, despite this continuity and complementarity, dissonances that are never completely reconcilable and yet stimulate creativity persist at both levels, such as those between the methods of description and transcendental reflection. Similarly, a philosophy whose purpose involves continual reacquaintance with the Other's easily overlooked height and resistance to totalization will not easily be at peace with a philosophy intent on tirelessly reminding interlocutors of the necessary conditions they implicitly presuppose every time they speak. Tensions will always flare between a more critically oriented philosophy that conceives its role as vigilantly struggling to reduce the betrayal of the saying in the said and a more constructively oriented philosophy whose role is to uphold the meta-institution of speech and the rational conversation of all humanity. While transcendental pragmatics strives for that solidarity and openness to the Other characteristic of the philosophy of liberation (and so itself deserves to be called *a* philosophy of liberation), the Dusselian-Levinasian philosophy of liberation, functioning at a different level of the architectonic and utilizing a different methodology, in the end cannot be replaced without losses. Without the philosophy of liberation, one would lose sight of an account of origins and of the constant and rigorous challenge that the Other, precisely by being exterior to every totality, poses for every hermeneutical interpretation: namely, that in the end it be ethical; for every claim to rationality, that in the end it be all the more rational; and for every reciprocal accord, that in the end it not be merely strategic. Finally, the philosophy of liberation fosters the motivation upon which selfless, daring, and heroic emancipation relies.

IS DUSSEL'S REAPPROPRIATION OF MARX ANACHRONISTIC?

Apel's criticism of Dussel's reappropriation of Marx occurs in his essay "Die Diskursethik vor der Herausforderung der Dritten Welt," in *Diskursethik oder Befreiungsethik.* In that essay, Apel distinguishes between Dussel's claim that the poverty-stricken 75 percent of the world is excluded from the real communication community of humanity—a claim with which Apel agrees—and the claim that Apel has not read Marx's *Capital* carefully enough and so cannot understand Marx's significance for the liberation

THE CRITIQUE OF KARL-OTTO APEL

of the "Third World"—a claim to which Apel takes exception. Apel admits, though, that there might be some significance to Dussel's appeal to Marx, given Dussel's Latin American context and background, in spite of the failure of the state-socialist alternative to capitalism in Eastern Europe.[21]

Marx, in Apel's opinion, basing himself on the dialectical laws of history and strengthened by his scientific transformation in later life, considered the market economy irreformable and was willing to substitute a social utopia for that economy and its accompanying system of liberal rights. Because of Dussel's rejection of similar reformist possibilities in his *Philosophy of Liberation* (1977), he appears anachronistic in the face of the European experience, in which the social democracies of Western Europe, with their welfare provisions and democratic procedures, have developed a better alternative to "real existing socialism" itself. Latin Americans have responded to such charges of anachronism by dubbing this a *Eurocentric* approach and offering their own "dependence theory," according to which wealthy nations control the framework conditions of the world economy, establishing the terms of trade and originating and defining the debt crisis in such a way that an overcoming of the progressive impoverishment of the Third World masses has become in principle impossible.[22]

Apel, though, believes that the interrelations among individual lands of Latin America, Africa, Asia, and the North are considerably more diverse than the "grand theories of the left" recognize, with their talk of the Third World depending on the First World. The great differences in adaptation to the capitalist system throughout the Third World (the economic success of former Japanese colonies such as Korea, Hong Kong, and Singapore, for example) suggest that poverty results in part from avoidable failures of development politics, social experiments, civil wars, and sufficient or insufficient inherited sociocultural dispositions. If the historical-geographical presuppositions of dependence theory are oversimplified, so are its economic premises. Citing the Marxist-inspired Thomas Hurtienne, Apel argues that many of the structural features attributed to peripheral capitalism these days (for example, high luxury consumption among the wealthy, exports driven by the needs of foreign markets instead of the inner one, great heterogeneity in income distribution, and massivization of poverty) also characterized England and Germany at the beginning of their development, such that it took workers and farmers in those lands a hundred years to be able to share in the fruit of their productivity.[23]

Before raising three major and final objections to Dussel's espousal of Marx, Apel points out the socioeconomic facts that would justify Dussel's *ethical* demand upon the North if that were all that his philosophy of liberation were issuing. Apel cites the destruction and enslavement of cultures at the time of colonialization, the subsequent economic domination of formerly colonized countries, the problem of overpopulation, the debt crisis, and disastrous ecological exploitation. But in order to solve these problems, Apel, concurring with earlier criticisms raised in particular by Cerutti, insists that what is called for is not "metaphysical-rhetorical oversimplifications, but rather the critical collaboration of philosophy with the empirical sciences in an ethically relevant form." But Apel also turns his criticisms on the West when he asserts that any effort to reduce ethics to the preservation or strengthening of the customariness of the West's cultural tradition in the face of this world crisis is nothing but irresponsible escapism. A universalistic macroethics of humanity—along the lines of Apel's own transcendental pragmatics—alone can ground the ethical norms necessary for transforming this world.[24]

Apel objects more specifically to Marx's theory of alienation, his labor theory of value, and his historical determinism. Marx's theory of alienation developed within the philosophical paradigm of the subject-object relationship prevalent in German idealism without giving sufficient attention to the reciprocity relationships of acting subjects and the linguistic communication. In the tradition of recent critical theory, Apel prefers to conceive economic systems as quasi-automatically functioning action-systems entailing a necessary alienation and yet susceptible to limited practical control and organizational interventions agreed to in argumentative discourse and directed toward reform (and not total revolution).[25]

As regards Marx's theory of surplus value, Apel believes that Marx resorted to a "hyperabstraction" in order to show how the exchange values of objects could be equilibrated, in spite of their diverse use values. In Marx's view, these exchange values were determined according to the common standard of human labor-time invested in them and without regard for natural endowments, use value, or the play of supply and demand. Apel believes that Marx engaged in this hyperabstraction because he focused on the subject acting on the object and investing it with value rather than on the reciprocal exchange relations between seller and buyer, dependent on the supply and demand and generated in part by the usefulness of the object to the buyer. Had Marx focused on these relations, he would have placed his emphasis on communicative relations in the life-world, whose obligation it is to restrain the systemic alienation that is never totally eliminable. As a consequence, Marxism would not have turned, as it did, to either a regressive-utopian elimination of culture or the bureaucratization and paralysis of a state system.[26]

Apel's final critique of Marx focuses on his scientific prognosis of history on the basis of a dialectical theory of history. This "met-aposition" enables the Marxist to explain (*erklären*) away opposing positions as context-determined phases of bourgeois thinking—with the result that truth and goodness are finally determined, not through argumentative discourse, but through the Politburo's insight into the necessary course of history. In Apel's view, Dussel has distanced himself from this interpretation of Marx by reading him as an ethician guided by Kant's categorical imperative, and such an ethical interpretation is incompatible with historicism, whether of the Marxist or the postmodern brand.[27]

In order to grasp and assess a possible Dusselian response to these criticisms, it is important to recall that Dussel's immersion in the manuscripts underlying *Capital* has led him to understand the late Marx in a different way from the antiphilosophical "scientific" economist that Engels or Althusser portrays. For Dussel, Marx is constructing an ontology of economics, a blend of anthropological, ethical, and metaphysical elements that I have dubbed an "ethical hermeneutics" of the economy, which interprets the entire capitalist system from the viewpoint of that system's exterior, that is, living labor. As we have seen, Marx did conceive his work as "scientific," not in a naturalist, empiricist sense, but, rather, according to German idealism's notion of *Wissenschaft*, which moves beyond phenomena to seek out at a different level the underlying essence, that is, the mutual connections—and thus thinks from the phenomena back to the essence. According to Dussel, the "rationality" of Marx's discourse depends upon just this "scientific" explanation, in a systematic and fundamental way, of the development of the concept of capital, even if some of Marx's affirmations at the phenomenal level may be falsified or shown to be impossible. Marx's ethical ontology of capitalism provides a framework from which one can interpret facts without contradicting them, generate concrete scientific investigations open to empirical verification or refutation, and develop joint political decisions.[28]

But a question arises: How can one reconcile this ethical-hermeneutical view of economic science with prevailing notions of empirical economic science which demand that hypotheses be capable of withstanding tests of falsifiability, notions that implicitly underlie Apel's critique of both Marx and Dussel? Following modern empirical economics, Apel chides Marx for neglecting that the laws of supply and demand are constitutive for the value of goods. But Apel does not seem to observe the distinctions that Dussel and Marx make, in particular, that surplus value is created *in the sphere of production* through labor's unpaid investment of time, even though supply and demand *in the sphere of circulation* affect the amount of profit a capitalist will realize from the surplus value of the goods he or she brings to the market. Marx never denies that supply and demand play a key role, but, according to Marx's interpretive distinctions, their function is to distribute surplus value, not create it.[29]

However, a central question remains: namely, whether Dussel's and Marx's interpretation of economic facts is falsifiable. Factually, while both Dussel and the bourgeois economist can agree that the capitalist's sales on the market net him or her a profit after expenses are deducted and in relation to the current supply and demand, Dussel, as ethical hermeneuticist dedicated to capitalism's Other in the tradition of Marx, seeks the "hidden fundament" behind these empirical phenomena. In order to keep the economic theorist vividly aware that exploited living labor and nothing else (supply and demand, for example) lies at the origin of value in capitalism, Dussel insists that the surplus value created by unpaid labor in the originary relationship between capitalist and worker establishes the reserve on which supply and demand exercise their influence and from which profit eventually results. What conceivable empirical data could disprove this ethically oriented conception of surplus value and its origin? By reverting from the empirically observed phenomena to the underlying essence—here the surplus value created in the sphere of production through exploited labor—Dussel and Marx furnish an ethical framework for economic science in much the same way as Dussel's ethical hermeneutics in the field of history involved adopting a heuristic or interpretive preference for the forgotten Other. Dussel appropriates Marx's categorical framework, although more elaborate than the simple resolve in history to interpret events from the view of the Other, in order never to allow one to lose sight of the forgotten Other of the capitalist economy, living labor, which, even as it creates value for capitalism, suffers most acutely its unforeseen consequences (for example, crises). No empirical phenomenal facts about the economy can refute this hermeneutical framework, any more than individual historical facts can abolish the decision to interpret history by focusing on the suppressed Other. Ethical hermeneutics does not contradict empirical phenomena; it situates them within an interpretation that begins with these phenomena and immediately moves to a more abstract plane.[30]

Similarly, regarding the dependence theory, there can certainly be empirical agreement that the merging of goods toward a common average price on the international market will benefit those who produce goods more cheaply (those of central capital) or of less value (in Marx's terms); that even those who produce goods more expensively (peripheral capitalism) or of greater value (again according to Marx) can still make some profit; and that peripheral capitalism, in spite of its gains, seems destined to lag *relative to* central capitalism. But Dussel, given his ethical-hermeneutical account of the origin of profit in the more encompassing surplus value, interprets these facts by arguing that less-developed capital thereby transfers some of its surplus value (from which it might have taken a greater profit) to developed capital (which extracts its greater profit from this transferred surplus value). While both Dussel and the bourgeois economist can admit that peripheral capitalism in spite of its slow progress is handicapped relative to a stronger capitalism, Dussel's interpretation of these phenomena in terms of transferred surplus value connects them to an underlying ethical concern for the exploited (here the workers of developing nations) and to his project of studying capitalism from their viewpoint and in terms of its impact upon them. In conclusion, Apel's reading of Dussel as engaging in "metaphysical-rhetorical oversimplifications" instead of collaborating with the empirical sciences seems to me to ignore that Dussel does not compete with the empirical sciences, but rather engages in an ethical hermeneutics that begins with empirical economic phenomena and interprets them within an ethical categorical framework.[31]

In response to Apel's and Cerutti's objection that the dependence theory and he ignore the diversity of nations and the multicausal nature of world poverty, Dussel admits that his analysis of the law of dependence proceeds at an abstract level (more concrete than that of capital in general, but more abstract than that of the concrete social formation) that should not be confused with the investigations of concrete, multiple, phenomenal, and historical appearances of dependence and the many concrete variables interacting at this level. Indeed, economics itself, in order to clarify the economic laws that would function if everyone were to be solely economically motivated, forms constructs of actors, similar to Weberian types, in abstraction from the multiple motivations characterizing agents in everyday life. Dussel admits that counteracting influences may interfere with the action of a law in general and seem to annul it, giving it the character of only a tendency whose effects are manifest in impressive form under determinate circumstances and in the course of prolonged periods. As an instance of phenomena seeming to contradict the law of dependence, Dussel cites a counterexample raised by Samir Amin: namely, that the exports of peripheral countries, such as coffee, are produced by companies with high organic composition (more similar to those of central capitalism). Dussel counterargues that such goods really do not enter into competition with the goods of central capitalism—a key feature of the dependence theory—because they are not produced in central capitalist countries and central capitalism exercises a monopoly as a buyer in such cases. Tendentially, the law of dependence is fulfilled in spite of the phenomenal factors that only appear to annul it. While Apel accuses Dussel of naïve neglect of the diverse, concrete, historical, geographical, social, and cultural factors affecting dependence, Dussel's bracketing of these factors seems part of a highly self-conscious methodology not all that different from the methods of Weberian-type construction or economic science. In addition, while allowing for a methodological abstraction from cultural factors, Dussel evidences his awareness of their importance in his mistrust of Marxist internationalism's tendency to overlook distinctive nationalist resources for liberation and his preference for social analysis based on the *pueblo* instead of class. Moreover, Dussel himself explicitly rejects the idea that one could explain all the concrete levels of different national histories through the theory of dependence, and hence one ought not to ask more from that theory than it can deliver. Furthermore, though Dussel is not opposed to Hurtienne's view that peripheral capitalism may attain in a hundred years the standard of living in present-day central capitalism, he believes that such development exacts its toll in large transfers of surplus value (and human life), and even then, a century from now, central capitalism ought to be relatively far ahead of its later-starting counterpart.[32]

Dussel seems to confirm Apel's suspicion that he rejects reformist approaches to the international market economy. After two treatments of the theory of dependence in *La producción teórica de Marx* and *Hacia un Marx desconocido*, Dussel concludes with discussions of "national" and "popular" liberation in which he makes the following point:

> The process of national and popular liberation is the only response to destroy the mechanisms of the *transference of surplus value*, in constant and increasing manner, away from less-developed global national capital. But this presupposes that one transcend capitalism as such, since the extraction of surplus value (the relationship of capital to living labor) is articulated in terms of the transference of surplus value in competition between global national capitals at different stages of development. Because of the fact of the *weakness* of peripheral capitalism (due to the structural transference of surplus value), the entire population cannot be subsumed within the class of salaried labor: for this reason, the great *popular* [*populares*]

marginal masses play a protagonist function in the process of change. The popular movement and organization becomes a political priority.[33]

It does not clearly follow from the transference of surplus value that popular national revolutions are the only solution. One might recommend patience to developing nations, pointing out that, in spite of transferred surplus value, developing nations can still make *a* profit, that development is occurring, and that some developing nations such as China, Mexico, or those of southeast Asia seem on verge of surpassing their current status as developing nations. But Dussel would no doubt find this appeal for patience on the part of developing nations highly *Eurocentric,* particularly since it overlooks or downplays the deep misery "the great *popular* [*populares*] marginal masses" must undergo until that future moment arrives—a misery outweighing even the immense sufferings inflicted on those nations Dussel praises for seeking to leave the dialectic of the international competition of capitalism and facing internal economic problems and external pressures (for example, from the United States), such as Cuba and Nicaragua. Apel would probably object that all developing nations, even those who seek to escape the competition, must inevitably take account of the systemic imperatives of the market economy. Hence, while Apel might consider revolution utopian, he would place his hope in the communicative processes curbing the deleterious effects visited upon the life-world by the blind, merely technical functioning of the capitalist economic system and overly bureaucratized socialism as well, as has occurred in the Western social democracies. Given the grave inequities in the distribution of wealth and power in many developing nations, one wonders if some other level B tactics—along the lines that Dussel suggests—might not be necessary to realize this ideal of life-world communities checking systemic incursions.[34]

Given the tendency of critical theory at this practical level (Part B, to be sure) to allow systemic forces some free play in dialectical relationship to the life-world, some critical theorists, such as James Marsh, have shown more sympathy for Dussel's position. Marsh has attempted to implant requirements for material conditions, such as adequate food, housing, and education, within the norm of the ideal communication community itself (Part A) by arguing that these conditions constitute the conditions of the possibility of communication and therefore of communicative ethics. Some Apelians, though, intent on maintaining the priority of communicative ethics over any solutions derived from it, might protest that communicative ethics itself constitutes the condition of the possibility for establishing these conditions of its own possibility that Marsh spells out. They might charge Marsh with transferring issues of the B level, regarding the implementation of communication ethics through removal of obstacles to it, to the A level. Dussel and the philosophy of liberation would no doubt mistrust such a distinction *on the level of justification* since it would tend to privilege *at a practical level* democratic dialogic processes. Dussel undoubtedly would be reluctant to entrust the practical resolution of urgent questions regarding malnutrition, starvation, and massive unemployment in developing nations to slow-working, haphazard democratic procedures, which so often have shown themselves indifferent to the pain of those on their periphery. This debate, now returned to the practical level, raises the question of what comes first, dialogic, democratic decision procedures requisite for nontotalitarian conflict-resolution or the socialist provision of the basic needs requisite for participating in such procedures. As such, the debate encapsulates differences between democracy and socialism, between the West and the former Eastern bloc, between the developed nations, where capitalism's irrationalities do not produce as much misery, and those developing.[35]

There might be grounds for rapprochement, however, at this practical level when one considers Apel's condemnation of the recommendation (attributed to von Hayek) that humanity maintain the equilibrium of the world's biosphere by allowing those in the overpopulated Third World who cannot help themselves to starve. In the light of Apel's denunciation of sacrificing human life as a means to ecological ends, it would not seem consistent for him to tolerate at this practical level the immense suffering of peripheral capitalism, far more extreme than that of the Western social democracies, just because gradual and unpredictable democratic procedures ought to take their course or just because some *real* communication communities have not as yet come to recognize the immorality of the current arrangements. To think otherwise would subordinate the Third World starving to the liberalist *telos* of an unobstructed exchange of ideas—an equivalent to sacrificing them for the world's biosphere. The extreme plight of Third World nations might constitute one of those situations in which an ethics of responsibility might, regrettably, require strategic, violent action or some coercive supervision of the economy by the state, in order to put in place and ensure the material conditions necessary for the communicative action called for by communicative ethics itself and necessary if one ever hopes to realize the higher-level ideal that the life-world restrain encroaching systems.[36]

If communicative ethics would espouse this practical position—which seems highly plausible—it would converge with the view defended in Franz Hinkelammert's *Crítica a la razón utópica*—a treatise in theoretical economics endorsed by Dussel. Hinkelammert, equally offended by Hayek's comments on sacrificing lives, nevertheless admits, on the one hand, that a market economy with autonomous businesses is necessary because mercantile relations supply for the limitations of knowledge befalling any economic planner. However, state planning of the economy is also indispensable, to ensure full employment and the satisfaction of basic needs, which are the center of institutionality. While Apel, if I might construe him as in accord in with Hinkelammert, would be conceding something here to the socialist position of Dussel, would not Dussel also have to allow something of a market economy with some of the systemic alienation that Apel and Hinkelammert claim is unavoidable? When it comes to the dire situations of the Third World, Apel's reformism would have to approach revolution, just as Dussel's revolution can never be total.[37]

In regard to Marx's theory of alienation, insofar as some form of market would be preserved even after a popular, national revolution, I do not see how Dussel can hope to achieve any utopian overcoming of all alienation, as Apel suggests. Yet Dussel's new reading of Marx would seem to offset the old interpretations that Marx's view is developed within the paradigm of the subject-object relationship prevalent in German idealism. In Dussel's view, Marx, motivated by his concern for the Other of capitalism—that is, living labor—begins his analysis of capital with the social relationship between living labor and the capitalist, whose profiting off of unrecompensed labor Marx characterizes as "robbery." Indeed, the relationship between capitalism and its Other is at least co-originary with the labor theory of value, and, as Dussel reads Marx, it seems preeminent in importance. For Dussel, Marx's focus on surplus value throughout *Capital* has little to do with Marx's, German idealism's, and particularly Hegel's admiration of the human power to bestow value triumphantly on inert matter through labor, and everything to do with tracing all of capitalism's categories back to that originary relationship in which the Other of capitalism was treated unfairly and subsequently forgotten. Even though Apel recognizes Dussel's basic intersubjective paradigm and cites his works on Marx, Apel still seems to read Marx through the eyes of Hegel, as if Marx were materializing Hegelian idealism. How different is Dussel's reading of Marx through the eyes of Levinas, as if Marx were doing an ethical hermeneutics of the economy, beginning with the excluded Other![38]

Similarly, Apel argues that Marx, unwittingly under the influence of German idealism and its philosophy of the subject, sought the origin of surplus value in labor's investment in the object—"hyperabstracting" from other factors such as supply and demand, which reflect reciprocal-exchange *human relationships.* Here Apel seems to lack a clear understanding of the distinctions Marx makes between production and circulation and of the function of supply and demand in his thought. Moreover, Dussel never would allow such a neat separation of *poesis* (as action on nature) from *praxis* (political interrelationships). If Marx's economics constitute an ethical hermeneutics beginning from the system's excluded Other, living labor, then the theory of surplus value serves as a constant reminder of the originary exploitative human relationship that exists when the totally dispossessed faces a prospective employer. Apel seems to neglect how human relationships, albeit distorted ones, enter the capitalist picture at the level of production long before goods are placed in circulation on the market—perhaps because he is so under the sway of a German idealist reading of Marx instead of a Levinasian one. In fact, it was Marx's attention to the ethical demands of human communicative relationships, not his neglect of them, as Apel suggests, that led him to hope for an total overcoming of alienation, however unachievable such a dream might be.[39]

Finally, it is obvious that Dussel no longer partakes of the scientific prognosis of history, falsely attributed to Marx, who never believed that Russia would have to pass inevitably through capitalism on its way to socialism. Furthermore, it is significant that, after he has described the transfer of surplus value from less-developed to developed economies, Dussel resorts to a *political* solution that does not rigorously follow from its economic antecedents, instead of predicting *economically* that Third World nations will pass from capitalism directly and inevitably into socialism. Furthermore, in light of his focus on the exteriority that submits even socialist regimes to question, Dussel could never accept a mechanistic view of history or a Politburo defining all truth and goodness—these would be nothing more than new totalities closed against the Infinity beyond them.[40]

CONCLUSION

In response to charges from Schutte and Cerutti that Dussel's philosophy is irrationalist, I have argued that they have not taken sufficient account of his Levinasian presuppositions, due in part to the fact that Dussel often does not present them fully. The charge that Dussel promotes blind worship of the Other fails to pay attention to Dussel's own texts and to such key Levinasian concepts as separation, apology, and discourse. My interpretation of Levinas as a phenomenologist, but in a new key, can help defend Dussel from the criticisms that he refuses to test validity claims, dogmatically affirms his own foundationalism instead of giving an account of his own philosophizing, and arrogantly claims to have overcome all European rationality. With this emphasis on his Levinasian roots, Dussel's "foundation" should lead not to pomposity but to self-undermining, opening the philosopher of liberation to questions and to cooperation with the empirical sciences. The early ambiguous relationship of the philosophy of liberation with Peronism does not destroy its rational credentials, precisely because the relationship was ambiguous and because the criticism itself seems to commit the genetic fallacy.

Finally, I have concurred with Schutte that Dussel's sexual ethics in particular do not adequately break with the natural law ethics with which he began. This does not weaken his present Levinasian position; it merely suggests that he needs to take it more seriously.

In regard to Apel's attacks on Dussel, I have argued that Dussel's philosophy, self-denominated as "transmodern," is not in opposition to Apel's rational transcendental pragmatics. Though Dussel's Levinasian method cannot provide a rational grounding for ethics as Apel has, Dussel can locate Apel's enterprise and concur with it as taking place after the entrance of the Third, in Levinasian terminology. Dussel's own work, like Levinas's, attempts to return to a preoriginary moment beneath the level of the Third, revivify the height of the Other that Apel's transcendental pragmatics inevitably levels, and thus explain how the beginning of discursive rationality unfolds in the presence of the Other, whose questions challenge and renew rationality, making it all the more rational. I have suggested that Dussel and Apel belong within a common philosophical architectonic, utilizing different but complementary methods. Both can be conceived as carrying on the work of a single reason, owning up to what it often ignores, exploring the horizons prior to the origin of theory in Dussel's case and uncovering the presuppositions of all ongoing theory and argumentation in Apel's.

I have also argued that Dussel's Marxism must be understood in terms of German idealism's *Wissenschaft*, seeking the underlying essence beyond phenomena and not competing with the empirical sciences, even though it is capable of generating testable claims at the phenomenal level. The "essence" Dussel finds, though, is the ethical framework, the relationship with capitalism's Other, through which he interprets empirical economic phenomena. Empirical phenomena can no more jeopardize this ethical hermeneutics than individual historical facts can dissolve a framework or heuristic for doing history that would focus itself on allowing the voice of the excluded Other to be heard. I have also made the case that Apel fails to understand the abstractive level of Dussel's "law of dependence." I have tried to show that in the face of the plight of developing nations, Apel would be moved toward a planned economy, as Hinkelammert describes it, while Dussel would be unable to deny the need for a market econ-

omy with some inescapable alienation. Finally, I have explained
how Dussel's ethical hermeneutics of the economy in the pattern
of Marx need not partake of the presuppositions of the philosophy of the subject in accounting for alienation and surplus value,
or endorse any mechanistic theory of history that would relativize
any claims to validity except those of the Politburo.

NOTES

1. Karl-Otto Apel, *Diskurs und Verantwortung*, pp. 98, 198, 371; *Transformation der Philosophie* I (English translation, *Towards a Transformation of
Philosophy*, indicated after slashes), pp. 19, 80, 88–104, 115–36, 141–57,
173–74, 243, 288, 307, 313, 317, 320–21, 334, 358–60/20–22, 371/33;
"Die Entfaltung der 'sprachanalytischen' Philosophie," in *Transformation der Philosophie. II. Das Apriori der Kommunikationsgemeinschaft* (Frankfurt am Main: Suhrkamp, 1973) [English translation after slash: *Analytic
Philosophy of Language and the Geisteswissenschaften*, trans. Harald Holstelilie (Dordrecht, The Netherlands: D. Reidel, 1967], pp. 40–46/12–17.
*Transformation der Philosophie. II. Das Apriori der Kommunikationsgemein-
schaft* [English translation, *Towards a Transformation of Philosophy*, henceforth indicated after slashes], pp. 102/50, 108/55, 149/00, 181–85/
96–98, 202/113, 233/147, 242–45, 286–88/197–98, 375–76/239,
398–99/258, 413–14/269; *Understanding and Explanation: A Transcendental-Pragmatic Perspective*, trans. Georgia Warnke (Cambridge, Mass., and
London: The MIT Press, 1984), pp. 37, 150, 197, 202, 249; Karl-Otto
Apel, *Charles S. Peirce: From Pragmatism to Pragmaticism*, trans. John Michael Krois (Amherst: University of Massachusetts Press, 1981), p. 159;
Razón comunicativa y responsabilidad solidaria, ed. Adela Cortina, 2d ed.
(Salamanca: Ediciones Sigueme, 1988), pp. 32, 54–55, 127.
    2. Apel, *Charles S. Peirce: From Pragmatism to Pragmaticism*, pp. 25, 60;
Transformation der Philosophie, 1:202–21, 272–73; 2:18; *Diskurs und Verantwortung*, pp. 102, 170, 202, 383–84, 405.
    3. *Diskurs und Verantwortung*, p. 353.
    4. *Transformation der Philosophie*, 2:411–14/267–70. This last point
sounds very similar to a position of Jürgen Habermas's that while the
arguing skeptic cannot be contradicted, the skeptic *living in everyday life*
cannot deny the discourse principles implicit in communicative action
except under pain of self-destruction. Apel rejects this argument as insufficient because it does not reach beyond Kohlberg's conventional
level to a level of rational discourse. Apel prefers to point to the way the

meaningfulness of action depends on language games which in turn depend on transcendental presuppositions. It would seem to me that both Apel and Habermas are doing a similar thing, eliciting presuppositions from the meaningful activity of the skeptic apart from the skeptic's involvement in formal philosophical argument. Cf. Karl-Otto Apel, "Normative Begründung der 'Kritischen Theorie' durch Rekurs auf lebensweltliche Sittlichkeit? Ein transzendentalpragmatisch orientierte Versuch, mit Habermas gegen Habermas zu denken," in *Zwischenbetrachtungen im Prozess der Aufklärung zum 60 Geburtstag J. Habermas*, ed. Axel Honneth and Thomas McCarthy (Frankfurt am Main: Suhrkamp, 1989), pp. 58–59; *Razón comunicativa y responsibilidad solidaria*, ed. Adela Cortina. (Salamanca: Ediciones Sigueme, 1988), pp. 94–95.

5. Apel, "Normative Begründung der 'Kritischen Theorie' durch Rekurs auf lebensweltliche Sittlichkeit?" pp. 37–38; *Understanding and Explanation*, pp. 79, 222; *Diskurs und Verantwortung*, pp. 36, 46, 50, 53, 66, 94–95, 116, 145, 202, 354; Karl-Otto Apel, *Teoría de la verdad y ética del discurso*, trans. Norberto Smilg (Barcelona: Paidos Iberica, 1987), pp. 120–22, 133, 143; *Transformation der Philosophie*, 1:63–67, 76; 2:149, 400/ 259.

6. *Transformation der Philosophie*, 1:60, 63, 307, 363–65/32–34, 2:146, 183/97, 202/113, 243, 247–48, 206, 299–300/206, 373–74/237–38, 395–400/256–60, 413–14/269, 423–35/276–85; *Understanding and Explanation*, pp. 57, 67, 78, 92, 197; *Diskurs und Verantwortung*, pp. 30, 36, 98, 120–45, 198, 200, 220, 233, 271; *Razón comunicativa y responsabilidad solidaria*, pp. 54–55, 212, 253, 259.

7. *Transformation der Philosophie*, 2:424/277–78; *Diskurs und Verantwortung*, pp. 37, 110–11, 202–203, 206–207, 236–37, 285, 338, 350, 360; *Teoría de la verdad y ética del discurso*, p. 145.

8. Karl-Otto Apel, "Die Diskursethik von der Herausforderung der Dritten Welt: Versuch einer Antwort an Enrique Dussel," in *Diskursethik oder Befreiungsethik? Dokumentation des Seminars: Die Transzendentalpragmatik und die ethischen Probleme im Nord-Sud-Konflikt*, ed. Raúl Fornet-Betancourt (Aachen: Verlag der Augustinus-Buchhandlung, 1992), pp. 18–21.

9. *Diskurs und Verantwortung*, pp. 114, 156–59, 389–91; Enrique Dussel, "Die Vernunft des Anderen: Die 'Interpellation' als Sprechackt," in *Diskursethik oder Befreiungsethik? Dokumentation des Seminars: Die Transzendentalpragmatik und die ethischen Probleme im Nord-Sud-Konflikt*, ed. Raul Fornet-Betancourt (Aachen: Verlag der Augustinus-Buchhandlung, 1992), pp. 106–107; *1492: El encubrimiento del Otro*, pp. 9–13, 203, 208–13; see above, chap. 5, pp. 00–00.

10. *Totality and Infinity*, pp. 22–30, 35–36, 80–81, 289–90; "Die Entfal-

tung der 'sprachanalytischen' Philosophie," pp. 45–46/17–18, 50–92/ 20–55; *Transformation der Philosophie*, 1:55, 66–69, 307, 316; 149, 238–63/ 151–72, 286/197–98, 400/259; *Understanding and Explanation*, pp. 151, 152, 222.

11. *Totality and Infinity*, pp. 43–44, 49, 84, 103–104, 194–97, 201, 210–12, 219, 292, 295; Enrique Dussel, "Vom Skeptiker zum Zyniker (Vom Gegner der 'Diskursethik' zu dem der 'Befreiungsphilosophie')," Lecture at the Neurod Symposium of the North-South Dialogue, April 12, 1992, pp. 2, 8–16.

12. "La introducción de la 'Transformatión de la Filosofía' de K.-O. Apel y la filosofía de la liberación," pp. 76–77; see above, chap. 1, pp. 11–12.

13. *Otherwise Than Being*, pp. 128, 157, 161, 193, pp. 196–97; *Totality and Infinity*, p. 300; see above, chap. 1, pp. 10–12, and above, at note 10.

14. *Totality and Infinity*, p. 214.

15. Ibid., pp. 213–14. Again, Levinas recommends no blind servility toward the Other here. As I have said, the demand of the Other for service in the face-to-face, made on the phenomenologically self-reflective and autonomous I, does not preclude apology or disagreement with the Other. Also, in the face-to-face, Levinas describes only the experience of normativity coming from the Other and does not set out to determine which specific norms are valid. In the situation of the Third, Levinas attempts to explain how the norm of reciprocity and equality is generated through interpersonal dynamics motivated by the claim of the Other on me (a claim not yet elaborated into a norm or not yet justified as a norm). And once that norm is in place, it can be used to assess whether specific claims of the Other are justifiable—of course, one must repeatedly return to the face-to-face to ensure that one's assessment is not totalizing. At every stage, then, there is always the sense that one is responsible for the Other, but not that one ought to do whatever the Other bids.

16. *Otherwise Than Being*, pp. 159–60, see also p. 128; *Emmanuel Lévinas*, ed. Jacques Rolland, Les Cahiers de la Nuit Surveillée (Paris: Editiones Verdier, 1984), pp. 345–45.

17. *Para una ética de la liberación*, 2:107–27; *Transformation der Philosophie*, 2:427–28/279; *Diskurs und Verantwortung*, pp. 122–28, 134, 241, 266, 367; Karl-Otto Apel, "La ética del discurso como ética de la responsibilidad: Una transformación posmetafísica de la ética de Kant," in *Fundamentación de la ética y filosofía de la liberación* (Mexico: Siglo Veintiuno Editores, 1992), pp. 40–42.

18. *Totality and Infinity*, p. 246.

19. *Teoría de la verdad*, p. 157; *Transformation der Philosophie*, 2:385–89/

248–51; "La ética del discurso como ética de la responsibilidad," pp. 16–19, 29–30, 41; "Normative Begründung der 'Kritischen Theorie' durch Rekurs auf lebensweltliche Sittlichkeit," pp. 21–58. In this latter essay, Apel chides Habermas for not keeping these levels distinct and for seeking ultimate grounding in the life-world instead of at a transcendental level.

20. *Transformation der Philosophie*, 2:423–35/267–85; *Diskurs und Verantwortung*, pp. 202–203, 215, 235–36, 266. Dussel, as already mentioned (see above, p. 42), does not always observe the distinctiveness of these levels. His *Ética de la liberación* articulates philosophy of liberation principles. These principles could be fashioned out of exposure to the face of the Other at the pretranscendental level, but the experience of the face, the critical counterpole to all principles, always needs to be distinguished from the denotative issuing of principles. Because his philosophy of liberation encompasses these two poles while keeping them distinct, Dussel is entitled to situate the philosophy of liberation, as he does in his recently published *The Underside of Modernity*, as lying in-between Apel's universalism and Richard Rorty's skepticism and in-between Apel's formalism and Charles Taylor's *Sittlichkeit*. See *Underside of Modernity*, pp. 114, 147–48.

21. Apel, "Die Diskursethik von der Herausforderung der Dritten Welt," pp. 18–21.

22. Ibid., pp. 22–26.

23. Ibid., pp. 27–32.

24. Ibid., pp. 32–38, see above, chap. 5, pp. 115–116.

25. Apel, "Die Diskursethik von der Herausforderung der Dritten Welt," pp. 39–44.

26. Ibid., pp. 44–50, 53.

27. Ibid., pp. 50–53.

28. See above, chap. 4, pp. 90–105; *El último Marx*, pp. 119, 361, 405. To see Dussel's own response to Apel's critique of his Marxism—a response that became available only after this volume was in press—see *Underside of Modernity*, pp. 213–39.

29. See above, chap. 4, pp. 90–97.

30. See above, chap. 4, pp. 101–102; Apel, "Die Diskursethik von der Herausforderung der Dritten Welt," pp. 44–50.

31. See above, chap. 5, pp. 115–116, *Hacia un Marx desconocido*, pp. 313–30, 340, 341, 347–48; *La producción teoríca de Marx*, pp. 386, 396; Cerutti, *Filosofía de la liberación latinoamericana*, pp. 69–86.

32. *Hacia un Marx desconocido*, pp. 340–41, 344–46, 350–52, 356; *La producción teoríca de Marx*, p. 386; see above, chap. 4, pp. 104–105, and chap. 5, pp. 115–116.

33. *Hacia un Marx desconocido*, pp. 358, see also pp. 357–61; *La producción teoríca de Marx*, pp. 400–13.

34. "Die Diskursethik von der Herausforderung der Dritten Welt," p. 24.

35. James Marsh, *Critique, Action, and Liberation* (Albany: State University of New York Press, 1995), pp. 124–47.

36. *Diskurs und Verantwortung*, pp. 62–63. Dussel admits that Marx's "realm of freedom" and the "perfect community of producers" is only a regulative ideal, which, like the ideal of perfect economic planning according to Hinkelammert, cannot be realized completely. Cf. *Underside of Modernity*, p. 222.

37. Franz J. Hinkelammert, *Crítica de la razón utópica* (San Jose, Costa Rica: Departamento Ecuménico de Investigaciones, 1984), pp. 88, 243–53, 265–66; Dussel, "La introducción de la 'Transformación de la Filosofía' de K.-O. Apel y la Filosofia de la Liberacion," p. 80.

38. Apel, "Die Diskursethik von der Herausforderung der Dritten Welt," pp. 39–44; see above, chap. 4, pp. 91–102.

39. *Filosofía de la producción*, pp. 39–40, 21; Apel, "Die Diskursethik von der Herausforderung der Dritten Welt," pp. 19, 40, 44–50; see above, chap. 4, pp. 94–105.

40. See above, chap. 4, pp. 104–105.

BIBLIOGRAPHY

WORKS BY DUSSEL

Books

Dussel, Enrique D. *América Latina: Dependencia y liberación*. Buenos Aires: Fernando García Cambiero, 1973.

———. *Cultura latinoamericana e historia de la Iglesia*. Buenos Aires: Ediciones de la Facultad de Teología de la Pontificia Universidad Católica Argentina, 1968.

———. *De Medellín a Puebla: Una década de sangre y esperanza (1968–1979)*. Mexico City: Editorial Edicol, 1979.

———. *Desintegración de la cristiandad colonial y liberación: Perspectiva latinoamericana*. Salamanca: Ediciones Sigueme, 1978.

———. *La dialéctica hegeliana: Supuestos y superación o del inicio originario del filosofar*. Mendoza, Argentina: Editorial Ser y Tiempo, 1972.

———. *El dualismo en la antropología de la cristiandad: Desde el origen del cristianismo hasta antes de la conquista de América*. Buenos Aires: Editorial Guadalupe, 1974.

———. *El episcopado latinoamericano y la liberación de los pobres, 1504–1620*. Mexico City: Centro de Reflexión Teológica, 1979.

———. *Ethics and the Theology of Liberation*. Trans. Bernard F. McWilliam, C.SS.R. Maryknoll, N.Y.: Orbis Books, 1978.

———. *Ética comunitaria*. Madrid: Ediciones Paulinas, 1986.

———. *Ética de la liberación en la edad de la globalización y de la exclusión*. Mexico City: Editorial Trotta, 1998.

———. *Les évèques hispano-américains: Défenseurs et évangélisateurs de l'Indien, 1504–1620*. Wiesbaden: Franz Steiner Verlag, 1970.

———. *Filosofía de la producción*. Bogotá: Editorial Nueva América, 1984.

———. *1492: El encubrimiento del Otro—Hacia el origen del "Mito de la modernidad": Conferencias de Frankfurt, Octobre de 1992*. Madrid: Editorial Nueva Utopia, 1992. English translation: *The Invention of the Americas: Eclipse of "the Other" and the Myth of Modernity*. Trans. Michael D. Barber. New York: Continuum, 1998.

———. *Hacía un Marx desconocido: Un comentario de manuscritos del 61–63*. Iztapalapa, Mexico: Siglo Veintiuno Editores, 1988.

————. *Hipótesis para una historia de la Iglesia en América Latina.* Barcelona: Editorial Estela, 1967.

————. *Hipótesis para una historia de la teología en América Latina.* Chapinero, Bogotá: Indo-American Press Service, 1986.

————. *History and the Theology of Liberation: A Latin American Perspective.* Trans. John Drury. Maryknoll, N.Y.: Orbis Books, 1976.

————. *A History of the Church in Latin America: Colonialism to Liberation (1492–1979).* Trans. and rev. Alan Neely. Grand Rapids, Mich.: William B. Eerdmans, 1981.

————. *El humanismo helénico.* Buenos Aires: Editorial Universitaria de Buenos Aires, 1975.

————. *El humanismo semita: Estructuras intencionales radicales del pueblo de Israel y otros semitas.* Buenos Aires: Editorial Universitaria de Buenos Aires, 1969.

————. *Liberación de la mujer y erótica latinoamericana: Ensayo filosófico.* Bogotá: Editorial Nueva América, 1983.

————. *Método para una filosofía de la liberación: Superación analéctica de la dialéctica hegeliana.* 2nd ed. Salamanca: Ediciones Sigueme, 1974. 3rd ed. Guadalajara: Editorial Universidad de Guadalajara, 1991.

————. *Para una de-strucción de la historia de la ética.* Mendoza, Argentina: Editores Ser y Tiempo, 1970.

————. *Para una ética de la liberación latinoamericana.* 5 vols. Vol. 1: *Acceso al punto de partida de la ética.* Buenos Aires: Siglo Vientiuno Argentina Editores, 1973. Vol. 2: *Eticidad y moralidad.* Buenos Aires: Siglo Vientiuno Argentina Editores, 1973. Vol. 3: *Filosofía ética latinoamericana: De la erótica a la pedagógica de la liberación.* Mexico City: Editorial Edicol, 1977. Vol. 4: *Filosofía ética latinoamericana: La política latinoamericana.* Bogotá: Universidad Santo Tomas, Centro de Enseñanza Desescolarizada, 1979. Vol. 5: *Filosofía ética latinoamericana: Arqueológica latinoamericana—Una filosofía de la religión antifetichista.* Bogotá: Universidad Santo Tomás, Centro de Enseñanza Desescolarizada, 1980.

————. *Philosophy of Liberation.* Trans. Aquilina Martínez and Christine Morkovsky. Maryknoll, N.Y.: Orbis Books, 1985.

————. *Praxis latinoamericana y filosofía de la liberación.* Bogotá: Editorial Nueva América, 1983.

————. *La producción teórica de Marx: Un comentario a los Grundrisse.* Iztapalapa, Mexico: Siglo Veintiuno Editores, 1985.

————. *Religión.* Mexico City: Editorial Edicol, 1977.

————. *Teología de la liberación y ética: Caminos de liberación latinoamericana.* Buenos Aires: Latinoamérica Libros, 1975.

————. *El último Marx (1863–1882) y la liberación latinoamericana: Un comentario a la tercera y a la cuarta redacción de "El Capital."* Iztapalapa, Mexico: Siglo Veintiuno Editores, 1990.

———. *Los últimos 50 años, 1930–1985, en la historia de la Iglesia en América Latina.* Bogotá: Indo-American Press Service, 1986.
———.*The Underside of Modernity: Apel, Ricoeur, Taylor, and the Philosophy of Liberation.* Trans. and ed. Eduardo Mendieta. Atlantic Highlands, N.J.: Humanities Press, 1996.
Dussell, Enrique, and María Mercedes Esandi. *El catolicismo popular en la Argentina.* Buenos Aires: Editorial Bonum, 1970.
Dussel, Enrique, and Daniel E. Guillot. *Liberación latinoamericana y Emmanuel Levinas.* Buenos Aires: Editorial Bonum, 1975.

Articles

Dussel, Enrique. "Algunos aspectos de la antropología cristiana hasta fines del siglo XIV." *Eidos* [Cordoba], 2 (1970), 16–46.
———. "Arte cristiano del oprimido en América Latina." *Concilium*, 152 (1980), 215–31.
———. "Auf dem Weg zur Geschichte der ganzen Kirche—Neue Horizonte." *Theologische Zeitschrift*, 38 (1982), 367–98.
———. "Die Ausbreitung der Christenheit und ihre heutige Krise." *Consilium*, 164 (1981), 307–316.
———. "La 'Base' en la teología del la liberación." *Concilium*, 104 (1975), 76–89.
———. "Claude Tresmontant." *Sapientia* [Buenos Aires], 76 (1965), 128–39.
———. "El concepto de fetichismo en el pensamiento de Marx: Elementos para una teoría general marxista de la religión." *Cristianismo y Sociedad* [Mexico], 85 (1985), 7–59.
———. "Conversación con Enrique Dussel." In *Conversaciones sobre la fe.* Ed. Teofilo Cabestrero. Salamanca: Ediciones Sigueme, 1977. Pp. 61–82.
———. "Cristiandad moderna ante el Otro: De Indio 'Rudo' al Bon Sauvage." *Concilium*, 150 (1979), 498–506.
———. "Criterios generales y periodificación de una historia de la Iglesia en América Latina." *Cristianismo y Sociedad* [Mexico], 82 (1984), 7–24.
———. "Cuatro temas en torno a teología y economía." *Cristianismo y Sociedad* [Mexico], 87 (1986), 67–91.
———. "La 'Cuestion Popular.'" *Cristianismo y Sociedad* [Mexico], 84 (1985), 81–90.
———. "Cultura imperial, cultura ilustrada y liberación de la cultura popular." *Stromata* [Argentina], 30 (1974), 93–123.
———. "Cultura latinoamericana y filosofía de la liberación: Cultura

popular revolucionaria más allá del populismo y del dogmatismo." *Cristianismo y Sociedad* [Mexico], 80 (1984), 9–45.

———. "Del descubrimiento al desencubrimiento: Hacía un desagravio historico." *Misiones Extranjeras*, 86 (1985), 105–14.

———. "Discernimiento: Cuestión de ortodoxía u ortopraxis?" *Concilium*, 139 (1978), 552–67.

———. "Ekklesiologie des christlichen Gemeinschaften des Volkes." In *Herausgefordert durch die Armen: Dokumente der Oekumenischen Vereinigung von Dritte-Welt-Theologen.* Freiburg, Basel, Vienna: Herder, 1983. Pp. 79–84.

———. "En torno a la obra de Teilhard de Chardin." *Punto Omega* [Buenos Aires], (1964), 1–14.

———. "Estética y ser." *Artes Plasticos* [Mendoza], 2 (1969), 15–18.

———. "An Ethics of Liberation: Fundamental Hypotheses." *Consilium*, 192 (1984), 54–63.

———. "La ética definitiva de Aristoteles o el Tratado moral contemporáneo del alma." *Cuadernos de Filosofía* [Buenos Aires], 11 (1969), 75–89.

———. "Ética de la liberación." *Iglesia Viva*, 102 (1982), 591–99.

———. "Existen 'Dos Morales' en Argentina? Limites éticos de una orden oficial superior." *Iglesias*, 2 (1985), 14–15.

———. "La filosofía de la liberación en Argentina: Irrupción de una nueva generación filosófica." *Praxis latinoamericana y filosofía de la liberación.* Bogotá: Editorial Nueva América, 1983. Pp. 47–56.

———. "Filosofía y liberación latinoamericana." *Latinoamerica* [Mexico], 10 (1977), 83–91.

———. "Francisco Romero: Filosofía de la modernidad en la Argentina." *Cuyo* [Mendoza], 6 (1970), 79–106.

———. "Fundamentación analéctica de la liberación." *Método para una filosofía de la liberación: Superación analéctica de la dialéctica hegeliana.* 2nd ed. Salamanca: Ediciones Sigueme, 1974. Pp. 259–88.

———. "Hacia una historia de la Iglesia latinoamericana." *Stromata* [Argentina], 21 (1965), 483–505.

———. "Hacia una teología del pan y trabajo." In *Experiencia latinoamericana de formación en la vida religiosa mercedaria.* Mexico City: Gulani, 1982. Pp. 141–54.

———. "Hermeneutica y liberación." Dialogue with Paul Ricoeur, April 1991. Pp. 1–50.

———. "Hernando Arias de Ugarte, obispo de Quito y arzobispo de Santa Fe de Bogotá, Charcas, y Lima (1561–1638)." In *XXXVI Congreso Internacional de Americanistas.* Seville, 1966. Pp. 167–78.

———. "Hipotésis para elaborar un marco teórico de la historia del pensamiento latinoamericano." *Praxis latinoamericana y filosofía de la liberación.* Bogotá: Editorial Nueva América, 1983. Pp. 261–305.

——. "Hipotésis para una historia de la filosofía en América Latina." In *Perspectivas de la filosofía.* III. *Simposio de filosofía contemporánea.* Iztapalapa, Mexico: Universidad Autónoma Metropolitana, 1990. Pp. 229–69.

——. "Historia y praxis (Ortopraxia y objectividad)." *Praxis latinoamericana y filosofía de la liberación.* Bogotá: Editorial Nueva América, 1983. Pp. 307–29.

——. "The History of the Church in Latin America: An Interpretation." In *Church History in an Ecumenical Perspective:.* Bern: Evangelische Arbeitsstelle Oekumene Schweiz, 1982. Pp. 29–50.

——. "An International Division of Theological Labor." *Foundations* [Arlington], 4 (1980), 332–54.

——. "La introducción de la 'Transformación de la filosofía' de K.-O. Apel y la filosofía de la liberación: Reflexiones desde una perspectiva latinoamericana." In Karl-Otto Apel, Enrique Dussel, and Raúl Betancourt-Fornet. *Fundamentación de la ética y filosofía de la liberación.* Iztapalapa, Mexico: Siglo Veintiuno Editores, 1992. Pp. 45–104.

——. "The Kingdom of God and the Poor." Consultation on the History of the Church in Latin America, Bossey, Switzerland, October, 1978. Pp. 10–13.

——. "Liberación latinoamericana y filosofía." In *Praxis latinoamericana y filosofía de la liberación.* Bogotá: Editorial Nueva América, 1983. Pp. 7–19.

——. "El martirio en América Latina (Palabras Preliminarias)." In P. Ferrari. *El martirio en América Latina.* Mexico City: Misiones Culturales de B. C., 1982. Pp. 3–7.

——. "Origenes del episcopado." *Servir* [Mexico], 99 (1982), 393–415.

——. "The People of El Salvador, The Communal Suffering of Job: A Theological Reflection Based on Documentary Evidence." Trans. Paul Bern. Pp. 61–65.

——. "Pierre Teilhard de Chardin, Questio Disputata." *Estudios* [Buenos Aires], 561 (1965), 121–32.

——. "La política del Papa para América Latina, vista por teólogo de la liberación, Enrique Dussel." *Iglesias* [Mexico], 30 (1986), 19–24.

——. "The Political and Ecclesial Context of Liberation Theology in Latin America." In *The Emergent Gospel: Theology from the Underside of History.* Maryknoll, N.Y.: Orbis Books, 1978. Pp. 175–92.

——. "Primera sesión." In *Iglesia y estado en América Latina.* Mexico: Centro Reflexión Teológica, 1979. Pp. 11–20.

————. "Puede legitimarse 'una' ética ante la pluralidad histórica de las morales?" In *Praxis latinoamericana y filosofía de la liberación.* Bogotá: Editorial Nueva América, 1983. Pp. 117–32.

————. "Racismo, América Latina negra, y teología de la liberación." *Servir* [Mexico], 86 (1980), 163–210.

————. "Reflexiones sobre la metodología para una historia de la Iglesia en América Latina." In *Desintegración de la cristiandad colonial y liberación: Perspectiva latinoamericana.* Salamanca: Ediciones Sigueme, 1978. Pp. 91–194.

————. "Religiosidad popular latinoamericana: Hipóteses fundamentales." *Cristianismo y Sociedad* [Mexico], 88 (1986), 103–12.

————. "Respondiendo algunas preguntas y objeciones sobre filosofía de la liberación." *Praxis latinoamericana y filosofía de la liberación.* Bogotá: Editorial Nueva América, 1983. Pp. 85–98.

————. "Retos actuales a la filosofía de la liberación en América Latina." *Libertação/Liberación,* 1 (1989), 9–29.

————. "Sentido teológico de lo acontecido desde 1962 en América Latina." *Organización Internacional de Universitarios Católicos,* Pax Romana, Ref. doc. mind. No. 239 (September 30, 1971), 1–12.

————. "Situación problematica de la antropología filosófica." *Nordeste (Resistencia),* 7 (1965), 101–30.

————. "Sobre el 'Documento de Consulta' para Puebla." In *Puebla '78: Temores y esperanzas.* Ed. Clodovin Boff. Mexico City: Centro Reflexión Teológica, 1978. Pp. 81–101.

————. "Sobre el sentido de la traducción." *Actos del Primer Congreso de Estudios Clásicos.* Mendoza, Argentina: Universidad Nacional de Cuyo, 1972. Pp. 131–36.

————. "Sobre la actualidad de Carlos Marx." In *Dando razón de nuestra esperanza: Los cristianos latinoamericanos frente a la crisis del socialismo y la derrota sandinista.* Managua, Nicaragua: Ediciones Nicarao, 1992. Pp. 108–11.

————. "A Specious Alternative: The Third Way; The Present Temptation of the Church in Latin America. In *The Church at the Crossroads.* Ed. IDOC International. Rome: IDOC International, 1978. Pp. 92–98.

————. "Supuestos histórico-filosóficos de la teología desde América Latina." In *La nueva frontera de la teología en América Latina.* Ed. Gustavo Gutiérrez, Rosino Gibelli, and Raul Vidales. Salamanca: Ediciones Sigueme, 1977. Pp. 174–98.

————. "Théologie de la 'Périphérie' et du 'Centre': Rencontre ou confrontation?" *Concilium,* 191 (1984), 143–58.

————. "Tomismo y metafísica en América Latina?" *I Congreso Internacional de Filosofía Latinoamericana* [Bogotá], (1981), 219–35.

————. "Towards a History of the Church in the World Periphery: Some Hypotheses." In Ecumenical Association of Third World Theologians. *Towards a History of the Church in the Third World: The Issue of Periodization.* Bern: Evangelische Arbeitsstelle Oekumene Schweiz, 1985. Pp. 110–30.

————. "Una década argentina (1966–1976) y el origen de la 'Filosofía de la liberación.'" *Reflexão,* 38 (1987), 20–49.

————. "Die Vernunft des Anderen: Die 'Interpellation' als Sprechackt." In *Diskursethik oder Befreiungsethik? Dokumentation des Seminars: Die Transzendentalpragmatik und die ethischen Probleme im Nord-Sud-Konflikt.* Ed. Raúl Fornet-Betancourt. Aachen: Verlag der Augustinus Buchhandlung, 1992. Pp. 96–102.

————. "Vom Skeptiker zum Zyniker (Vom Gegner der 'Diskursethik' zu dem der 'Befreiungsphilosophie." Lecture at Symposium of North–South Dialogue at Neurod, Germany, April 12, 1992. Pp. 1–18.

————. "Was Sozialisten lernen sollten." In *Der Papst in Mexico.* Dusseldorf: Patmos, 1979. Pp. 117–17.

Dussel, Enrique, and Antonio Blanch. "Fisionomía actual del catolicismo latinoamericano: Considerando su génesis histórica." *Fe cristiana y cambio social en América Latina.* Salamanca: Ediciones Sigueme, 1973. Pp. 345–51.

————, and Felipe Espinoza, s.j. "Puebla: Crónica e historia." *Cristus* [Mexico], (1979), 520–21.

————, and J. Meier. "Die kirchlichen Basisgemeinden in Brasilien." In *Die Basisgemeinden: Ein Schritt auf dem Weg zur Kirche des Konzils.* Ed. Elmar Klinger and Rolf Zerfass. Würzburg: Echter Verlag, 1984. Pp. 11–31.

RELATED WORKS

Apel, Karl-Otto. *Analytic Philosophy of Language and the Geisteswissenschaften.* Trans. Harald Holstelilie. Dordrecht: D. Reidel, 1967. Originally published as "Die Entfaltung der 'sprachanalytischen' Philosophie und das Problem der 'Geisteswissenschaften.'" In *Transformation der Philosophie.* II. *Das Apriori der Kommunkationsgemeinschaft.* Frankfurt am Main: Suhrkamp, 1973. Pp. 28–95.

————. *Charles S. Peirce: From Pragmatism to Pragmaticism.* Trans. John Michael Krois. Amherst: University of Massachusetts Press, 1981. Originally published as *Der Denkweg von Charles S. Peirce: Eine Einfuhrung in den amerikanischen Pragmatismus.* Frankfurt am Main: Suhrkamp, 1970.

————. "Die Diskursethik von der Herausforderung der Dritten Welt:

Versuch einer Antwort an Enrique Dussel." In *Diskursethik oder Befrei-ungsethik?* *Dokumentation des Seminars: Die Transzendentalpragmatik und die ethischen Probleme im Nord-Sud-Konflikt.* Ed. Raúl Fornet-Betancourt. Aachen: Verlag der Augustinus-Buchhandlung, 1992. Pp. 16–54.

———. *Diskurs und Verantwortung: Das Problem des Übergangs zur postkon-ventionellen Moral.* Frankfurt am Main: Suhrkamp, 1990.

———. "Epílogo: Limites de la ética discursiva?" In *Razón comunicativa y responsibilidad solidaria.* Ed. Adela Cortina. Salamanca: Ediciones Si-gueme, 1988. Pp. 233–62.

———. "La ética del discurso como ética de la responsibilidad: Una transformación postmetafísica de la ética de Kant." In Karl-Otto Apel, Enrique Dussel, and Raúl Fornet-Betancourt. *Fundamentación de la ética y filosofía de la liberación.* Iztapalapa, Mexico: Siglo Veintiuno Edi-tores, 1992. Pp. 11–44.

———. "Normative Begründung der 'Kritischen Theorie' durch Rekurs auf lebensweltliche Sittlichkeit? Ein transzendentalpragmatisch ori-entierte Versuch, mit Habermas gegen Habermas zu denken." In *Zwi-schenbetrachtungen im Prozess der Aufklärung zum 60. Geburtstag J. Habermas.* Ed. Axel Honnet and Thomas McCarthy. Frankfurt am Main: Suhrkamp Verlag, 1989. Pp. 15–65.

———. *Teoría de la verdad y ética del discurso.* Trans. Norberto Smilg. Bar-celona: Paidos Ibérica, 1987. Originally published as "Fallibilismus, Konsenstheorie der Wahrheit und Letztbegründung." In *Philosophie und Bergrundung.* Frankfurt am Main: Suhrkamp Verlag, 1987.

———. *Transformation der Philosophie.* 2 vols. Vol. 1: *Sprachanalytik, Semio-tik, Hermeneutik.* Frankfurt am Main, Suhrkamp Verlag, 1973. Vol. 2: *Das Apriori der Kommunikationsgemeinschaft.* Frankfurt am Main: Suhr-kamp, 1973. Trans. Glyn Adey and David Frisby, in parts, as *Towards a Transformation of Philosophy.* London and Boston: Routledge & Kegan Paul, 1980.

———. *Understanding and Explanation: A Transcendental-Pragmatic Perspec-tive.* Trans. Georgia Warnke. Cambridge, Mass, and London: The MIT Press, 1984. Originally published as *Die Erklären-Verstehen-Kontroverse in transzendental-pragmatischer Sicht.* Frankfurt am Main: Suhrkamp Ver-lag, 1979.

Apel, Karl-Otto, Enrique Dussel, and Raúl Fornet-Betancourt. *Funda-mentación de la ética y filosofía de la liberación.* Iztapalapa, Mexico: Siglo Veintiuno Editores, 1992.

Berger, Peter, and Thomas Luckmann. *The Social Construction of Reality: A Treatise in the Sociology of Knowledge.* Garden City, N.Y.: Doubleday Anchor, 1966.

Bernasconi, Robert. "Scepticism in the Face of Philosophy." In *Re-read-*

ing Levinas. Ed. Robert Bernasconi and Simon Critchley. Bloomington and Indianapolis: Indiana University Press, 1991. Pp. 149–61.

Bernasconi, Robert, and Simon Critchley, eds. *Re-reading Levinas*. Bloomington and Indianapolis: Indiana University Press, 1991.

Butler, Judith. *Gender Trouble: Feminism and the Subversion of Identity*. New York and London: Routledge, 1990.

Cerutti Guldberg, Horacio. *Filosofía de la liberación latinoamericana*. Mexico City: Fondo de Cultura Económica, 1983.

Cohen, Richard A., ed. *Face to Face with Levinas*. Albany: State University of New York Press, 1986.

Cortina, Adela, ed.. *Razón comunicativa y responsabilidad solidaria*. 2nd ed. Salamanca: Ediciones Sigueme, 1988.

De Boer, Theodore. "An Ethical Transcendental Philosophy." In *Face to Face with Levinas*. Ed. Richard A. Cohen. Albany: State University of New York Press, 1986. Pp. 83–115.

Derrida, Jacques. "Violence and Metaphysics." *Writing and Difference*. Trans. Alan Bass. Chicago and London: The University of Chicago Press, 1978. Pp. 79–153.

———. *Writing and Difference*. Trans. Alan Bass. Chicago and London: The University of Chicago Press, 1978.

Evans, J. Claude. *Strategies of Deconstruction: Derrida and the Myth of the Voice*. Minneapolis: University of Minnesota Press, 1991.

Fisher, Eugene J. "A New Maturity in Christian–Jewish Dialogue: An Annotated Bibliography, 1975–1989." In *In Our Time: The Flowering of Jewish–Catholic Dialogue*. Ed. Eugene E. Fisher and Leon Klenicki. New York and Mahwah, N.J.: Paulist Press, 1990. Pp. 107–61.

Fisher, Eugene J., and Leon Klenicki, eds. *In Our Time: The Flowering of Jewish–Catholic Dialogue*. New York and Mahwah, N.J.: Paulist Press, 1990.

Fournet-Betancourt, Raúl, ed. *Diskursethik oder Befreiungsethik? Dokumentation des Seminars: Die Transzendentalpragmatik und die ethischen Probleme im Nord-Sud-Konflikt*. Aachen: Verlag der Augustinus-Buchhandlung, 1992.

Gaos, José. "Filosofía 'Americana'?" Mexico City: UNAM, Coordinación de Humanidades, Centro de Estudios Latinoamericanos. No. 32 (1942), 5–17.

———. *Obras completas*. VII. *Filosofía de la filosofía e historia de la filosofía*. Mexico City: UNAM, 1987.

García Bacca, Juan David. *Cosas y personas*. Caracas: Fondo de Cultura Económica, 1977.

Gellner, Ernest. "Concepts and Society." In *Rationality*. Ed. Bryan R. Wilson. London: Basil Blackwell, 1970. Pp. 18–49.

Gorostiaga, Xavier, et al. *Dando razón de nuestra esperanza: Los cristianos latinoamericanos frente a la crisis del socialismo y la derrota sandinista*. Managua, Nicaragua: Nicarao, 1992.

Greef, Jan de. "Scepticism and Reason." In *Face to Face with Levinas*. Ed. Richard A. Cohen. Albany: State University of New York Press, 1986. Pp. 159–79.

Habermas, Jürgen. *Erläuterungen zur Diskursethik*. Frankfurt am Main: Suhrkamp Verlag, 1991.

————. *Moral Consciousness and Communicative Action*. Trans. Christian Lenhardt and Shierry Weber Nicholsen. Boston: The MIT Press, 1990.

————. *The Philosophical Discourse of Modernity*. Trans. Frederick Lawrence. Cambridge, Mass: The MIT Press, 1987.

————. *The Theory of Communicative Action*. I. *Reason and the Rationalization of Society*. Trans. Thomas McCarthy. Boston: Beacon Press, 1984.

Hand, Sean, ed. *The Levinas Reader*. Oxford and Cambridge, Mass.: Basil Blackwell, 1992.

Heidegger, Martin. *Basic Writings*. Ed. David Farrell Krell. New York: Harper & Row, 1977.

————. *Being and Time*. Trans. John Macquarrie and Edward Robinson. New York: Harper & Row, 1962.

————. *Discourse on Thinking: A Translation of Gelassenheit*. Trans. John M. Anderson and E. Hans Freund. New York: Harper & Row, 1966.

————. *Identity and Difference*. Trans. Joan Stambaugh. New York and London: Harper & Row, 1969.

————. *Kant and the Problem of Metaphysics*. Trans. James S. Churchill. Bloomington: Indiana University Press, 1962.

————. "My Way to Phenomenology." In *On Time and Being*. Trans. Joan Stambaugh. New York: Harper & Row, 1972. Pp. 74–82.

Hinkelammert, Franz J. *Las armas ideológicas de la muerte*. Salamanca: Ediciones Sigueme, 1978.

————. *Crítica de la razón utópica*. San José, Costa Rica: Departamento Ecuménico de Investigaciones, 1984.

Hollis, Martin, and Steven Lukes, eds. *Rationality and Relativism*. Cambridge, Mass.: The MIT Press, 1982.

Honnet, Axel, and Thomas McCarthy, eds. *Zwischenbetrachtungen im Prozess der Aufklärung zum 60. Geburtstag J. Habermas*. Frankfurt am Main: Suhrkamp Verlag, 1989.

Husserl, Edmund. *Cartesian Meditations: An Introduction to Phenomenology*. Trans. Dorion Cairns. The Hague: Martinus Nijhoff, 1960.

————. *The Crisis of European Sciences and Transcendental Phenomenology: An Introduction to Phenomenological Philosophy*. Trans. David Carr. Evanston, Ill.: Northwestern University Press, 1970.

————. *Ideas: General Introduction to Pure Phenomenology.* Trans. W. R. Boyce Gibson. New York: Collier Books; London: Collier Macmillan, 1931.

————. "The Vienna Lecture." In *The Crisis of European Sciences and Transcendental Phenomenology.* Trans. David Carr. Evanston, Ill.: Northwestern University Press, 1970. Pp. 269–99.

Kant, Immanuel. *Grounding for the Metaphysics of Morals.* Trans. James W. Ellington. Indianapolis, Ind: Hackett, 1981.

Klemm, David E. "Levinas's Phenomenology of the Other and Language as the Other of Phenomenology." *Man and World,* 22 (1989), 427–59.

León-Portilla, Miguel. *Das vorspanische Denken Mexicos: Die Náhuatl-Philosophie.* Cologne: Botschaft der Vereinigten Mexikanischen Staaten, Gerdt Kutscher, 1970.

————, ed. *Visión de los vencidos: Relaciones indígenas de la conquista.* 10th ed. Mexico City: Universidad Nacional Autónoma de México, 1984.

Levinas, Emmanuel. *Collected Philosophical Papers.* Trans. Alphonso Lingis. Dordrecht, The Netherlands: Martinus Nijhoff, 1987.

————. *De Dieu qui vient à l'idée.* Paris: J. Vrin, 1982.

————. *En découvrant l'existence avec Husserl et Heidegger.* Paris: J. Vrin, 1982.

————. "Ethics as First Philosophy." In *The Levinas Reader.* Ed. Sean Hand. Oxford and Cambridge, Mass.: Basil Blackwell, 1992. Pp. 75–87.

————. "God and Philosophy." In *The Levinas Reader.* Ed. Sean Hand. Oxford and Cambridge, Mass.: Basil Blackwell, 1992. Pp. 166–89.

————. "Martin Buber and the Theory of Knowledge." In *The Levinas Reader.* Ed. Sean Hand. Oxford and Cambridge, Mass.: Basil Blackwell, 1992. Pp. 59–74.

————. *Otherwise Than Being, or, Beyond Essence.* Trans. Alphonso Lingis. The Hague: Martinus Nijhoff, 1981.

————. "Phenomenon and Enigma." *Collected Philosophical Papers.* Trans. Alphonso Lingis. Dordrecht, The Netherlands: Martinus Nijhoff, 1987. Pp. 61–73.

————. "Time and the Other." In *The Levinas Reader.* Ed. Sean Hand. Oxford and Cambridge, Mass.: Basil Blackwell, 1992. Pp. 37–58.

————. *Totality and Infinity: An Essay on Exteriority.* Trans. Alphonso Lingis. The Hague: Martinus Nijhoff, 1979.

Levinas, Emmanuel, and Richard Kearney. "Dialogue with Emmanuel Levinas." In *Face to Face with Levinas.* Ed. Richard A. Cohen. Albany: State University of New York Press, 1986. Pp. 13–33.

Lingis, Alphonso. "The Sensuality and the Sensitivity." In *Face to Face with Levinas.* Ed. Richard A. Cohen. Albany: State University of New York Press, 1986. Pp. 219–30.

Lukes, Steven. "Relativism in Its Place." In *Rationality and Relativism.* Ed. Martin Hollis and Steven Lukes. Cambridge, Mass.: The MIT Press, 1982. Pp. 261–305.

Lyotard, Jean-François. "Levinas' Logic." In *Face to Face with Levinas.* Ed. Richard A. Cohen. Albany: State University of New York Press, 1986. Pp. 117–58.

McCarthy, Thomas. *The Critical Theory of Jürgen Habermas.* Cambridge, Mass.: The MIT Press, 1978.

McCarthy, Thomas, and Axel Honneth, eds. *Zwischenbetrachtungen im Prozess der Aufklärung zum 60. Geburtstag J. Habermas.* Frankfurt am Main: Suhrkamp Verlag, 1989.

MacDonald, Michael J. "Jewgreek and Greekjew: The Concept of the Trace in Derrida and Levinas." *Philosophy Today,* 35 (Fall 1991), 215–27.

Mariategui, José Carlos. "Existe un pensamiento hispanoamericano?" Mexico City: Universidad Nacional Autónoma de México, Coordinación de Humanidades, Centro de Estudios Latinoamericanos, Facultad de Filosofía y Letras, Uníon de Universidades de América Latina, 1979.

―――. *Seven Interpretive Essays on Peruvian Reality.* Trans. Marjory Urquidi. Austin: University of Texas Press, 1971.

Marsh, James. *Critique, Action, and Liberation.* Albany: State University of New York Press, 1995.

Martí, José. *Nuestra América.* Mexico City: Partido Revolucionario Institucional, Comisión Nacional Editorial, 1976.

Marx, Karl. *Capital: A Critique of Political Economy.* 2 vols. Vol. 1: *The Process of Capital Production.* Ed. Friedrich Engels. Trans. Samuel Moore and Edward Avelig. New York: International Publishers, 1967. Vol. 2: *Process of Circulation of Capital.* Ed. Friedrich Engels. Trans. Samuel Moore and Edward Avelig. New York: International Publishers, 1967.

Mayz Vallenilla, Ernesto. *El problema de América.* Caracas: Dirección de Cultura, Universidad de Venezuela, 1969.

Miro Quesada, Francisco. *Despertar y proyecto del filosofar latinoamericano.* Mexico City: Fondo de Cultura Económica, 1974.

Nicol, Eduardo. *Crítica de la razón simbólica: La revolución en la filosofía.* Mexico City: Fondo de Cultura Económica, 1982.

―――. *Ideas de vario linaje.* México: Universidad Nacional de Mexico, Facultad de Filosofía y Letras, 1990.

―――. *El porvenir de la filosofía.* Mexico City: Fondo de Cultura Económica, 1972.

————. *La reforma de la filosofía.* Mexico City: Fondo de Cultura Económica, 1980.

Peperzak, Adriaan. "Some Remarks on Hegel, Kant, and Levinas." In *Face to Face with Levinas.* Ed. Richard A. Cohen. Albany: State University of New York Press, 1986. Pp. 205–17.

Rand, Ayn. *For the New Intellectual: The Philosophy of Ayn Rand.* New York: Random House, 1961.

Roig, Arturo Andrés. "Función actual de la filosofía en América Latina." In Coloquio Nacional de Filosofía. *La filosofía actual en América Latina.* Mexico City: Editorial Grijalbo, 1976. Pp. 4–9.

————. "De la historia de las ideas a la filosofía de la liberación." In Coloquio Nacional de Filosofía. *La filosofía actual en América Latina.* Mexico City: Editorial Grijalbo, 1976. Pp. 45–72.

————. *Teoría y crítica del pensamiento latinoamericano.* Mexico City: Fondo de Cultura Económica, 1981.

Rolland, Jacques, ed. *Emmanuel Levinas.* Les Cahiers de la Nuit Surveillée. France: Éditions Verdier, 1984.

Ruether, Rosemary Radford. *Faith and Fratricide: The Theological Roots of Anti-Semitism.* New York: Seabury, 1974.

Salazar Bondy, Augusto. *Existe una filosofía de nuestra América?* Iztapalapa, Mexico: Siglo Veintiuno Editores, 1975.

————. "Filosofía de la dominación y filosofía de la liberación." *Stromata* [Argentina], 29 (1973), 393–97.

————. "The Meaning and Problem of Hispanic American Philosophical Thought." Trans. Donald L. Schmidt. Lawrence, Kans.: Center of Latin American Studies, 1969.

Scannone, Juan Carlos. "Liberación latinoamericana: Ontología del proceso auténticamente libertador." *Stromata* [Argentina], 28 (1972), 107–50.

————. "La pregunta por el Ser en la filosofía actual." *Stromata* [Argentina], 28 (1972), 593–96.

Schelkshorn, Hans. *Ethik der Befreiung: Einführung in die Philosophie Enrique Dussels.* Freiburg im Breisgau: Herder, 1992.

Schutte, Ofelia. "Origins and Tendencies of the Philosophy of Liberation in Latin American Thought: A Critique of Dussel's Ethics." *The Philosophical Forum*, 22 (1991), 270–95.

Schutz, Alfred. *Collected Papers. I. The Problem of Social Reality.* Ed. Maurice Natanson. The Hague: Martinus Nijhoff, 1962.

————. *The Phenomenology of the Social World.* Trans. George Walsh and Frederick Lehnert. Evanston, Ill.: Northwestern University Press, 1967.

Secretariat for Catholic–Jewish Relations, NCCB; Adult Education Department, USCC; Interfaith Affairs Department, ADL. "Within Context: Guidelines for the Catechetical Presentation of Jews and Judaism in the New Testament [1986]." In *In Our Time: The Flowering of Jewish-Catholic Dialogue*. Ed. Eugene J. Fisher and Leon Klenicki. New York and Mahwah, N.J.: Paulist Press, 1990. Pp. 59–74.

Smith, Steven G. "Reason as One for Another: Moral and Theoretical Argument in the Philosophy of Levinas." In *Face to Face with Levinas*. Ed. Richard A. Cohen. Albany: State University of New York Press, 1986. Pp. 53–71.

Spiegelberg, Herbert. *Doing Phenomenology: Essays on and in Phenomenology*. The Hague: Martinus Nijhoff, 1975.

Strasser, Stephan. *Jenseits von Sein und Zeit: Eine Einführung in Emmanuel Levinas' Philosophie*. The Hague: Martinus Nijhoff, 1978.

Todorov, Tzvetan. *La conquista de América: El problema del Otro*. Iztapalapa, Mexico: Siglo Veintiuno Editores, 1991.

Vargas Lozano, Gabriel. *Marx y su crítica de la filosofía*. Iztapalapa, Mexico: Universidad Autónoma Metropolitana, 1984.

Waelhens, Alfonse de. *La philosophie et les expériences naturelles*. The Hague: Martinus Nijhoff, 1961.

Zea, Leopoldo. *Conciencia y posibilidad del Mexicano*. Mexico City: Porrúa y Obregón, 1952.

———. "Dependencia y liberación en la filosofía latinoamericana." *Dianoia*, 20 (1974), 172–88.

———. *La filosofía americana como filosofía sin más*. Iztaplapa, Mexico: Siglo Veintiuno Editores, 1969.

———. *El positivismo y la circunstancia mexicana*. Mexico City: Fondo de Cultura Económica, 1985.

Zubiri, Xavier. *Inteligencia sentiente: Inteligencia y realidad*. Madrid: Alianza, Sociedad de Estudios y Publicaciones, 1984.

INDEX

revolution, 94, 103, 105, 115, 144, 150, 152
Ricardo, D., 93
Ricoeur, Paul, ix
Rodbertus, K., 93
Romero, Oscar, 122, 139
Rorty, Richard, ix
Rosenzweig, Franz, 1, 3
Rousseau, Jean-Jacques, xvii, 59
Russia, 66, 94, 105, 154

said, the, xvi, 5, 14, 52–53, 142
salary, 98–100, 103–104, 149
Salazar Bondy, Augusto, 61
El Salvador, 122
same, the, 66, 68, 75, 86, 98, 119, 134, 137
Sandinistas, 64, 105
Sandino, A. C., 70
San Salvador, 86
Sarmiento, D. F., 58
Sartre, J.-P., 29, 31–32, 36, 64
saying, xvi, 5, 14–15, 52, 142
Scannone, Juan Carlos, 115
sceptic, the, 129–30, 133–35, 156n4
Scheler, Max, 30, 41
Schelling, Friedrich, xi, xx, xxii, 27, 50, 96, 98, 100
Scholasticism, 18
Schutte, Ofelia, xi, xx–xxi, 67, 113–20, 123–24, 125n5, 133, 154–55
Schutz, Alfred, 53–54
science, xi–xii, xviii, xx–xxi, 2–3, 6, 14–15, 30–31, 38, 42, 57, 62–68, 71–72, 75, 85–86, 97, 100–102, 114–17, 127–29, 131, 139, 140–41, 143–49, 154–55
scientism, 63, 115, 139
secularization, 39
self-critique, 6–8, 15, 39, 44, 71, 85, 106, 119–21, 124, 131, 133, 135, 141
semantics, 127–28
Semitism, xvi, 19–21, 24–25, 28, 46n7, 57, 83
Sepúlveda, Gines de, 65, 75, 87
ser-americano, 84
shepherd of being, 33
signs, 53
"Situación problemática de la antropología filosófica," 18

Sixth Sun, 88
slavery, 87, 103, 106, 144
Smith, Adam, 93, 99
socialism, xii,xxi, 94, 98, 102, 105, 143, 150–52, 154
socialization, 71
Socrates, 134
solidarity, 133, 141–42
solipsism, 37, 66, 69, 128, 131, 137, 141
Sombart, Werner, 30, 41
Somocism, 64
Sorge, 48n29,
Spain, ix, xix, 18, 25, 57–58, 60, 65, 74, 82–84, 86, 87–88, 90, 103
speech, metainstitution of, 129, 142
Spiegelberg, Herbert, 118
spontaneity, 4, 6, 73, 120, 122
Stalin, Joseph, 51, 105
Stern der Erlösung, 3
Steuart, J., 92
subject, 9, 12–13, 26, 30–33, 38, 40–45, 59, 63, 67–68, 72–73, 79n26, 89, 91, 95–96, 99, 101, 121–22, 128, 130, 132, 134, 136, 144–45, 152–53, 156
super-accumulation, 103
supply and demand, 93, 97, 145–47, 153
surplus value, xxii, 93–94, 96–97, 99–100, 102–104, 144, 146–47, 153–54, 156; absolute, 91, 103; rate of, 94, 97; relative, 92, 103; transfer of, 93–94, 104, 147–50, 154
Symposium, 66
synchrony, 13
syncretism, 18, 57
syntactics, 127–28
system, 7, 13, 21, 27, 43–44, 50, 53–54, 56, 59, 62–65, 72, 79n.26, 87, 90, 92, 94, 96–98, 102–103, 105–106, 113, 120–21, 123, 134, 136, 140, 143–45, 146, 150, 152–53

tabula rasa, 57
temporality, 22
thematization, 4, 8, 13, 14, 22, 33, 36, 39, 68, 117, 136
"Théologie de la 'Péripherie' et du 'Centre,'" 60
theology, ix–xii, xviii–xx, xxii, 18, 20, 27, 31, 39, 42, 45, 57, 60–61, 65, 68–